CASES IN RURAL MARKETING

An Integrated Approach

Books of related interest:

Rural Marketing: Text and Cases	by Krishnamacharyulu & Ramakrishnan
Marketing Management, 11e	by Kotler
Marketing: An Introduction, 5e	by Armstrong & Kotler
Consumer Behavior, 7e	by Schiffman
Marketing Research, 3e	by Malhotra

CASES IN RURAL MARKETING

An Integrated Approach

C. S. G. Krishnamacharyulu
Professor and Chairman, BOS
School of Business Management
Sri Venkateswara University
Tirupati

Lalitha Ramakrishnan
Academic Coordinator
Sri Padmavathi Women's University
Tirupati

PEARSON

ISBN 978-81-317-0188-1

First Impression, 2007

Published by Pearson India Education Services Pvt.Ltd,CIN:U72200TN2005PTC057128.
Formerly known as TutorVista Global Pvt Ltd, licensees of Pearson Education in South Asia

Head Office: 7th Floor, knowledge Boulevard, A-8(A) Sector-62, Noida (U.P) 201309, India

Registered Office: Module G4, Ground Floor, Elnet Software City, TS -140,Block 2 & 9
Rajiv Gandhi Salai, Taramani, Chennai, Tamil Nadu 600113.,Fax: 080-30461003,
Phone: 080-30461060, www.pearson.co.in email id: companysecretary.india@pearson.com

Digitally Printed in India by Repro India Ltd. in the year of 2016.

PREFACE

Rural marketing has emerged as an exciting and dynamic discipline. One way of learning this discipline is through case method. Cases provide the students an opportunity to develop an appreciation to the real-life problem-situations, help unfold challenges and sharpen the skills of analysis and decision-making. Like other managerial skills, analytical and evaluation skills are difficult to acquire and perfect. However, 'practice makes one perfect' is a reliable advice. By exposing to a variety of cases one can improve the skills so necessary for success in marketing and other areas of business.

The oft-expressed dissatisfaction of marketing executives is that the classroom teaching of marketing is unrealistic and overly theoretical, leaving the students inadequately prepared for management careers. Keeping in mind this point, the book is compiled with several contemporary, real-life business situations.

The cases in this book represent a broad range of marketing problems in the context of either urban and/or rural markets, emphasising rural marketing. Each case is designed to fit into a specific section of the course. There are long and short cases with varying levels of difficulty. Teachers like improving or testing comprehension, analytical and diagnostic skills to meet one or more of the goals of case method will find the book useful.

Another interesting point is the cases are developed to facilitate professors to use the book for discussing not only rural marketing but also urban marketing strategies. An effort has been made to provide role models in the case content for the increasing number of women entering into business world. The main features of the book are:

1. Helpful hints on how to analyse cases
2. Guidance on preparing case analysis and written and oral presentations of case analysis
3. Two model case analyses
4. Forty cases, drawn mostly from real world marketing useful to teach rural as well as urban marketing.

The book is divided into eight parts.

Part I — Orients the students to case analysis. A brief discussion on case method and marketing decisions and models is followed by a presentation of rural marketing opportunities, strategies and statistical data. Also two illustrative case analyses are given in this section.

Part II — Presents three cases on rural markets to discuss their emergence as a new opportunity and what corporate enterprises can do.

Part III — Provides five cases on rural market analysis and information system. The concerned issues are consumer behaviour analysis, marketing research information system design and demand forecasting.

Part IV–VI — Bring to you five cases on each of the marketing mix elements—product, price, promotion and distribution in that order.

Part VIII — Provides 12 comprehensive cases that expose students to strategy making for agri-products and consumer goods.

It is important to note that the cases were prepared as a basis for classroom discussion rather than to illustrate either effective or ineffective handling of administrative situations.

We hope the book will be of use to young executives and management students in improving their managerial skills and understanding of marketing dynamics. Also, we welcome suggestions from professors, trainers, managers and students for improving the content of the book in future.

C.S.G. Krishnamacharyulu
Lalitha Ramakrishnan

ACKNOWLEDGEMENTS

The inspiration for writing the book has come from Mr. Sanjay K. Singh, Managing Editor—Higher Education, Pearson Education. We are thankful to him and his team for their support.

The senior author expresses his deep sense of gratitude to his teachers:

- Prof. K. V. Sivayya, MBA (Bradley), Ph.D (Illinois. Tech), Retired Professor, Andhra University and presently Director, Dr. N. S. Kolla School of Business, Visakhapatnam, who taught the basics of case analysis
- Prof. D. Dakshina Murthy, M.Com. Ph.D (New York) at Nagarjuna University, who imparted skills of inquiry and analysis as a research supervisor.

We place on record our gratefulness to:

- Prof. P. Murali, Vice-Chancellor, Sri Venkateswara University, Tirupati
- Prof. R. Madhavi, Vice-Chancellor, Sri Padmavathi Mahila University, Tirupati
- Prof. V. Jayarami Reddy, Secretary, AP State Council for Higher Education, Hyderabad who in their pursuit of academic excellence in universities have given us the right atmosphere, facilities and support in our endeavours.

Our special thanks are due to Dr. Rajeswari, Assistant Librarian, Sri Padmavathi Mahila University and the staff of the library for their kind cooperation.

Finally, our appreciation is to our little decision makers, Srikrishna and Srivalli, who inspire us in our problem solving by saying 'I've got an idea' and 'I have a plan'.

C.S.G. Krishnamacharyulu
Lalitha Ramakrishnan

CONTENTS

PART

1

Orientation

- Case Method
- Marketing Decisions and Models
- Rural Marketing
- Model Case Analysis
  1. A Stitch in Time Saves Nine
  2. Where Eagles Dare

CHAPTER

1

Case Method

It goes without saying that the case method is one of the most popular techniques in management training. The case method is different from lecture-cum discussion method. Cases provide an opportunity to simulate actual experience by analysing problems and making decisions. This method is known as experiential learning or learning by doing. In experiential learning, a four-step process is involved as given below.

Analysis A pre-class preparation and analysis of the case often including library research, determining percentages, ratios, etc.

Presentation and Discussion Students are involved either as a presenter or discussant in the case presentation and ideas are subject to open debates and criticism.

Critique Students compare their analyses with others, evaluate approaches and compare the results of different decisions.

Generalisation Through numerous encounters, students evolve common approaches to problems.

WHAT IS A CASE?

A case is a descriptive portrayal of some episode in an organisational activity. A typical case consists of a number of pages of prose description. It often includes some quantitative material, either interspersed with the qualitative prose or presented as charts, graphs or tables. Other exhibits such as maps, organisation charts, pictures may also be included. Case analysis is prescriptive, the analyst must specify what should be done. To define it, a case is:

> "Typically a record of a business issue which actually has been faced by business executives, together with surrounding facts, opinions and prejudices upon which the executives had to depend. These real and particularized cases are presented to students for considered analysis, open discussion, and final decision as to the type of action which should be taken".

RATIONALE OF CASE METHOD

Why should one use the case method as a substitute or complement to traditional lecture method?

Real Knowledge is action-oriented

Knowledge acquired by reading text books and listening to lecture is static. When one applies it, its power will be known and experienced. Peter F. Drucker says: "Achievement rather than knowledge, is both proof and aim of management". What management students need is real knowledge—the knowledge of action and application. Real knowledge cannot be conferred; it has to be acquired by painstaking effort. Real education is hard work.

Wisdom cannot be told

No amount of information, whether of theory or fact, in itself improves insight and judgement or increases ability to act wisely under condition of responsibility. There are two popular beliefs: (1) It is possible to learn to act wisely only by experience—in the school of hard knocks. (2) The act of listening to wise statements and sound advice makes one wise. Both the beliefs have their own limitations requiring teachers to use both of them appropriately. Case method provides an ample opportunity to mix them. Under the case method, the student plays an active role. He thinks situationally, applies his knowledge and arrives at a decision. The instructor plays a passive role. He does not tell the student, he encourages the student to act and questions him to logically justify his stand. He makes him realize that one cannot effectively use the insight and knowledge of others, it must be his own.

CHARACTERISTICS OF A CASE

A case presents to the student, a real-life situation that requires understanding, critiquing and decision making.

Descriptive

A case is descriptive in nature. It presents an episode as it has evolved over a time period. In the narration, one finds event by event occurrence, of course not necessarily in a chronological order.

Lengthy

Cases vary in their length. There is no standardized length or form. Some cases are fairly lengthy, fifteen to thirty pages or more. Some cases are short, one to three pages. Whatever may be the length of the case, the intent of the case is to provide the student with an intellectually challenging material.

Form

In form, cases differ. Some cases may be quantitative. They may present little or no quantitative data. Other cases may carry a large amount of data requiring the use of mathematical or statistical tools for analysis and decision making.

Not a law case

Business cases are like law cases only in rare instances. In fact, they are different both in nature and purpose. A law case presents a decision that has already been made; a history. It is based on precedents and sets another precedent for lawyers to quote in the future. In a business case, a manager can disregard a precedent unless that precedent has been blessed as an organization policy. Even in this situation also, the manager has ample opportunity to overturn the policy by objectively showing that it does not suffice. Business situations are dynamic, the manifold factors of the situations in the business world change so rapidly that old solutions to uncertainties may furnish useful analogies but rarely definitive answers. In a sense, business cases are more like medical cases—diagnostic and prescriptive. Trainee doctors examine the patients, prepare case history and carry out investigations to produce a diagnosis. Based on the diagnosis they prescribe a specific treatment and administer it.

BENEFITS

It is not primarily to help the students to accumulate a store of knowledge or to acquaint them with current business practices. These may come as side benefits. The primary purpose is to sharpen the students' skills in working through a problem. It requires that student take an active role of a thinker, analyzer, evaluator, decider and implementer in place of a passive listener. Precisely the benefits are:

Trains as a manager The case method places the students in a simulated business environment and substitutes the students in the place of the manager or a consultant. It gives them an opportunity to think and act like a manager or a consultant, particularly when role playing is employed for case development.

Promotes analytical skills In the case method, the emphasis is not on solution. The process of arriving at a solution is what is more important. The student is expected to move stage by stage from problem identification to solution implementation. Also, the goal is not to develop a set of right answers, but to learn to reason well with the data available. In fact, there is no single right answer to a case. As such, a student can learn how to think critically and effectively reason when dealing with specific problems.

Improves communication skills Case method encourages, presentation and discussion. The students would learn to write and present their analysis in a cogent and convincing manner. The written case report should be complete in all respects, reflecting the thought processes of the student. In presentation, it should be clear for others to appreciate the thought process and give their critical view points.

Develops team work Case discussion provides opportunities to develop group work through intellectual encounters. As one presents his or her view points, others criticize them constructively. In turn, the presenters shall defend their analysis and plan of action against the criticism of others in the class. In the process, students shall learn the following:

- How they have overlooked some points or overweighed other points or got swayed by some other points.
- How opinions and values of other members of the class differ from their own.

As a result, this leads to a clearer perception of problems, and recognition of many and often conflicting interpretations of the facts and events in the case. Also, students learn to work with others, when problems particularly are multi-faceted and complex.

Expands knowledge horizons Case technique is not a substitute for learning theory. It does not attack the place of theories and facts in the students' training. Rather it combines these with practical business problems or issues and develops a task integrating theory and practice, called a case. Its aim is to provide a more fruitful learning situation.

Fosters creativity A conscientious student improves his or her creative skills in decision making by transferring analytical problem solving skills from the given setting to any number of other settings. Analogy is a good approach to creativity. Another source of creativity is participation. As case discussions are participative, a student is exposed to divergent thinking.

Enhances empathy The realistic orientation to life where differences are natural may stimulate the students to work harder for the gift of seeing others as they see themselves and visualizing their solutions.

Prepares for a career Practice in analyzing the cases will help the student to prepare for a career in decision making. Most persons start out their careers with little authority in decision making. At this level, the problem could be relatively simple being routine type. For problem solving, programmed decision making is required. Remember, persons with sharp analytical mind climb the ladder faster. As they occupy positions of more authority they will have complex problems—which require heuristic approaches and team work. The case analysis assists in preparing the students for the first job, but more importantly, for positions of higher level to facilitate rapid rise in career.

Helps deal with uncertainties Business decision making is rarely based on perfect information. Good cases, like real-world situations, do not usually come neatly packaged. Too much data with too little information. In case analysis, often students complain about the low level of availability of information—"The picture is vague; facts are inadequate". The students will very likely become frustrated by the lack of certain data which, in their view, must be available to fully understand the case and to render a meaningful solution. Such patent lack of real data should not turn off a manager. What is required in those situations is making reasonable assumptions and learning to make decisions under uncertainty. There is often a strong reluctance or helplessness on the part of the student to do this, but ability to make decisions based on well reasoned assumptions is a skill that must be developed for a manager, tc be truly effective.

Improves social relationships A significant benefit of case method is the democratic atmosphere which provides a new axis for personal relationships. The students find their attention transferred from the teacher to each other. It is no longer a question of dealing with an elder but dealing with a large number of equals and contemporaries whose criticism is to be faced and whose contributions need be comprehended and appreciated. The art of exchanging zeroes the ego and other idiosyncrasies and instills confidence with humility.

CASE ANALYSIS DEMANDS SKILLS

In the class room learning situation, the role of the student is always active. However, the lecture-cum discussion method provides less opportunities to the student to open up. A case method is student-centric. It is a participative method and its success depends on the contribution of the student. The case is raw material, thinking is process and development is output. The student's benefit from the case method will be proportional to the effort he or she puts into his or her analysis of the case. Superficial treatment of the case will result in a superficial learning experience.

A student may have to employ the following skills in analyzing the case:

Skills	*Tasks*
Comprehension	Understand the whole situation—the past and the present.
Analytical	Clearly identify facts, problems, symptoms, opportunities and actionable plans.
Computational	Perform computations using appropriate quantitative tools.

Conceptual and Design	Visualize future situations. Set up in clear terms objectives and alternative approaches to attain the objectives.
Technical	Use knowledge and techniques related to the problem on hand.
Evaluative	Evaluate the alternative courses of action using suitable criteria. Evaluating without criteria is like steering a ship without the compass.
Judgement	Select the appropriate alternative.
Conceptual and Design	Visualise future situations and develop an action plan for implementation.

TYPES OF CASES

Cases used in class rooms may be categorised into three types based on the purpose as given below.

Purpose	*Type*	*Method of Case Writing*	*Analyst Tasks*
Improve comprehension	Case history	Library research	Study and Appreciate
Improve evaluation	Appraisal cases	Library research and interviews	Analyse and evaluate
Improve decision making	Problem or Decision cases	Field research	Analyse, evaluate, and decide

The underlying purpose of case histories seems to be for students to learn how a particular organization made a successful or unsuccessful decision. Appraisal cases have largely to do with analyzing and assimilating the situation or decision already taken. Decision making cases require problem solving or opportunity grabbing plans of action.

The typical questions at the end of these cases are:

A. Histories:

1. Briefly describe the marketing model of HLL.
2. What lessons do you draw from the successful experiments of Colgate?

B. Appraisal type:

1. Identify the major issues in the situation.
2. Analyse the situation and define the problem.
3. Do you agree with the views and actions of CavinKare ?.

C. Decision type:

1. Is Philips right in its decision to penetrate into rural areas?
2. What action would you take if you were the marketing manager of BPL?
3. Evaluate the strategies of Dabur India?

READING THE CASE

The case will have to be read a number of times before the analysis is completed. It is seldom possible to assimilate the facts in a first reading; indeed the first reading is useful primarily as a means of isolating learning issues and sketching the background. In many cases, the issue will be quite simple and direct. In others, it will be complex and obscure. In many cases what seems like an issue on reading may upon reflection be only a symptom of some deeper basic problem.

Quick reading

First, read the case quickly. Read the case by underlining or making notes in the margin on important facts. Try to get a feel of the overall content of the case. Also, read the questions given at the end. The purpose of quick reading is to have answers to the following questions relating to the situation.

- What type of organization is it?
- Where it happened?
- When it happened?
- Which functional area relates to it?
- Who are involved?
- What has happened?
- What is the problem?

Thorough reading

From a preliminary understanding, move to a complete understanding. Thorough reading is necessary for mastering the situational factors and dimensions. Therefore, read the text again. This time forming a logical outline collecting common elements and examining in detail goals, policies, symptoms of problems, unresolved issues, managerial roles, etc. As a part of this reading,

- Recognise the actors and their characteristics.
- Identify the events and their cause and effect relationships.
- Trace the sequence in chronological order and if necessary rearrange in any other logical order.
- Note the problems.
- Examine all the exhibits carefully. These may include sales data, market shares, demand forecasts, budgets, costs, etc. It is safe to assume that these items have been included for a purpose.

Check reading

There is a need to thoroughly verify and understand the situation before pròceeding to make analysis. You should not blindly accept all the data presented, as not all information is equally reliable and relevant.

- Check whether all the facts are relevant and understood.
- Identify data gaps and data processing needs.

PLAYING THE ROLE

Immerse yourself in the case; get to know the details. Mull the case over; put yourself in the role of the decision maker; consider how you would see things and how you would feel, were you required to reach a decision not as a mere exercise but in real life.

CASE ANALYSIS PROCEDURE

There is no standard formula or ideal methodology that is appropriate for all cases. Case analysis may vary influenced by factors like the type of the case, the purpose for which it is used, the level of students, etc. Accordingly, case analyses also differ in terms of approach and depth. Also, students come across two types of cases:

(i) Those which specify questions at the end.
(ii) Those which indicate the dilemma faced by a company or an executive.

The questions at the end of the case do not always focus directly on the principal issue. They are designed to help the student to start the analysis. In no way are the questions designed to limit the scope and breadth of the discussion. Case analysis is a decision making exercise. As such, the procedure involved in case analysis is very much similar to that of decision making. Figure –1.1 gives a logical frame-work for case analysis and Table –1.1 lists the tasks.

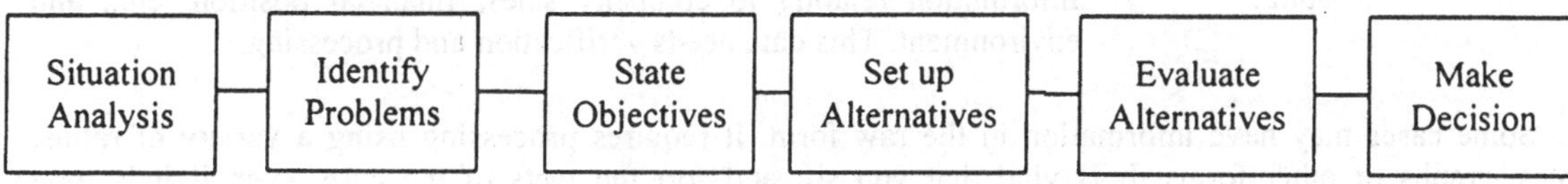

Fig. 1.1 Frame-work for Case Analysis

Table 1.1 Tasks in Case Analysis

Step	*Analysis Tasks*	*Judgmental Tasks*
1	Situation—past and present (Expectations and actuals)	Identify central problems
2	Situation—future (Opportunities and threats)	State objectives and acceptable solutions
3	Ways of achieving objectives	Set up alternatives
4	Applying criteria for selection (Feasibility analysis)	Evaluate alternatives
5	Analysing reasons for selection	Make decision
6	Analysing situation for implementation	Decide action plan

Analyse the situation

The first step in case analysis is understanding the situation in which the problem is located. A situation is never complete in its description. All marketing decisions are made on the basis of incomplete information. Also, it is wrong to view the situation as a bunch of facts. A situation is complex of facts, views, assumptions, inferences and predictions. Sort out the relevant from the irrelevant, facts from the assumptions and goals from actions, and organize the issues into a clear exposition of the problems at hand.

The useful steps are:

1. List all the past and current events. In listing the events, look for relationships and order. The order may be chronological or otherwise.
2. Note the characters and their attitudes. You must be alert to personal characteristics and relationships among the principals of the case. Given their personality and disposition and other factors what kind of stand have they taken? What will be their actions and reactions? What surprises or shocks could they spring in future? Can we expect consistency in their behaviours?
3. Look for facts. Evidence in the case may come in three forms :

Fact :	XYZ company was set up in 1992
Opinion :	They appear in two forms: Direct opinions in quotations or attributed opinions in statements like "the boss believes that advertising will be of no help in this situation".
Data :	Information relating to company sales, financial position, etc., and environment. This data needs verification and processing.

Some cases may have information in the raw form. It requires processing using a variety of ratios, tables, graphs or other forms. It is vital that you sift and sort the facts of the case, even if it is time consuming. List the most important facts first and the least ones last. Between them fill in various facts in descending order of importance.

Always ask : What do I need to know in order to answer the question or solve the problem?

Use your judgement in building the list of facts. Revise and restructure the facts, using your logic, commonsense and intuition until you feel you are saturated.

- Some data may look irrelevant. Care should be exercised in discarding them. Let your imagination play with the fact and see if you can fit it in your structure of analysis. Sometimes a seemingly irrelevant fact may become relevant.
- Sometimes important facts are buried in some chance remark or seemingly minor statistical exhibit.
- Sometimes cases contain errors (either by accident or by design) and the instructor may prefer to remain silent.
- In some cases information designed to distract and confuse the imperceptive reader may be included.
- Some cases may have information gaps. Either collect more information or make assumptions.

Categorise: Now categorise the facts. A necessary categorisation is to separate objective facts from subjective information (opinions, assumption and speculations). The latter are by no means unimportant, but they should be correctly labeled for future use and suitable weighting.

4. Make realistic assumptions to fill in the gaps of information.
5. Process quantitative data using appropriate techniques to gain meaningful information.
6. Draw inferences wherever necessary. Facts do not have meaning without interpretation.

   Eg: The current ratio is 1:1. What does this mean? A poor liquidity position when the required current ratio is 2:1.This inference is important.
7. Put the system or situation in perspective. Think of any theoretical material that would help in understanding the case, put it to work in your analysis. Sketch an appropriate model representing the situation or the system like Consumer Behaviour Model or AIDA model. Since effective analysis is based on a systematic frame-work, picture the overall system with the subsystems involved and specify the relationships of their interaction.

SITUATION = FACTS + INFERENCES + ASSUMPTIONS + PREDICTIONS

Identify the central problem

A well identified problem is a problem half solved. A problem is a deviation from standard, or a gap between expected and actual outcomes or a short fall from the budgeted figures or performance.

In identifying problem, one should not confuse symptoms with problems. We illustrate how one can identify the root cause of the problem and avoid seeing apparent symptoms as problems. Say, if the sales of a company are falling then what is the problem? Probe with whys to locate the problem as shown below.

Apparent	*Areas of Concern*	*Finding*
Sales are down—Why?	Competition. Consumer preferences. Product price. Promotion, Distribution	Salesperson's failure
Salespersons failure—Why?	Sales supervision. Poor product presentation. Consumer attitudes, Low sales expenditures. Low allowances compensation	Poor training
Poor training—Why?	Training methods, Trainer. Trainees, Budget	Low budget

Finally, state the problem. It is possible to state the problem in different ways.

(i) In agreement or disagreement with a person's suggestions given in the case. Do you agree with Dr. Jyoti's proposed price change?

(ii) In expectation of an independent proposal. What should the price be?

Objectives and constraints

'Managing an organisation is managing by objectives and results expected' says Peter F. Drucker. Without objectives, decisions may become misdirected missiles. One has to clearly state what is expected of the situation in the short and long term interests of the organisation. Objectives must be clear and measurable.

Vague	*Clear*
To achieve large volume of sales	To achieve 10 percent rise over the previous year sales in the next fiscal year.
To maximize profits	To recoup investment within three years.
To cut costs	To reduce costs by 15 per cent level within two years.

Objectives must specify the level of achievement and while stating the time frame for the objectives, one must take into cognizance not only the opportunities but also constraints. A useful analytical tool is SWOT (strengths weaknesses, opportunities and threats) analysis. It helps to convert wish statements into concrete attainable objectives. An example of SWOT is:

STRENGTHS: Strong distribution network
WEAKNESS: Limited company resources
OPPORTUNITIES: Growing market at a rate of 5 per cent
THREATS: Competition from MNCs
CONSTRAINTS: The goal of 10 per cent rise in sales is to be achieved under the following set of conditions.

1. Advertising will be 1 per cent of past sales.
2. No further addition to sales force.

Formulate alternatives

A good analysis is a sort of 'construct-destruct' exercise. Develop alternatives explicit and implicit in the case, and generate more by applying some of the creative thinking methods. One should not be content with the alternatives stated in the case. One must go beyond to find new information and new alternatives. Once a list of alternatives is constructed, the analyst will go about dismissing the unfeasible, apparently irrelevant ones. It is always better, if the list of alternatives are reduced to three or four to receive the most careful, detailed consideration. Remember, one alternative that should always be considered is the maintenance of *status-quo*. Sometimes doing nothing is the best course of action to follow.

Evaluate alternatives

Consider the alternatives along with the criteria for selection. The criteria are to be derived from the objectives and constraints and state them explicitly.

The criteria may relate to the following:

(1) Profitability—Level of profits desired.

(2) Sales growth—Level of sales revenues', percentage of market share.

(3) Risk—Degree of risk acceptable.

(4) Time—Time frame of action.

(5) Resources—Level of expenditure desirable. Availability of resources.

For example, a company may want to achieve a 10 per cent rise in sales in the next year with a budget constraint of Rs. 3 crore, and no changes in the existing system of distribution. Obviously, alternatives involving financial burden of more than Rs. 3 crore and change in distribution system are ruled out.

To examine the efficacy of the alternatives, make effective use of financial and other quantitative information. Techniques like NPV, Break Even Analysis, Bayesian Analysis, and ANOVA can be employed to ascertain the value of the alternatives. Then analyse the pros and cons of the alternatives as illustrated below.

Pros	*Cons*
1. Opens up new market	1. Risk of failure
2. Combats competition	2. Imitation can be very fast

Make decision

Reach a clearcut decision and avoid qualifications and other hedges. Select the action alternative that provides the best answer to the problem under the given constraints. The choice should be logically consistent with the situation analysis that was done. Sometimes students recommend that the decision be postponed to get more information. This is not an acceptable solution in a business case. Delay in decision may mean loss of markets and research may not really produce required information.

Other students may disagree with your situation analysis and thus your resultant conclusion, but they should not be able to fault the logical connection between your situation analysis and decision. If they can, you have a poor case analysis.

Your decision is not complete until you prepare gross operational plans at least for its implementation. Draw up a statement of:

(i) What must be done to carry out your decision?

(ii) What personnel must be assigned to do it?

(iii) When the act(s) should be carried out?

(iv) How much will it cost?

Develop a plan of action to deal with existing acts, or new personnel, as you might like to hedge your bets and say 'may be this, may be that'. However, gross estimates are infinitely better than no estimates at all, for they force you to bring to a logical conclusion, a logical process of thinking.

Before you finish your case analysis, review it one last time and check whether everything is considered and you have gone beyond the initial confines of the case study ,if necessary.

Role of a Teacher

The teacher has to perform the following in order to make case method of study a useful pedagogical tool.

(i) Decide whether to use the case method

(ii) Prepare in advance how to conduct the discussion

(iii) Ensure preparation by students

(iv) Organise class room discussion

(v) Evaluate oral and written case analyses

Decision to use To start with, the teacher has to decide whether to use the case method. The decision is contingent upon factors like the quality of the case, capabilities of self and maturity of students. Exhibit–1.1 aids in the evaluation of these factors and in making a decision to use the case method.

Exhibit: 1.1 Evaluation to Use Case Method

1. Is the student sufficiently oriented to case philosophy?
2. Is the student well prepared for class room discussion?
3. Is the student free from inhibitions to present his /her arguments and listen to others?
4. Is the student too conscious of right and wrong solutions?
5. Is the student willing to think and argue independently without much intervention from the instructor?
6. Does the instructor have the open-mindedness and tolerance to listen to the views of students?
7. Does he have the breadth of knowledge across areas either to relate or handle a case?
8. Is the instructor prepared to hold a case discussion in a class room?
9. Does the instructor have capabilities to moderate—to direct discussion, to become devil advocate, to relieve tension, to pull up students when they fail?
10. Is the instructor well versed with the use of learning methods like role play and aids like overhead transparencies?
11. Whether the case serves the purpose of learning—analysis, examination and decision making?
12. Whether the case is good in terms of clarity and length?
13. Whether the case can be used at this level? Does it match the maturity level of the students?

Preparation The instructor to be effective must do some homework. He should prepare his teaching note which may contain the following:

- Positioning of the course in the case he is handling.
- Cross reference to the cases handled. Past experiences in the class room, the knowledge base and skill development.
- Objectives of the case. Its linkages to past learning and contribution to further learning.
- Class room strategies that can be adopted.
- Major issues to be covered.
- Student preparation tasks—specifying information to be gathered by the student.
- Quantitative or qualitative analysis to be made.

Making students to prepare Though students are expected to base their analysis on the evidence presented in the case, but this does not mean that other information cannot be used. Appropriate information about environment or industry may be gathered and used. The teacher may guide the students in this regard. Distribution of case material in advance, fixing date for discussion and giving specific assignments if any will naturally stimulate interest in the students to come prepared for discussion.

Organising Discussion Case development may take several forms such as group discussion, recitation, written work at home, a timed written analysis in class, an individual or group oral report, a debate between teams or role playing. Combinations of these forms are also used.

Classroom discussion may occur in different ways depending upon the contributions of instructor and participants as shown in Figure 1.2.

Participant Contribution	Instructor Contribution: High	Instructor Contribution: Low
High	Controlled Discussion	Democratic Discussion
Low	Monologue	Dialogue

Fig. 1.2 Classroom Discussion Types

Monologue:

What happens when the 'underprepared' students and the 'overprepared' instructor come together to discuss the case? The actual process is not really a 'discussion', but a question-answer session. Disappointed by the incoherent responses from the students, the instructor analyses the case and closes the session with a piece of advice to the students.

Dialogue:

The teacher as well as the students may come unprepared. As a result neither of them will be in a position to raise questions or make presentations. The whole process drags painfully and dysfunctionally, not able to serve any of the purposes of case method.

Democratic discussion:

The ideal democratic discussion takes place when contribution by the teacher is less and that of participants is high. It will be a functional and fructifying experience to all those involved.

Controlled discussion:

A slight variation to the democratic discussion comes in the form of high contribution by an over zealous instructor. It mars partly the atmosphere, robs student's time and initiative and lowers the benefits of case discussion.

Though democratic discussion is preferred, a teacher cannot ask for it all the time. Styles of interaction and direction vary depending on time or stage in course being taught, purpose of the case and level of students as shown in Table 1.2.

Table 1.2 Teacher-Student Involvements

Variable	*More Teacher Direction*	*More Student Direction*
Time in course	Early	Late
Teacher's purpose	Illustrate a concept	Make a decision
Students' level:		
Participation	Less prepared	Well prepared
Experience	Less experienced	Well experienced

In a matured class the expectation is that students exhibit leadership roles and facilitate democratic and cooperative effort. If every member of each study group takes some share in leading, what is the role of teacher?

> "It should be the chief aim of a university professor to exhibit himself in his own true character that is, an ignorant man thinking actively utilising his small share of knowledge". (A.N.Whitehead, 1929)

The role of a teacher is passive but important. He or she can be an enabler or a facilitator. By being 'on tap not on top' he or she can avoid the undesirable extremes of doing things which students could profitably do for each other, and of doing nothing. By being sparing in what he or she says or does, a teacher can earn a tribute like this:

> "Of a good leader, who talks little,
> When his work is done, his aim fulfilled
> They will all say, "we did this ourselves". (Writter Bynner, 1944)

Effective Group Discussion

Group discussion method can be productive when the following specifications are met.

- Discussion should always be focused.
- Discussion should always be sufficiently specific.
- Discussion should get us some where in promoting agreement and mutual understanding.

Group discussion can be productive only when all the participants fulfil the following leadership responsibilities. The atmosphere of discussion should be free, informal and experimental. Four freedoms which promote productive group discussions are:

(a) To try out ideas for size
(b) To cite experience
(c) To speak one's mind (even in disagreement)
(d) To propose and try experiments

The students have to perform the following tasks to make a discussion productive.

- Helping a group to get started.
- Helping to establish a friendly atmosphere.
- Keeping group talk going.
- Playing the role of partner.
- Introducing procedures which facilitate productive interactions.
- Allowing others to take lead.
- Raising thought provoking questions to focus group attention on important tasks.
- Discouraging private conversation.

EFFECTIVE WRITING GUIDELINES

A well written case is a reflection of the competence of the analyst. The following factors require consideration in writing a report.

Objective

Instructors like to see papers that are objective and structured. Nothing upsets an instructor more than reading a paper that repeats the statements that appear in the cases with no interpretation and explanation of implications.

Structure

Students will begin with the first thought that comes into their heads, continue in almost random fashion, until they run out of ideas. The end result is a paper that has no beginning, and no end, and often consists of one long paragraph. The report is to be structured logically using suitable subheads.

Balance

Balancing the presentation requires judgment on matters like length, content and emphasis. The situation analysis should be elaborate and complete. The problem statement should be brief; it rarely runs to more than one or two sentences.

Focus

The recommendations section should be relatively short and concise. This is not a place to evaluate the facts or to hedge your position.

Length

There is no optimum length for a written case analysis. It depends on the amount of data provided in the case and the preferences of the instructor. The report should be long enough to adequately cover the subject but not so long as to bore the instructor and the class.

Grammatical

It is fairly obvious that written reports must be neat, legible and free of errors in grammar and spelling. Business professors are not hired to teach English composition, but they do expect certain minimum standards of performance in written expression. Their standards for written work are reflections of what the business community expects from college graduates.

Clarity

The presentation should be simple and illustrative. Using models for depicting the situation and statistical tools for analyzing and presenting information, will go a long way in enhancing clarity of the reports.

EFFECTIVE CASE ANALYSES

In this section, features of a good case analysis are discussed. They serve two purposes:

1. Direct students in producing good case analysis.
2. Aid instructors in evaluating the case reports.

A student may be intelligent, enthusiastic and participative in decision making. Yet, he may fail in producing good case analysis, if he or she has no clear idea as to what constitutes a good case analysis. While there are no right and wrong answers to the case, there is definitely a right way of thinking based on ones own logic. A sort of checklist is therefore necessary, to guide the students in making a good case analysis.

The checklist also helps instructors to evaluate either an oral or written case analysis. Without a checklist, there can be no common understanding between the instructor and the student on what is to be expected of a case analysis.

The important features of a good case analysis are:

(i) *Complete*—in understanding, analysis, and solution.

(ii) *Objective*—avoids rehash or repetition.

(iii) *Realistic*—imaginative with reference to attainable objectives; constructively chooses an appropriate course of action with reference to constraints.

(iv) *Creative*—generates alternatives beyond normal thinking.

(v) *Critical*—questions the situation and inferences and argues in different ways. Discusses pros and cons of alternatives. Tries to destroy alternative solutions.

(vi) *Logical*—entire thought process has a sequence, and approach in using intuitive, scientific and creative thinking methods. As a result inferences, assumptions, alternatives and decisions sound logical in the frame-work of thinking adopted by the student.

(vii) *Clear*—presentation is simple, methodical, and easy to understand. It does not confuse problems with symptoms and opportunities to taking actions.

(viii) *Analytical*—makes effective data classifications and computations and presents analysis with the help of suitable presentation techniques.

EVALUATION OF CASE ANALYSES

While you are presenting a case analysis for academic assignments, you may have another opportunity to improve your analysis. In business, however, a 'second chance' may not be forth-coming, particularly, when a market estimate is based on inaccurate use of figures, or when your recommendations are couched in hazy, ambiguous language so that a special order is unnecessarily delayed. A temporary transition from the position of 'analyst' to one of 'evaluator' will allow the student to develop some appreciation of those points which determine satisfactory analyses. Exhibit 1.2 presents such evaluation questions.

Exhibit 1.2 Self Evaluation of Case Analysis

- Is the central problem, well defined? Are the objectives well stated? Are the criteria for attaining objectives identified?
- Have you presented sufficient evidence to support your analysis convincingly?
- Have you utilized evidence which supports positions other than your own?
- Did you examine the reliability of the evidence you used?
- Did you draw sound conclusions from the case evidence?.
- Are your interpretations free from bias and subjectivity?
- Have you explored the significance of the evidence you consider?
- Have you avoided making contradictory statements?
- Did you make clear the relative weight or importance which you attached to the evidence that you considered?
- Have you been decisive throughout your analysis?
- Have you adequately used the available quantitative evidence?
- Have you taken advantage of the useful possibilities for reworking the quantitative data?
- Did you use the right method of analysis and computation?
- Did you recognise the main elements of the situation?
- Have you demonstrated the relationships of the major elements?
- Did you reach a definite decision?
- Does your decision follow from analysis?
- Have you spelled out your recommendations with sufficiently complete directions?
- Have you considered other possibilities?
- Have you considered the various important effects of your recommended action?

A teacher may use the case evaluation sheet given in Exhibit 1.3 for rating the case analysis done by the students. This is based on the steps involved in case analysis. Alternatively, or as a complement to this, a teacher may employ the evaluation sheet useful for rating oral or written presentation of case analysis given in Exhibit 1.4.

Exhibit 1.3 Case Analysis Evaluation Sheet

Title of the Case:
Name of the Student:
Course: Roll No:

S. No	Criteria	Rating		
1.	Analysis of situation	A	B	C
2.	Statement of objectives and constraints	A	B	C
3.	Formulation of central problem	A	B	C
4.	Generation of alternatives	A	B	C
5.	Evaluation of alternatives	A	B	C
6.	Selection of alternative-Reaching decision	A	B	C
7.	Action plan for implementation of decision.	A	B	C
	Overall Appraisal	A	B	C

A: Good B: Average C: Poor

Date: Signature of Evaluator

Exhibit 1.4 Case Report or Presentation Evaluation

Title of the Case:
Name of the Student:
Course: Roll No.:

S. No	Criteria	Rating		
1.	Objective	A	B	C
2.	Realistic	A	B	C
3.	Creative	A	B	C
4.	Critical	A	B	C
5.	Logical	A	B	C
6.	Analytical	A	B	C
7.	Clear	A	B	C
8.	Structured	A	B	C
9.	Balanced	A	B	C
10.	Grammatical	A	B	C
11.	Length of presentation	A	B	C
	Overall Appraisal	A	B	C

A: Good B: Average C: Poor

Date: Signature of Evaluator

Limitation

The actual results achieved by case method have not always equalled what seems theoretically possible for students to learn. The following factors may be responsible for the gap between expectations and accomplishments.

(i) *Slow learning process* Progress in developing administrative skills is slow among students and the teacher may feel thwarted, especially in the early periods of introduction of case method. It takes time to gain a foothold on the hardway of learning through this experiential method.

(ii) *Low maturity levels of participants* The assumption that a student has a basic knowledge of facts as well as maturity and a readiness for acceptance of responsibility is not right at least for some time.

(iii) *Oversimplified real life situation* A case is a snap shot of a situation. It captures the events and presents an episodic version of them. As such, the dynamic, evolving situation is fitted in a framework or defined boundaries. Also, the situation, which may be vague in reality may be improved in clarity by the case writer, with the addition of assumptions or facts. As such students end up learning how to act in a defined situation.

The different approaches to case analysis have their own limitations.

(A) Solitary case analysis:

1. *Inadequate preparation* Many people don't like to think by themselves, for hours at a time, a level of concentration is required. Even students at school, skip such home work, if they are expected to do it entirely alone.
2. *Inability to think clearly* Many people face difficulty in clarifying vague impressions and unformulated ideas when thinking solitarily. In order to think clearly they wish to communicate with someone preferably, in a face-to-face talk.
3. *Lopsided view* When any one studies a case by himself or herself, he or she is likely to be unaware of the prejudices and preconceptions that slant his or her view in some places, and shut it off in other places.

(B) Group discussion:

(i) *Intellectual* No one can give his or her whole attention simultaneously to several kinds of mental activity. Many find it distracting to alternate rapidly between listening to others, interpreting what is said, thinking out their own opinion, and expressing it.

(ii) *Time* Time during which a whole group can work together is too short to permit any one to get all the food for thought, that is provided by a case.

(iii) *Psychological* The personality differences of individuals can be another source of limitation. An aggressive person may try to impose his ideas on others by not allowing others to express their views. An introvert finds it difficult to think out loud in public. Some think faster than others. Some may be less capable and may worry about the idea that whatever they say won't compare well with what other people contribute. Some may be dogmatic and try to stall the discussion to win their point.

FINAL WORD

Like any pedagogical tool, case method has its own advantages and limitations. It requires a wise teacher, committed students, good cases and suitably furnished class room, to be a potent tool of learning.

REFERENCES

1. A N Whitehead, *The Aims of Education and other Essays*, The Macmillan Co., New York, 1929, p.58.
2. Writer Bynner, *The Way of Life According to Latzu; An American Version*, John Day Co., New York, 1944, pp. 34–35.
3. Hinkle L. Charles and Stineman F. Esther, *Cases in Marketing Management,* Prentice Hall Inc., New Jersey, 1984.
4. O 'Dell, Ruppes, Trent, Kehoe, *Marketing Decision Making—Analytic Frame Work and Cases Manual,* South Western Pub. Co., USA, 1984.
5. Greer V. Thomas, *Cases in Marketing: Orientation, Analysis and Problems,* Macmillan Pub. Co., Inc., New York, 1979.

6. Bernhandt L. Kenneth and Kinnear C. Thomas, *Cases in Marketing Management,* Business Pub. Inc., Texas, 1981.
7. Gross W. Charles and Peterson T. Robin, *Marketing,* West Pub. Co., New York, 1987.
8. Boyd, Westfall and Stasch, *Marketing Research: Text and Cases*, Richard D. Irwin, Inc., Illinois, 1985.
9. Shan and Semenik, *Marketing,* South Western Pub. Co., Ohio, 1985.

CHAPTER 2

Marketing Decisions and Models

As Paul Mazur very rightly described "Marketing's role is delivery of standard of living to people in the society". A simple marketing system may be as shown in Figure 2.1.

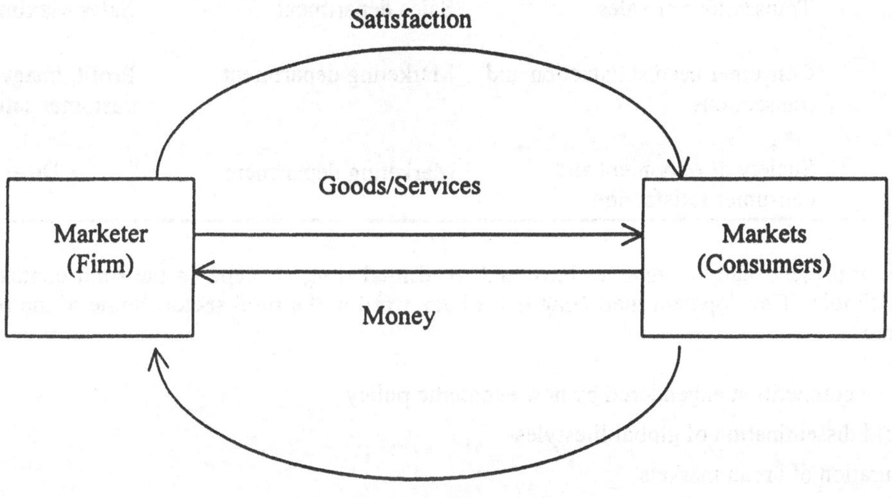

Fig. 2.1 A Simple Marketing System

TASKS AND GOALS

Marketing is essentially demand management. The task of marketer is to proact and react to the different demand situations. (Table 2.1)

Table 2.1 Types of Marketing

Situation	*Types of Marketing*
Latent demand	Creative marketing
Unwholesome demand	Demarketing, Social marketing
Negative demand	Conversion marketing
No demand	Stimulational marketing
Regular demand	Aggressive marketing
Irregular demand	Syncho marketing

When undertaking marketing, a firm has to consider its philosophy. Five philosophical alternatives are identified in practice. Table 2.2 depicts them.

Table 2.2 Marketing Orientations

Concept	*Key Tasks*	*Marketing Organisation*	*Major Goal*
Production	Distribution	Part of production	Profit
Product	R&D, Design	Part of production	Image
Selling	Transactions or sales	Sales department	Sales Maximisation
Marketing	Consumer need satisfaction and transactions	Marketing department	Profit, image and customer satisfaction
Societal	Society development and consumer satisfaction	Marketing department	-- Do --

In India, at present many companies have embraced marketing concept. In the rural context, societal concept is desirable. Development marketing is the buzz word in the rural sector. Some of the reasons for this change are:

- Fierce competition engendered by new economic policy
- Rapid dissemination of global lifestyles
- Saturation of urban markets
- Emergence of rural markets with new expectations and raising standard of living.

Contemporary marketing makes organisations integrated within and with the environment. It is a coordinated marketing comprising two functions and one single goal viz., customer satisfaction.

(i) Internal marketing—It is the task of successfully developing people within the organization to serve customers.

(ii) External marketing—It is the task of offering products and services that satisfy individual needs and wants.

Coordinated marketing requires integration at two levels:

(1) Integration of various functions of marketing.

(2) Integration of marketing with other departments.

GOALS AND CONCERNS

Depending upon the opportunities and individual ambitions, companies may pursue one or more of the marketing goals as shown in Table 2.3.

Table 2.3 Goals of Marketing

Enterprise Goals	*Marketing Goals*
Profitability	• Sales revenue maximization • Cost minimization
Growth	• Sales growth maximization • Product development • Market penetration • Market development • Diversification
Market Standing	• Innovation • Market leadership • Consumer satisfaction
Image	• Brand image • Company image

The environmental factors or stake holders' concerns which influence marketing decisions are illustrated in Table 2.4.

Table 2.4 Marketing Environments

Socio-cultural	— Consumers and their preferences
Politico-legal	— Government policies and legislation
Technological	— R&D labs, science and technology associations and their innovations
Economic	— Competitors, suppliers, channel members, industry associations and business concerns, Government's economic policies, savings, consumptions, investments and employment levels

The environmental factors or stake holders' concerns may positively or negatively affect marketing decisions. Companies are gearing up to improve their effectiveness in the new environment of change and challenge. They are moving away from the conventional practices as highlighted in Table 2.5

Table 2.5 Responses to Challenges

S.No.	*Aspect*	*From*	*To*
1	Reengineering	Focus on functional departments	Key processes in organization and multi-discipline teams
2	Bench marking	Reliance on self-improvement	Study world class performers and adopt best practices
3	Total Quality Management	Quality control in select areas	Total quality is a company wide programme
4	Outsourcing	A physical company making every thing inside	A virtual company making everything outside
5	E-commerce	Attracting customers to stores and selling standardized products	Attracting customers to internet and delivering direct customized products
6	Alliances	Playing alone	Partnership teams
7	Supply chain	Many retailers, loosely controlled, less reliable intermediaries	Few retailers, closely controlled, highly reliable partners
8	Marketing	Transaction marketing, long range commercial relationship with focus on satisfaction	Relationship marketing, long range socio-commercial relationship with focus on delight and welfare
9	Markets	National—urban markets and exports	National—rural and global market

ORGANISING

Modern marketers find alternative approaches to design the structures of their organisations. Table 2.6 presents such alternative structures. Depending upon the benefit desired one can choose simple or hybrid structures.

Table 2.6 Marketing Organisation Structures

Type	*Key Benefit*
Function	Functional specialisation
Territory	Wider distribution
Product	Product management
Customer	Major accounts management
Project	Independent works management
Matrix	Benefits of function and project types

STRATEGIC MARKETING

Mckinsey 7-s frame work is a useful tool for marketers to initiate competitive decisions. The seven Ss are:

- Shared values
- Strategy
- Structure
- Systems
- Staff
- Skills
- Style

Strategic planning is a process of designing a plan of action to maintain viable organization-environment fit reactively, actively or proactively with changing situations. It involves two levels of activity.

Corporate Planning

- Defining the corporate mission
- Identifying company's strategic business units (SBUs)
- Evaluating the current portfolio businesses
- Scouting for new business arenas to enter

Business Strategic Planning

- Defining the mission of businesses
- Analyzing the external environment
- Analyzing the internal environment
- Goal formulation
- Strategy formulation
- Program formulation
- Implementation

The evaluation of SBUs can be done with the help of portfolio models like BCG Matrix and GEC Model presented in Figure 2.2 and Figure 2.3 respectively.

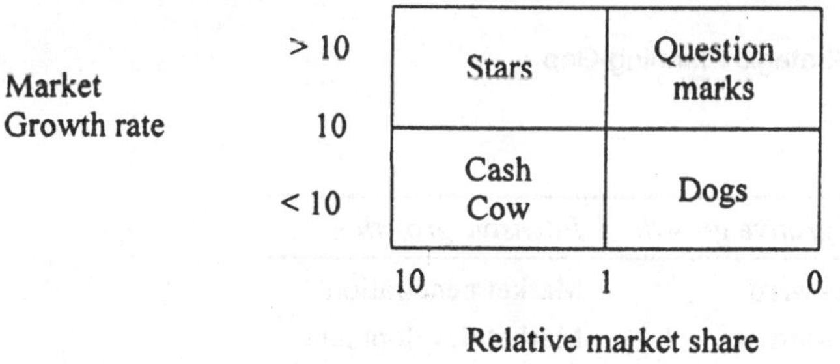

Fig. 2.2 BCG Matrix

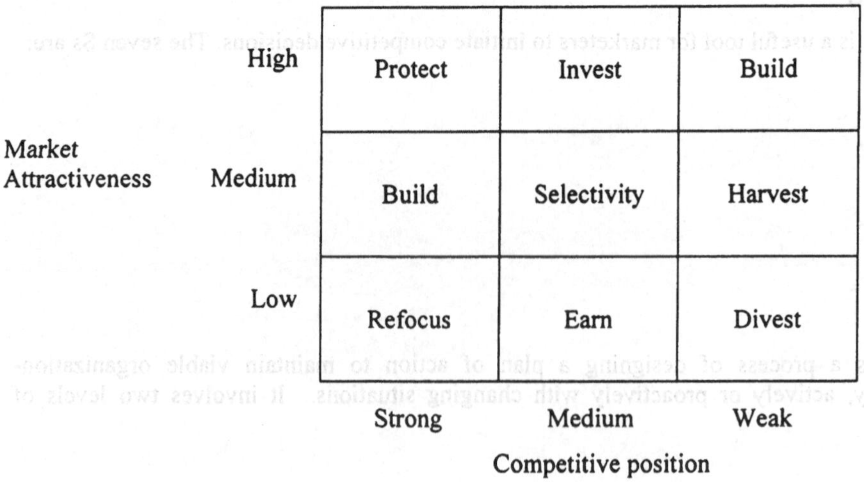

Fig. 2.3 GEC Model

Strategic planning gap can be identified depending upon the portfolio analysis as shown in Figure 2.4. The growth strategies that a company may adopt are listed in Table 2.7.

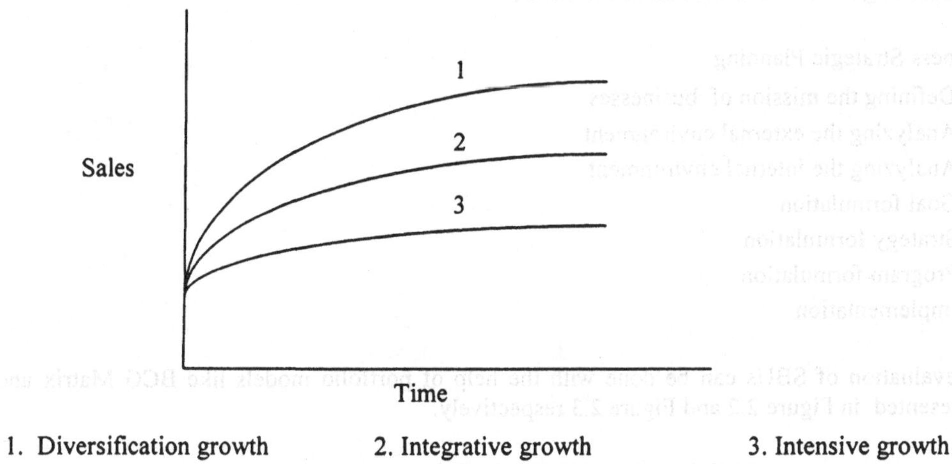

Fig. 2.4 Strategic Planning Gap

Table 2.7 Growth Strategies

Diversification growth	*Integrative growth*	*Intensive growth*
Concentric	Backward	Market penetration
Horizontal	Forward	Market development
Conglomerate	Horizontal	Product development

Strategic planning requires environmental scanning for opportunity or threat identification and internal environmental analysis to know strengths and weaknesses.

Opportunity	— attractive arena; actions here give advantages
Threat	— dangerous arena; actions here avoid failures
Strength	— a performance capability of importance
Weakness	— a performance incapability of importance

Categorizing opportunities, threats, strengths and weakness can be done by using models given in Figures 2.5, 2.6 and 2.7. I, II, III and IV indicate priorities in descending order of importance. Based on SWOT analysis, strategies are formulated, resources are allocated and implementation programmes are designed.

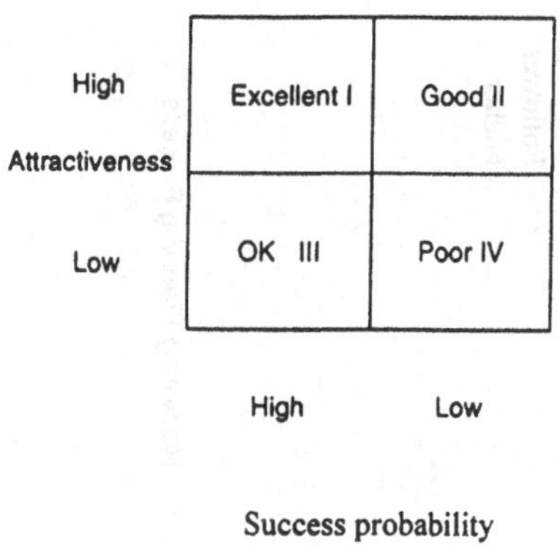

Fig. 2.5 Opportunity Matrix

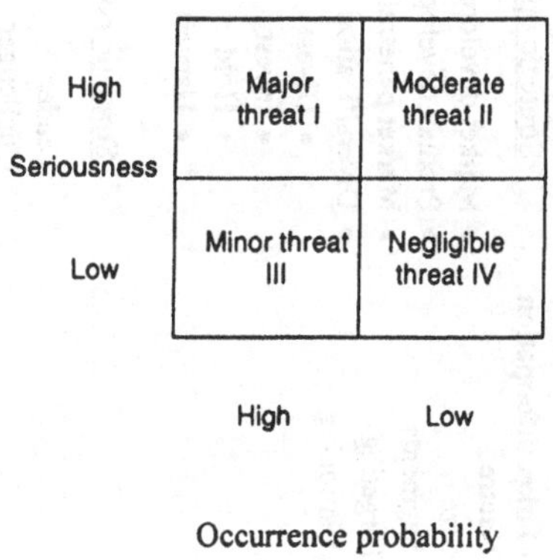

Fig. 2.6 Threat Matrix

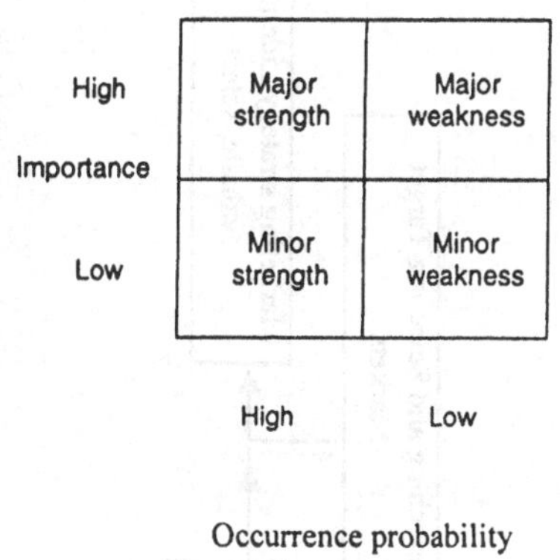

Fig. 2.7 Performance - Importance Matrix

MARKETING PLANNING

The marketing plan or strategy formulation is a rigorous, complex exercise and demands holistic or systemic thinking. Figure 2.8 depicts the planning process and related factors.

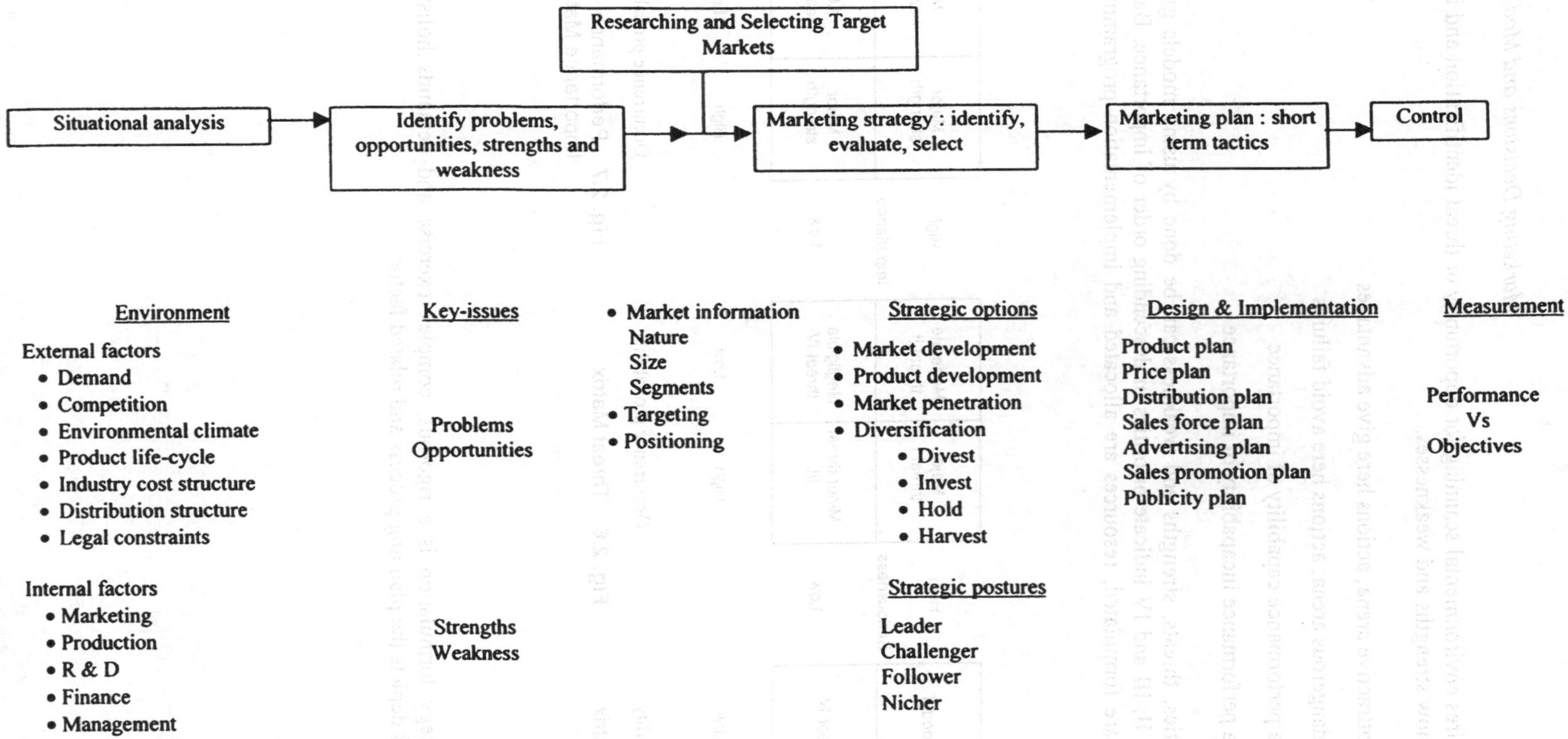

Fig. 2.8 Marketing Planning Process

SELECTING AND ATTRACTING MARKETS

A firm has to activate its marketing information system to get information from multiple sources. If such a system is not in operation, it should formalize and design an effective marketing information system. A typical marketing information system consists of four subsystems. Table 2.8 briefly describes them.

Table 2.8 Marketing Information System

Subsystem	*Information*
Internal Reporting System	Internal reports as orders, sales, deliveries, inventories, credit sales, etc. It is data on events occurred and results obtained.
Marketing Intelligence System	Information about relevant events or development external to the firm. The sources are news papers, magazines, journals and other publications, conferences, exhibitions, meetings, etc.
Marketing Research System	Systematic investigation of information about a phenomenon specific to marketing situation. Desk or field research, own research or through agency.
Decision Support System	A coordinated set of models and procedures with supporting computer software and hardware.

Marketing research may be necessary sometimes. When available information is not enough to make a decision, marketing manager has to employ marketing research. The important considerations are:

(i) Do we get the needed information, if we commission marketing research?
(ii) What is the value of information?
(iii) Is the value of information more than the costs of marketing research?

A cost-benefit analysis to assess value of information by research is to be done. Bayesian Analysis effectively serves the purpose of budgeting the research. The steps in marketing research process and the useful tools are given in Table 2.9.

Table 2.9 Marketing Research Process and Tools

S. No	*Steps*	*Task*	*Tools*
1	Problem definition	Identify and define problem	Funneling or narrow down method. Problem audit. Background Analysis. Situation analysis. Model development.
2	Research budget	Allocation of funds	Intuition. Expected value approach (Bayesian Analysis)
3	Research design	Choosing one of the designs • Exploratory	Survey, observation, case method, experiments.

		• Descriptive • Casual	
4	Sampling design	Random samples Non-random samples	Tippets numbers. Population lists. Geography maps.
5	Data collection	Designing instrument and field work	Questionnaire, interview, observation, etc., Scaling techniques, ladder, images, colours.
6	Data analysis	Classification analysis and interpretation	Averages, variances, Index numbers, growth rates, tests of significance .
7	Report writing and presentation	Presentation of findings and conclusions	Report formats, presentation aids like tables, graphs, diagrams and equipment like OHP and LCD projector.

Once markets are identified, the next step is demand forecasting. The useful techniques are:

- Survey of buyers' intentions
- Composite of sales force opinions
- Expert opinion
- Market-test method
- Time series analysis

Demand estimation will be followed by market coverage decision. The choice lies between two alternatives.

- Mass marketing
- Target marketing

Target marketing requires segmentation of the markets. Market segmentation variables include:

- Geographic (Region, country, state, etc.)
- Demographic (Sex, age, marital status, education, income, etc.)
- Psychographic (Social class, life style, personality)
- Behavioural (Occasions, usage rate, benefits, loyalty)

A firm may decide to cover one or all segments like rural and urban, high and low income groups, male or female or family. When dealing with more than one segment, one important decision is related to ways of marketing as shown in Figure 2.9.

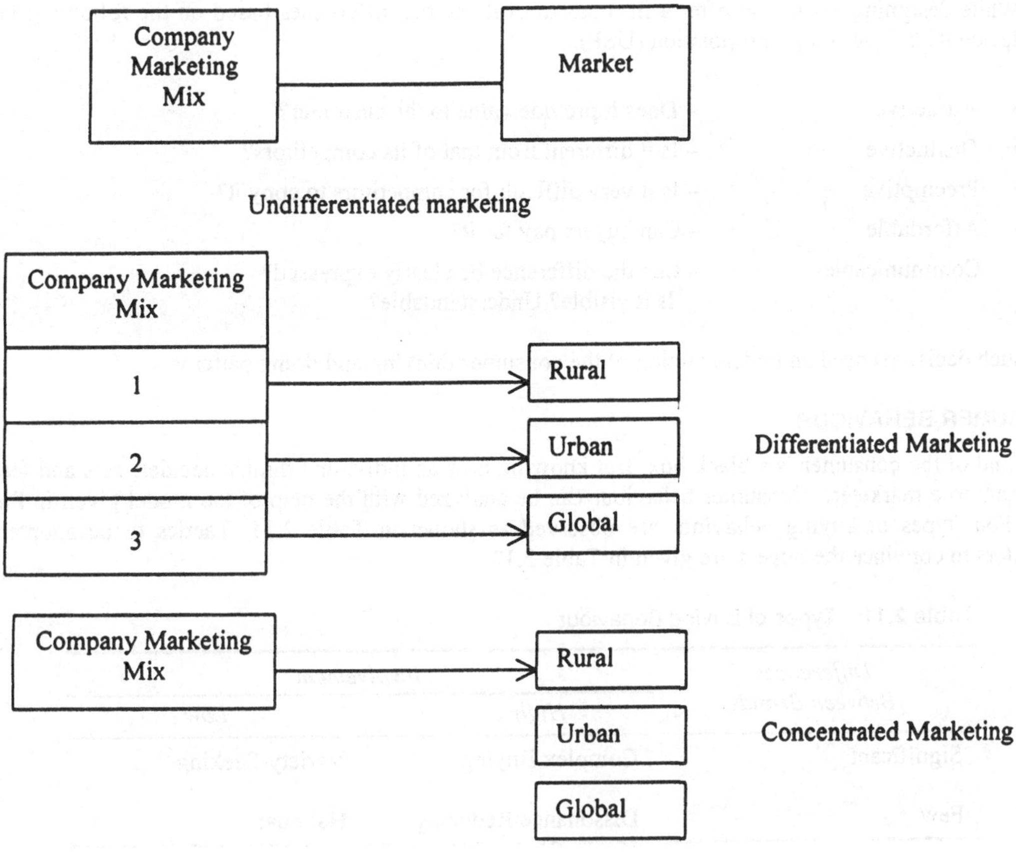

Fig. 2.9 Types of Coverage Strategies

The choice of the strategy is decided taking into consideration the resources, product and market. Table 2.10 explains how they influence the choice.

Table 2.10 Coverage Strategies

Variable	*Strategy*		
	Undifferentiated	*Differentiated*	*Concentrated*
Company resources	Moderate	Large	Limited
Product variability	Less	More	Less
Product life-cycle stage	Introduction	Growth	Introduction
Market variability	Less	High	High

While designing marketing offer a firm has to evaluate the differences based on the following factors and decide its unique selling proposition (USP).

- Attractive – Does it provide value to the customer?
- Distinctive – Is it different from that of its competitors?
- Preemptive – Is it very difficult for competitors to copy it?
- Affordable – Can buyers pay for it?
- Communicable – Can the difference be clearly expressed? Is it visible? Understandable?

Such decisions need an understanding of the consumer thinking and doing patterns.

CONSUMER BEHAVIOUR

The mind of the consumer is a black box. But knowing how an individual thinks, decides, acts and feels is important to a marketer. Consumer behaviour can be analyzed with the help of the model given in Figure 2.10. Four types of buying behaviour are observed as shown in Table 2.11. Tactics to be adopted by marketers to convince the buyers are given in Table 2.12.

Table 2.11 Types of Buying Behaviour

Differences Between Brands	*Involvement*	
	High	*Low*
Significant	Complex Buying	Variety-Seeking
Few	Dissonance Reducing	Habitual

Table 2.12 Buying Behaviours and Marketer Tactics

Types of Buying Behaviour	*Tactics*
Complex	Differentiate features, educative comparative ads, training retailers or sales force.
Dissonance Reducing	Convincing communications with statistics of buyers and endorsements, service, good relationships.
Habitual	Low price, sales promotion, repetitive ads, image by symbols, USP, unique features.
Variety Seeking	Wide distribution, window display, sales promotion.

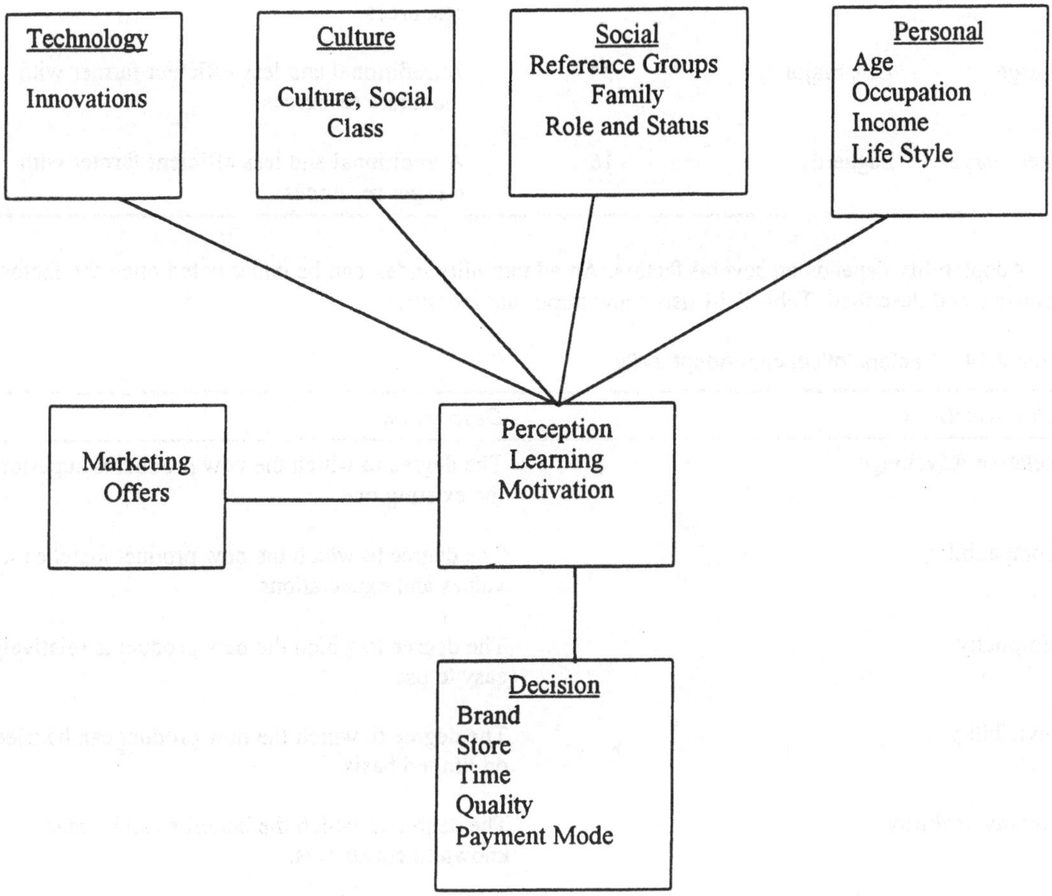

Fig. 2.10 Model of Buying Behaviour

The next question is : How do people adopt innovations? Table 2.13 shows different adopter groups as identified by Rogers.

Table 2.13 Adopter Groups

Time Lag in Adoption	*Groups*	*Percentage*	*Probable Consumer*
No	Innovator	2.5	A farmer, better educated and more efficient
Very less	Early adopter	13.5	An educated and efficiency conscious farmer with adequate resources

Less	Early majority	34	A hesitant but adaptive farmer with moderate resources
Large	Late majority	34	A traditional and less efficient farmer with moderate resources
Very large	Laggards	16	A traditional and less efficient farmer with meager resources

Adoptability depends on several factors. An adoptability index can be constructed once the factors are identified and described. Table 2.14 lists some important measures.

Table 2.14 Factors Influencing Adoptability

Characteristics	*Description*
Relative Advantage	The degree to which the new product is superior to the existing one.
Compatibility	The degree to which the new product matches with values and expectations.
Simplicity	The degree to which the new product is relatively easy to use.
Divisibility	The degree to which the new product can be tried on limited basis.
Communicability	The degree to which the benefits can be made known to consumers.
Affordability	The degree of economy in initial outlay and maintenance costs.
Social Approval	The degree to which it will gain social or community acceptance.

POSITIONING

Depending upon the consumer's attitudes and expectations in each segment, the firm has to develop appropriate product features and communicate them effectively to the consumers. The act of designing the offer to place it in the mind of the consumer and attract him to try the product is called positioning. Many positions are available to a firm. Marketers have been found to resort to more subtle ways to draw distinctions among different options available, such distinctions are identifiable with the help of perceptual maps–which portray positions of the competitors' brands in the mind of consumers in relation to two or more attributes. Figure 2.11 illustrates a typical perceptual map.

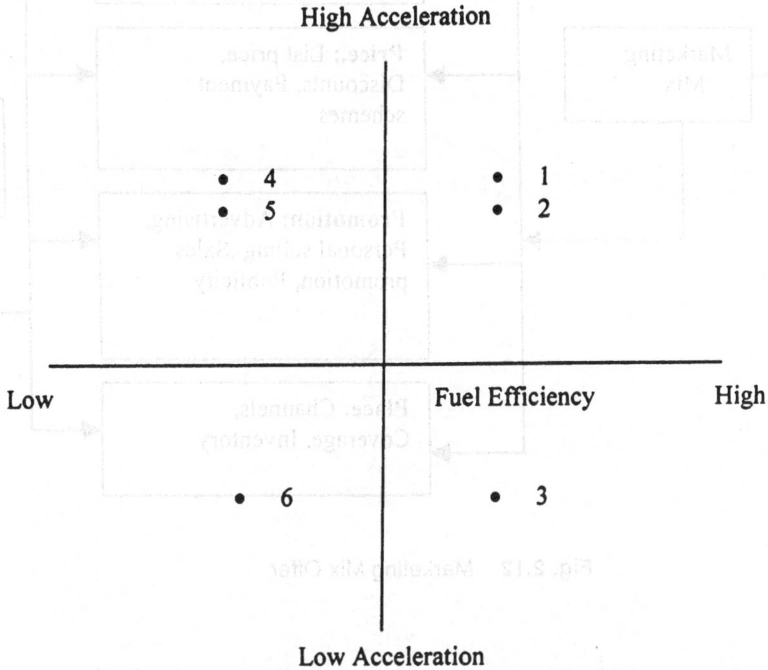

1. Hero Honda
2. Kawasaki Bajaj
3. Suraj
4. Yezdi 350
5. Bullet
6. Fury

Fig. 2.11 Perceptual Map

MARKETING MIX

Finally, the marketer has to formulate a marketing mix strategy. It is a set of marketing tools that the firm uses to pursue its marketing objectives in the target market. Marketing mix components are depicted in Figure 2.12.

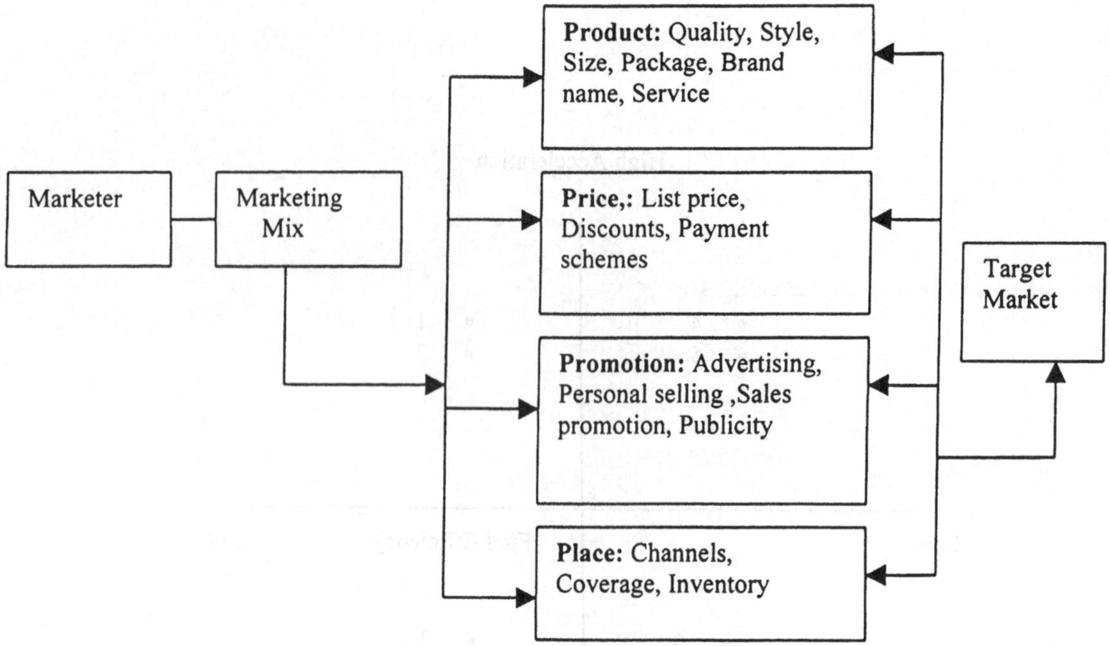

Fig. 2.12 Marketing Mix Offer

PRODUCT

We will now examine the decisions in each marketing mix element. A product is any tangible or intangible offer made by marketers to satisfy human needs and wants. The key decisions are:

(i) What should be our product item, product line and product mix?

(ii) Is there a need to change the product or product line or product mix?

Various product strategies adopted at the three levels are given in Table 2.15.

Table 2.15 Product Decisions

Level	*Strategy*
Product Mix	Width extension—New product lines Length extension—New product items Depth extension—New product variants
Product Line	Stretching—Upward, downward, both ways Line pruning, and Line modernization
Product Item	Quality, Features, Design, Brand and Package

Individual product decisions pertain to four aspects–attributes, branding, packaging and labelling. Table 2.16 identifies relevant questions for decision makers to understand the intricacies of product item decision.

Table 2.16 Product Item Decision

S. No	*Decision area*	*Questions*
1	Attributes	
	Quality	What is the level of quality? What are the performance criteria?
	Features	How many? What?
	Design	How much attractive? How much useful? How good the appearance?
2	Branding	Should we brand the product? How to name the brand? What procedure is to be followed? What should be the brand name? Which options to use—Individual vs family vs private? Is brand extension good?
3	Packaging	Material, size, shape, colour, text, brand name, trade marks, etc.
4	Labelling	Type of identification, description and grading information.

Next aspect that draws the attention of marketers is the product line. The key decision areas are given in the following Table 2.17.

Table 2.17 Product Line Decision

S. No	*Decision Area*	*Questions*
1	Line length	Should it be short or long?
2	Line stretching	Do we need downward or upward stretch? Or two way stretch?
3	Line filling	Do we need a line filler?
4	Line modernisation	Is our line outdated? Does it need modernisation?
5	Line featuring	Is it good if we promote our line with a flagship brand? If yes, which one?
6	Line pruning	Is our product line redundant? Does it need pruning to be effective? If yes, which items are to be dropped or modified?

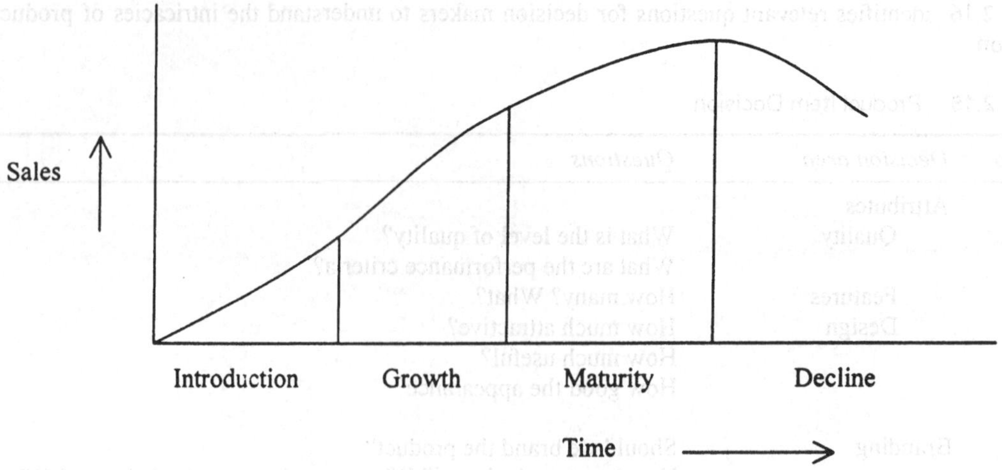

Fig. 2.13 Product Life-Cycle

Product decisions are dynamic. There is a need to continuously track the performance of the product at the market place and change the product to achieve right product-market fit. There are two tools in this regard.

(i) Product life-cycle

(ii) Customer satisfaction audit

Product life-cycle presents the four stages of product life, known as introduction, growth, maturity and decline as shown in Figure 2.13. The strategies that can be adopted at different stages of product life-cycle are discussed in Table 2.18.

Table 2.18 Product Life-Cycle Strategies

Introduction (Slow rise in sales)	A basic product, warranties, skimming or penetration price, selective distribution, advertisement to create awareness and sales promotion to entice trials
Growth (Quick rise in sales)	Product extensions or improvements, service, price changes competitively, intensive distribution, interest generating advertisements, and normal sales promotion to offset competition
Maturity (Slow rise in sales)	Diversify brands and models, competitive pricing, intensive distribution, advertising to create differentiation, sales promotion to encourage brand switching and promote user loyalty
Decline (Fall in sales)	Drop weak ones, low price to milch the cow, selective distribution, minimal advertising and sales promotion

The second important weapon in the armory of marketer to assess performance of a product is customer satisfaction audit. For this purpose, data are to be piled up through several methods. Some of them are listed here.

- Set up complaint and suggestion boxes.
- Gather consumer opinions immediately after service.
- Encourage correspondence.
- Read consumer opinions and reports in the media.
- Conduct satisfaction surveys.
- Make lost customer analysis—how many shifted and why?

When existing products are found vulnerable, a decision to develop and introduce new products becomes inevitable. Initially the decision focuses on:

- Modifying existing product and offer it to the existing market. (say urban)
- Introducing existing product in the new markets. (say rural)
- Developing a new product for the existing markets. (say urban)
- Developing a new product for new markets. (say rural)

New product development is a socio-technical process and requires involvement of a team of R & D and marketing personnel. Eight stages in new product development process are briefly presented in Table 2.19.

Table 2.19 Product Development Process

S. No	*Step*	*Tools*
1	Idea Generation	Attribute listing, Forced relationships Brainstorming, Synectics
2	Idea Screening	Product idea rating devices
3	Concept Development and Testing	Panel research, Focus group interview
4	Marketing Strategy Development	SWOT analysis, Perceptual maps
5	Business Analysis	Demand forecasting techniques, Cost-volume-profit analysis (a break-even technique), Capital budgeting tools, Projected income statements, Risk analysis, etc.
6	Product Development	Functional tests in laboratory, Consumer testing in firms or homes. (Scaling techniques)
7	Market Testing	Sales wave research. Simulated store technique.
8	Commercialisation	Controlled test marketing. Test marketing.

COMPETITIVE PRODUCT STRATEGIES

Several strategies are being developed by marketers. An illustrative list is given below.

(i) Leader

- Product innovation strategy
- Quality improvement strategy
- Multi-brand strategy
- Brand extension strategy
- Superior service strategy
- Image building strategy

(ii) Challenger

- Cheaper goods strategy
- Prestige goods strategy
- Economy goods strategy, and
- Reacting or proacting in the above strategies of a leader on a high or moderate level

(iii) Follower

- Innovative imitation strategy, and
- Other strategies of leader and challenger in a low profile

(iv) Nicher

- High/low quality strategy
- Narrow product line
- Superior service, and
- Indifference to other companies as none of them is a competitor.

The following strategies are for the consideration of rural marketers.	
• Identity strategies	Commodity strategy Branding strategy
• Innovation strategies	Rural-urban common Special for rural
• Customer value strategy	Mass product strategy Premium product strategy

• Quality strategies	Quality improvement strategy Spurious goods strategy
• Packaging strategies	Small unit packing
• Brand strategies	Brand extension strategy Multi-brand strategy Co-branding strategy Brand image/Equity management

PRICING

A price represents the market value of the product or service. Pricing is a key decision, as it is the major determinant of demand for a product and its sales revenues. Pricing objectives fall into four categories as shown in Table 2.20.

Table 2.20 Pricing Objectives

Objective	Types
Profit	Profit maximization. Target profit
Sales	Gain market share Growth in absolute sales Growth in market share Minimum sales necessary to survive Maintenance of sales volume or market share
Competition	Meet or prevent competition. Destroy competition
Development	Gain market share

A pricing policy is a standing answer to recurring questions. A marketer finds himself in different situations based on product life-cycle and competitor's moves. Table 2.21 identifies some of the pricing situations.

Table 2.21 Pricing Situations

S. No	*Situation*	*Major Factors*	*Approach*	*Method*
1	New product introduction	Demand Elastic Inelastic	Cost-oriented Demand-oriented	Cost-plus or mark-up. Penetration, Skimming
2	Product life-cycle (short)	Cost Demand Competition	Cost-oriented	Payback/capital recovery, Rate of return
3	Growing markets, Moderate competition	Cost Demand	Cost-oriented	Cost plus, mark-up, Experience curve

4	Mature markets, Stiff competition	Competition	Competition-oriented	Leader pricing, Competitive, pricing (bidding)
5	Growing/mature markets, Discerning buyers	Demand	Demand-oriented	Discriminatory, Differential, Perceived value, Psychological, Value pricing
6	Product-mix promotion	Demand Cost Competition Image	Demand-oriented	Product-line, Optional feature, Captive product, Two-part, Product bundling
7	Distribution to scattered customers	Geographical Cost	Cost-oriented	Geographic pricing
8	Motivating channel	Competition Channel members	Competition-oriented	Discount pricing

In accordance with the situations and objectives different operational pricing approaches and methods are in use. Table 2.22 shows the approaches and relevant pricing methods.

Table 2.22 Pricing Methods

Approach	*Methods*
Cost-based	Cost plus, or mark-up, marginal cost, target return, payback method, experience curve.
Competition-based	Leader pricing, competitive pricing, going rate, sealed bid.
Demand-based	Discrimination, perceived-value, psychological, value satisfaction (Everyday low pricing)

Price decisions depend upon a host of factors. The most important ones are: competition, consumers, distribution and government. A brief presentation of their influence is made here.

Competition: Competitively, based on the actions and reactions of the competitors, pricing, decisions are taken as shown below.

Competitor's Decision	*Company's Reactions*	*Justification*
Rise	Rise	Matching; when costs are on the rise and demand is growing.
	Maintain	Value-conscious markets.
	Cut	Benefit of technology or large scale economies.

Maintenance	Rise Maintain Cut	When quality improvements are made. Match. Benefit of technology or large scale economies.
Cut	Rise Maintain Cut	Unusual. May be when quality improvements are made. Ignore considering the action of competitor as a desperate step. Appeal value-conscious market. Match.

Consumers: Based on the consumer groups, pricing and the other elements of marketing mix need vary.

Category	*Annual Income*	*Lifestyle*	*Price*
Quality Conscious	Over Rs. 1,50,001	Very rich	High
Value Conscious	Rs. 45,001–150,000	Consuming class	
		Climbers	Moderate
Price Conscious	Rs. 22,001–Rs. 45,000	Aspirants	
	Rs. 16,001–Rs. 2,000	Destitute	Low
	Between Rs. 16,000		

Distribution: Pricing decisions require consideration of channel members, their interests and gains in a competitive market. Companies have to evolve to pricing policies as shown below.

Geographical Pricing	FOB mill, uniform delivered pricing, zone pricing; base point pricing, volume discounts, trade discounts, payment terms
Discount Pricing	Seasonal reductions, promotional reductions

Government: Government policies and legislations influence pricing decisions.

- Legal provisions like display of prices on packages, and sales counters
- Fixation of price considering subsidies, taxes and duties.

PROMOTION

Promotion is an important element in marketing mix. It has two components—information and incentives. Information may have one or more of the tasks:

- Inform — explain and educate
- Convince — analyse and impress
- Persuade — argue and activate
- Remind — refresh memory

Incentives may be financial or non-financial. It may be, a one rupee off coupon, a low price for a specific period, buy one take one free, like offers involving financial benefits. It may also be mere messages that enrich possession value like "we congratulate your wise decision of buying......" "Great people think alike", etc. They satisfy recognition, status and achievement needs of individuals. The well known communication tools are listed in Table 2.23.

Table 2.23 Promotools

Advertising	Sales Promotion	Publicity	Personal Selling
Print ads	Contests	Press release	Sales presentations
Radio ads	Gifts	Speeches	Fairs
TV ads	Sampling	Seminars	Tradeshows
Slides	Coupons	Annual reports	*Melas*
Short films	Installment schemes	Donations	Exhibitions
Bill boards	Low-interest financing	Public relations	*Haats*
Display signs			
Pop displays			
Symbols and logos			

The designing of promotion-mix is a very challenging job. It involves the following steps.

1. Profiling Target Audience

Promotion is to be tailored to suit the maturity levels, interests and expectations of target consumer groups. For this, the marketer has to probe and profile the target audience. Probing can be done by market research and motivation research. Image of product or firm, familiarity with the product, buying intentions, etc may be measured. Familiarity–Favourability analysis is illustrated in Figure 2.14. The possible communication objectives are identifiable from this.

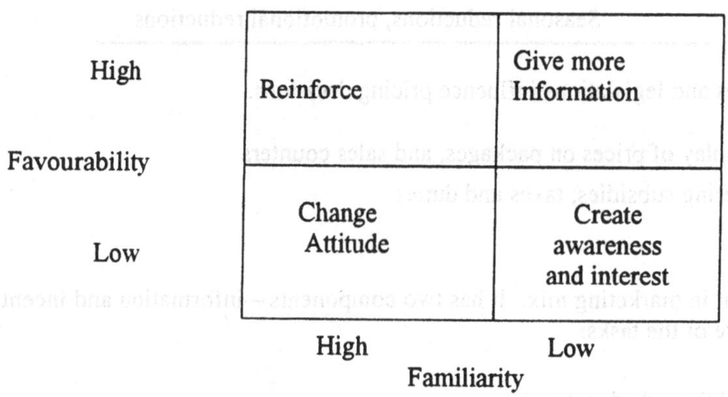

Fig. 2.14 Familiarity–Favourability Analysis

2. Determining Communication Objectives

The objectives can be defined by considering the cognitive, affective and behavioural response from the target audience. Here, the hierarchy models will be of help. Table 2.24 presents two such models.

Table 2.24 Promotion Models

Stages	AIDA model	Innovation Adoption model
Congnitive	Attention	Awareness
Affective	Interest Desire	Interest Evaluation
Behaviour	Action	Trial Adoption

3. Designing Message

Message is the vital part of the promotion as it requires creativity and technical competence. The decisions relate to the following aspects:

Message content	What to say? Rational, emotional, moral
Message structure	What is the logical order? Length or short, linear or non-linear
Message format	What is the arrangement? Layout and components, like picture, message, headline, logo, signature
Message source	Who should say? Celebrity, professional, common people

4. Selecting Communication Channel

Communication channels are of two types: Personal and non-personal. The non-personal media may further be categorised into local and mass media. How can one employ the media? Table 2.5 provides relevant information.

Table 2.25 Media Choices

Personal	Advocate	Sales people, social workers
	Expert	Professionals
	Social	Neighbours, friends, family members
Non-personal	Media	Print, TV, radio, direct mail, websites
	Atmosphere	Environment at sales point
	Events	Sports, music, festivals

Local media include cinema, hoardings, posters, video vans, leaflets, animal parade and transit media. (advertisements on carts, bullocks, buses, etc)

5. Establishing Budget

The funds required for implementing the promotional campaign can be determined using one of the following methods.

- All you can afford approach
- Percentage of sales method
- Competitive parity method
- Objective and task method

6. Deciding Promotion Mix

Distributing budget over the four promotools is a difficult task. Technically, it involves consideration of the following points:

(1) What are the objectives of the promotion?
(2) How much each one of the promotools individually and collectively can contribute to these objectives?

Politically, there will be a lot of bargaining. Since sound technical arguments are difficult to make, the decision may tilt favourably to the strong political side. Though expensive, experiments can lend credibility to one's arguments and aid in decision making.

7. Measuring Promotion Results

How effective the promotion has been? This is important to rationalize the promotion programme expenditure. Periodically, the results are to be monitored through correlations with sales data and opinion surveys of middlemen and consumers.

DISTRIBUTION

Several changes are taking place in the distribution philosophy and practices. Table 2.26 shows the trends.

Table 2.26 Distribution Trends

Element of Sales	*From*	*To*
Time	Restricted, limited timings	Unrestricted, anytime,
Place	Own retail outlet, occasionally public place for example, exhibitions	Anywhere
Choice	Limited to brands	Unlimited. Any product to any specification.
Sales	Products	Product's experiences, Relationships, Achievement
Result	Customer satisfaction	Customer participation and satisfaction

We will now take a look at the different levels of channels. Five levels are in vogue as shown in Table 2.27.

Table 2.27 Distribution Channels

Level	*Channel Measure*	*Place*
Level A	Company depot	National/State
Level B	Redistribution stockist, C&F agents, Semi-wholesalers and retailers	District headquarters *Tehsil* headquarters
Level C	Semi-wholesalers and retailers	Mofussil towns Industrial townships
Level D	Itinerant traders, Vans, Petrol bunks Semi wholesalers, retailers, Co-operative societies	*Haats* Large villages
Level E	Retailers, vans, sales people, NGOs, Government agencies	Villages

The players in the channels are

(1) Old – Wholesalers, retailers, vans, weekly *haats/bazaars/ shandies, melas* and fairs.

(2) New – Unofficial channels, cooperative society, public distribution system, agri-input dealers, NGOs, barefoot salesmen, syndicated distribution.

New approaches in distribution are:

(1) Relationship marketing
(2) Direct-to-Home selling
  - Network marketing
  - Internet marketing

The choice canvass, therefore, is very wide and exciting. Table 2.28 spreads the canvass.

Table 2.28 Distribution Choices

1.	Selling where? Home or work place	Door-to-door selling, mobile vans, mail order selling, tele-marketing
	Commercial places	Industrial exhibition, *haats/shandies*, fairs/*melas*
	Own place	*Malls*, super markets, showrooms/galleries, provision/fancy/

		kirana shops, medical stores, *paan* shops, cooperatives, petrolbunks, NGOs
	Anywhere	Internet selling
2.	Selling when?	Limited timings, anytime
3.	Selling who?	Company or its agents, syndicates, consumers
4.	Selling what?	Products and services Experiences Relationships Achievements Convenience
5.	Selling why?	Profit Images Business equity

CHANNEL DECISIONS

Deciding the type of channel, appointing channel members, and monitoring channel performance are the key tasks.

(1) Deciding the type of channel

Three alternative approaches merit consideration.

Type	*Coverage*	*Products*
Intensive	All outlets	Mass products like cigarettes, salt, beverages
Exclusive	Authorised showrooms, own retail shops, franchisees	Consumer durables like automobiles
Selective	Few outlets	Jewellery, greeting cards

(2) Selection of channel

Next decision pertains to selection of channels based on the following criteria:

Economic	– Level of sales and costs
Control	– Degree of commitment
Adaptivity	– Degree of flexibility

(3) Selecting channel members

After a company has chosen a channel alternative, individual middlemen must be selected. The selection depends on factors like years of experience, location, products handled, previous sales and profit record, solvency, cooperativeness, and reputation.

(4) Motivating channel members

Middlemen are to be motivated to perform their best. Motivation can be created by terms of appointment and enhanced by training, supervision and incentives.

(5) Evaluating channel members

The evaluation of channel members may consider the following factors.

- Sales—quota attainment
- Average inventory levels
- Treatment of damaged and lost goods
- Cooperation in company promotional and training programmes
- Customer service

CHAPTER

3

Rural Marketing

In a recent agro *mela* in a village near Delhi, the main attraction was small car giant Maruti and the Korean Daewoo much to the surprise of many participants. Stalls selling soaps, detergents and radios no longer hold the interest of rural buyers, who have shifted gear. And market men with drive are pushing their products in the dusty outback.

THE NEW MARKET

At a recent seminar on rural marketing, organised in New Delhi, by the International Development Enterprise, the speakers opined that the rural *bazaar* is displaying a market trend towards consumerism. The Indian rural tastes are changing fast, thereby reflecting a marked improvement in the purchasing power of village households. Rural incomes have changed drastically over the last few years, influencing market behaviour. The rural incomes are rising most probably because this sector is relatively free from direct taxes. In 1990–92 the lowest end of the rural market earned around Rs. 14,000 a year and today this segment's annual earning has shot up to around Rs. 24,000. Another emerging trend was the rural buyers' disenchantment for second-hand items, unless it was something like a radio, cassette recorder or a table fan.

Does the rural rush mean that urban market is slowing down? Some say it is. Others differ on this point. They argue that there has been a shift in demand not, a fall. In the past, rural purchases were made in urban markets, but now these purchases are made in rural markets.

NATURE OF MARKET

The market is characterised by 'large volumes but low margins'. High incomes combined with low cost of living in the villages have meant more money to spend. Sales volumes are growing rapidly but concurrently. Rural markets are also witnessing 'value growth'. That is, rural consumers are willing to go for premium brands in any product category. And with the market providing them options, tastes are also changing, old reliables like detergent cakes and single-edged blades have given way for detergent powders and twin blades. This slow but sure erosion of price sensitivity explains why shops have started stocking Whisper sanitary napkins, Kellogg's corn flakes and other premium products.

But the biggest problem in the rural market is the absence of a middle segment. There is a complete absence of middle class in the rural market. There are only the rich and the poor in the villages. The huge income disparity could well pose a problem for companies. They could exhaust the market potential sooner than they anticipate. In fact, in some product categories the penetration is already falling. For instance, the potential for colour TV sets in the lowest rural segment has already become negative (over 2 per cent, according to current NCAER reports), implying that stock penetration has peaked.

MARKET SIZE AND GROWTH

Gone are the days when companies used to consider rural sales a bonus to the total sales turnover. Today, markets are more than shoring up bottom lines. Exact figures are, however, hard to come by because a lot of sales is through retailers who buy from urban stockists making it difficult for most companies to keep track of product movement.

Estimates are that the rural market is growing twice as fast as the urban market for durable products like wrist-watches, fans, televisions, video cassette recorders, as also non-durables like nail polish, lipstick, ice-cream, shampoo and mosquito repellents witnessing a rise in sales of hitherto typical urban kitchen gadgets like refrigerators, mixer-grinders and pressure cookers. Among the items whose market share is on the rise in rural regions are colour and B&W television sets, cassette recorders, VCRs and VCPs, pressure cookers, ceiling and table fans, and sewing machines. Geysers, which had almost no takers in the countryside till the middle of 1980s, have made an inroad into this market with an estimated share of little less than 1 per cent.

Statistics presented at the meet assessed the market size for nail polish at around Rs. 270 million in rural areas as against only Rs. 81 million in the cities. Similarly, the market for lipsticks is worth around Rs. 250 million in rural areas, compared to only Rs. 131 million in the urban segment. Face cream demand in villages estimated at about 1,099 tonnes far outstrips that in the cities at about 426 tonnes, shampoo too has more potential in rural *bazaar* (about 2,257 tonnes) than urban markets (about 718 tonnes). The rural market for mosquito repellents is reckoned at around Rs. 173 million against a mere Rs. 79 million in urban centres.

Sales of Maruti have recorded a near hundred per cent jump in the countryside during 1996–97. Rural sales constituted more than 40 per cent of the combined sales for that year. VST's lowly-priced Charminar cigarettes continue to notch up impressive sales in the countryside. Thanks to the semi-urban market sales, the company managed a near 13.3 per cent market share by producing 1.36 billion cigarette sticks compared to market leader ITC's 6.89 billion sticks that guaranteed the Calcutta-based giant a whopping 67.4 per cent market share—more than 20 per cent of which is from the rural markets.

Asian Paints (more than 55 per cent market share) is experiencing a second revolution with the customers and these are customers from the countryside who have developed tastes matching that of the city for the 1,150 shades it is offering. Koshika plans to focus cellular services primarily on the country's rural belt. They have exclusive data that suggests more than 30 per cent of their customers are from the villages who have developed a certain taste and style.

The premium income from the eastern sector has been the highest among LIC's seven national zones. LIC has the largest number of agents deployed in the East. Almost 25 per cent of LIC's 7 lakh foot soldiers are in this region. LIC sold 39.56 lakh policies contributing a growth of 14.42 per cent in 2001–2002, about 25.15 per cent of this business from the East. Nearly 75 per cent of business in Eastern sector was from rural areas.

RURAL MARKET SEGMENTS

Rural market can be segmented using the concept of "urban orientation". Urban orientation is defined as the degree to which a rural consumer would like to replicate the urban lifestyle. The higher the urban orientation, the higher will be the requirements for goods and services consumed in urban India and vice versa.

Urban orientation will be influenced by connectivity and social links. Villages closer to the urban center will be higher on urban orientation as compared to far off villages. Similarly, villages connected by public transport will be higher on urban orientation as compared to villages not connected by public transport. Based on connectivity, villages can be divided into three groups (a) close to the urban centre (b) villages connected by public transport and (c) remote.

Social links are high when (a) incomes are high, (b) many of their relatives would have been staying in bigger cities/ metros for more than one generation and (c) they generally also send their children to bigger cities/ metros for education. They are medium when (a) incomes are high, (b) they are agriculture dependent, (c) they are the first generation to attain financial status, (d) relatives in urban centres would also be first generation migrants and (e) their children may go for studies in urban centers but the children are not completely detached from agriculture.

Table 3.1 Market Segments by Urban Orientation of Rurals

Physical Connectivity / *Social Links*	*Villages connected by local transport (Riksha, auto, city bus or local trains)*	*Villages connected by public transport (Bus or train)*	*Remote village (Not connected by public transport)*
High	Highest (Super premium goods)	High (Premium and value-for-money goods)	Moderate (Value-for-money goods)
Medium	High (Premium and value-for-money goods)	Moderate (Value-for-money goods)	Low (Duplicates)
Low	Moderate (Value-for-money goods)	Low (Duplicates)	Lowest (Not a market)

Broadly, the market can be segmented into three categories:

- Premium niche segment
- Premium and value-for-money segment
- Value-for-money segment

STRATEGIES

Several companies are drawing up strategies specifically for the rural markets. The most important aspect of the marketing mix in most of these categories is the value—the quality of the product and the price at which the quality is offered to consumers at the lower end. A-1 tea, Vendee edible oil (loose branded oil offered through vending machines), Vim, Lakhani footwear, Tiger biscuits, Haldirams, MTR snacks and Nirma detergent are some examples which have demonstrated the usefulness of the approach.

Product

Brand building and extensive distribution network is a key factor. A successful brand is a precious asset, which could fetch a price many times the cost of assets required to make that product. A study conducted by A&N-ORG-MARG reflects that the share of branded goods is high for a number of daily used products. Branded goods comprise 65 per cent of sales in villages and the share of non-branded products is shrinking dramatically. In the case of convenience goods, sachets or low unit packs have generated a new sales wave for branded products.

Decisions relating to products vary between modification to customization. Hindustan Motors launched a ten seater transport vehicle. C.K.Rao, Vice-President HM, said 'the rural transportation needs are met but not satisfactorily to the consumer's needs. Villages which are 60 to 70 km away from Delhi cannot be reached by general vehicles and the rural folk have to go to the nearest highway for transport'. So HM decided to come up with a vehicle that will meet the needs of the villagers. The vehicle manufactured in collaboration with OKA Motor Corporation of Australia, is designed with high ground clearance and is fitted with long travel suspension for rugged roads. The wheel assembly is so designed that if the vehicle is stuck in slush the entire torque is diverted to one wheel making it easier for the vehicle to get out.

Zee Telefilms Ltd., has done experiments to eliminate the keyboard from the personal computer (PC) and to have voice activation instead for the rural markets. The voice-activated PC would be a hit in the rural markets where literacy levels are not high and people have trouble operating the keyboard while BEST also would make interactive classrooms available to villagers where students young and old could interact with their teachers.

Reliance have also got into the fray to attract the rural customer. Rue-Rel, its latest product, is primarily intended to increase the penetration level of polyrich suiting segment. It was decided to create a fighting brand based on the assumption that Rue-Rel will partake some of the Reliance polyrich suitings market but the combined sale of the two brands would be greater than the sale of polyrich as it existed before the introduction of Rue-Rel. Marketers say the idea of the brand germinated from the survey reports which suggested a tremendous opportunity in the form of niche for a low-priced polyrich fabric particularly in the towns and smaller cities. Thus was born Rue-Rel. The suitings have been priced most competitively and with an aim to cater to the mass market. Over 900 designs which keep getting updated and added can satisfy just about any taste and pocket.

We will now examine briefly the product offerings for the premium segment and value-for-money segments. The middle segment is self-explanatory as it possesses characteristics of both these segments.

Premium Segment

There is a cross-section of consumers which is prepared to pay more for a better product and service. The success of some brands in both FMCG and durable categories emphasise the fact that good value (in comparison with competitive offerings) could deliver results at a higher price point, even against odds. This is because the niche segment is prepared to (and can afford to) pay a premium if there are brands which satisfy the fastidious needs of the segment.

Brands such as Colgate total and Ayurvedic Concepts are ones that are not targeted towards masses. Colgate total was repositioned as a toothpaste, which offers a 12-hour protection and Ayurvedic Concepts has been delivering value through the traditional herbal route in the cosmetics category as well as the OTC pharmaceutical category. The value in this case also is associated with a higher price point.

Whirpool, a recent brand in the Indian context, has a share of 37 per cent in the premium segment (above 300 liters) of the refrigerator market.

LG is another brand which has registered success in the recent times with its feature-benefit combination, which has been unique to the brand. LG positioned itself on benefits (by making use of technology) preservation of nutrition with regard to refrigerators, healthy air with regard to air-conditioners and easy viewing with regard to televisions.

Santro has met with success in spite of the deviation in design within the category of automobiles (tall boy). It's success is based on a good product and excellent service.

Value Segment

There seems to be a vast potential in a number of categories where value could be provided to the masses at the lower end of the pyramid. A lower-end offering has to be a no-frills offering whose performance would be perceived better than the existing substitutes. A distinguishing feature in the Indian marketing context is the presence of the unorganised sector in a host of product categories. If marketers could provide value, preferably at a lower price point in these markets (low priced variants or small pack offers) consumers are likely to upgrade to these products.

Hindustan Lever came out with brands such as Tiger (a combination of tea and tapioca) to upgrade consumers from the loose (unorganised) tea market and Aim was the toothpaste introduced by the company to bring in consumers from the toothpowder segment.

VIP came out with Alfa, initially to move the consumers from the unorganised to the branded market (with a superior product).

Videocon's low-priced semi-automatic washing machine targeted towards rural areas and the lower-end audio products from BPL are examples from the durable categories in which value was provided to the lower end offerings.

The Tiger brand from Britannia is an excellent example of a value-based offering in a market structure, which was full of substandard offerings in the unorganised sector.

Vendee edible oil (good quality edible oil distributed through vending machines) followed a unique concept, which appealed to the masses.

Price

It is obvious that rural marketers have to consider different price points as discussed above. Obviously, pricing is done keeping incomes in mind. Some more examples substantiate this observation. Companies like BPL use dual pricing policy. A litre of oil which costs Rs. 70 in towns in priced at Rs. 50 in the villages. A sachet of Pantene costs Rs.2 in Delhi but the same is available for around Re. 1.60 in a remote village in Ghaziabad. A jar of cold cream can be had for Rs. 11 against Rs. 13.50 in the city. Companies also often compete on pricing by offering discounts and freebies in a bid to increase penetration in the nascent market.

Hindustan Coca-Cola Beverages Pvt. Ltd. launched an instant and ready-to-mix Sunfill in a single-serve sachet of 25 gms and a multi-serve sachet of 200 gms priced at Rs. 2 and Rs. 15, respectively in Andhra Pradesh, Tamil Nadu, Delhi and Maharashtra. The idea behind the launch of Sunfill, according to Mr. Singh, was to initiate those who have hitherto not been able to afford bottled carbonated drinks, into soft drinks.

Place

Marketing strategies were recast for the rural areas and rustics were lapping up Pantene, Whisper, Ponds cold cream and Good Knight virtually at their doorsteps. But the fact remains that the options available to the rural consumer are nowhere near what they are in the urban supermarkets. And for obvious reasons. "It is physically impossible for a company to cover all the three million outlets in the country", said Sachin Gopal,Vice-President, Marketing, Gillette India Ltd. "At best a company can cover about 7 lakh outlets, which is barely around 20 per cent of the rural market. The rest of the market is served by retailers who buy the products from the urban markets".

Gillette and Nirma depend upon urban market to feed rural areas because distribution costs of serving the rural are prohibitive. "The costs would in turn affect product pricing making it either expensive or less profitable. Hence our reliance on wholesale network" said Nirma's Executive Director, Kalpesh Patel.

"Gillette is not shifting its sights to the rural market because our logic is that if we are well distributed in the urban areas, where there is a lot of untapped potential for our products, the products will find their way into the rural areas also through rural retailers" said Sachin Gopal.

In rural areas the market battle is between fewer brands because retailers feel shy of stocking too many brands of a product category. Obviously, one brand tends to dominate. HLL is trying to get round this problem by giving credit to the distributors. The quest is for higher volumes to offset marketing costs, be it transaction cost of distributors or low selling. Delhi based Sunstar Lubricants is using a combination of low pricing and incentives to distributors to extend its reach in the rural areas.

The enormity of the rural market, which constitutes 627,000 villages spread over 32,87,263 sq.km calls for a substantial allocation for distribution. The FMCG companies are weighing their distribution strengths and costs involved in setting it up. With industry's distribution focus becoming rural-centric, there is a growing trend whereby a number of companies like P&G Hygiene and Healthcare have disbanded their entire distribution team and decided to piggy back on another company's retail reach.

The distribution strengths of three FMCG majors are given below:

Particulars	*HLL*	*Colgate*	*Britannia*
Retail outlets services	10,00,000	2,500,000	400,000
cities/towns/villages	50,000	20,000	2,200
Distributors	7,500	2,000	2,500
Rural turnover	50.0%	35.0%	30.0%

Promotion

Advertising is what most companies are turning to for influencing rural consumer behaviour quickly. The rural advertising budget of companies is generally between Rs. 6 and 15 crore. Though it doesn't seem much, according to Videocon's Navin Gupta, Rs. 10 crore spent in villages achieves the same visibility as Rs. 50 crore in the towns and cities.

MNCs like Samsung are spending Rs. 40 crore on advertising in semi-urban areas. A significant part of this budget goes to Doordarshan, because no other mass media has as wide a reach across the country. Another key factor is radio and spot advertising in the villages. Sunstar Lubricants prints leaflets in regional languages, attends *panchayat* meetings and participates in agro meets to promote its products.

To attract rural buyers advertisers can use simple films showing how a product is to be used. Rajdoot Paints issues such functional advertising very effectively. "Sales promotion has to be customized and localized says Jagdeep Kapoor, Managing Director, Samsika Marketing. A company has to keep in mind religion, festivals and local sentiments. While Nirma makes extensive use of wall paintings, a soil conditioner called Terracare uses images of Sita, Luv and Kush to attract the rural consumer.

The rural market is a significant part of the marketing strategy of Coca-Cola India. It has painted the holy city of Haridwar red. It has found a unique tool for the Indian market. Metal boxes containing a base of ice, thereby eliminating the need for electricity and at a price of Rs. 5 for a 200 ml cup. As many as 3,000 of such 15 kg carts rolled out in the dusty, pot-holed streets of the price-conscious rural markets of Bihar, Uttar Pradesh, Gujarat and West Bengal this summer.

Going a step beyond selling its products, HLL is encouraging primary education in the villages through a V-Sat connection, beginning with Maharashtra. The underlying motive is to influence people's behaviour. HLL believes that such an effort will create more awareness of hygiene and cleanliness which will in turn have a direct impact on the sales of its toilettries. Events like the Kumbh Mela, where more than 10 million visit, are once in a lifetime marketing opportunities that enables a company—either Indian or multinational–to understand the importance of the rural market. Significantly, most of the purchases are made from the household's own income. Hire-purchase schemes and loans account for only around ten per cent of rural buying. As a result, an increasing number of companies are making a beeline for the villages and smaller towns.

Conclusion

Indian villagers are going to enter the twenty first century on par with their urban cousins. Marketing of the Indian industry is going to make it happen.

References

1. Business Time Research Bureau, Purchasing Power: Rural Areas Reveal Their Muscle, *Times of India*, September 27 1999.
2. Is the Urban Rural Divide a Myth: *Businessline*, October 7, 1999.
3. *The Economic Times*, Brand Equity September 22, 1999.
4. Neeraj Jha, Gunghoo on Rural Marketing, *The Financial Express*, June 19, 2002.
5. Rinku Pegu, Maya Bazar, *The Week*, May 30, 1999.
6. Joydeep Ghosh, The Great Rural Rush, *The Week*, October 19, 2001.
7. Sravanthi Chellapalli, Rural Riddle, Urban Quest, *Business Line, Catalyst*, October 11, 2001.
8. Ramesh Kumar, Selling Smartly Against Odds, *Business Line, Catalyst,* December 27, 2001.
9. Irfan Khan, Voice Activated PCs for Rural Markets, *Business Times Bureau*, Sunday, April 9, 2000.
10. www.indiainfoline.com.

APPENDIX - I

Strategies

Philip's Maha Strategy

Consumer durables major, Philips India has designed an innovative strategy called the 'Philips *Maha sangram* Integrated Marketing Programme'.

Aim

The Philips *Mahasangram* is aimed at taking Philips' new products to the semi-urban and rural customers and increasing their awareness where product knowledge, information and availability are concerned. Philips is targeting to increase the percentage contribution in terms of portable audio from rural/semi-urban areas to a total turnover of 50 per cent.by end-2003 from the current 28 per cent. For CTVs, the company is aiming to increase that figure to 45 per cent in the same period, from the current 22 per cent.

Target Market

The rural initiative will be taken across the country focusing on rural towns with a population of less than 5,000 and semi-urban towns with a population between 5,000 and 50,000. Philips will be spending about 4.5 per cent of its turnover from the rural semi-urban areas on the *Mahasangram* alone.

Why?

Meanwhile, the key reason behind this initiative lies in the growing potential of the rural market. According to an industry data, while in 1997–98, rural sales formed about 25 per cent of the total sales for CTVs, refrigerators and washing machines, it increased to 36 per cent in 2001–2002 and is expected to go up to as high as 41 per cent in 2006–07. Similarly, the radio segment is expected to grow from the current Rs. 160 crore to around Rs. 1,200 crore by fiscal 2005 and to Rs. 3,400 crore by fiscal 2010. Out of this at least 60 per cent of the growth is expected to come from the semi-urban and rural areas. In addition, the expected increase in FM services is also expected to boost demand for radio sets.

The Strategy

Product strategy Products to be pushed during the *Mahasangram* include the recently launched Free Power Radio, which does not require batteries or any external source of electricity for operation. A one-minute winding of the lever runs the radio for as long as 30 minutes. Research studies showed us that in semi-urban and rural India, an average household spends Rs. 1,000 to Rs. 2,000 annually on batteries for a radio set. The Free Power Radio, priced at Rs. 995, is ideal for this rural household as the household actually saves on costs incurred on batteries, and experiences a pay back of the money invested in the radio, in just one year. It also manages to save more than Rs. 1,000 every year for the next 12 years, the same amount which the household would have spent on batteries.

Philips also recently introduced a new CD portable system, at Rs. 4,000 in a bid to make the CD-based music system affordable to the semi-urban and rural customers. Philips will also be launching a range of new CTV products. These include special economy models in the 14-inch colour television (CTV) segment, starting at a price point of Rs. 8,000. Other new models to be introduced will include features such as a new 'Eye-fi technology which allows picture improvement under any cable signal condition, economy in electricity consumption and on-screen display in the regional language, among other things.

Promotion Philips plans to implement an innovative FMCG style marketing strategy to push its durables in the rural segment. The advertising and marketing strategy will be a combination of above-the-line and below-the-line/ on-ground activities. Various promotional activities planned during the *Mahasangram* include a series of on-ground activities such as point of sale material at retailers' counters, road-shows, mobile vans with Philips' products on display and games, innovative tactics like advertising on an inland letter form or postcard (a popular form of communication in rural areas) and sponsorship of local events, among other things.

Distribution Philips claims to have the biggest distribution network (as compared to other consumer electronic companies) and aims an extensive physical reach of 80 per cent plus. Steps that help in developing volume reach, geographical reach and counter share significantly are initiated. The company has carried out an extensive product-wise mapping exercise over 540 districts across India. It has developed a second line of activity in their distribution set-up. Also, in order to cater to volume drivers i.e., major retailers, they have identified the main retailers of each distributor and implemented the Key Account Management Approach with them, so that there is a focus on improving relations, trade with these retailers, and catering to their needs.

Source

Neha Kaushik, Philips' Mahastrategy, Catalyst, *Business Line,* June 20, 2002.

POLAR GLOBAL STRATEGY

Polar Latex (Rs. 400 crore) in its bid to reposition itself from being a major government supplier to a focused marketing organisation has launched domestic brands. The domestic market is expected to grow to 2,500 million pieces per annum by 2003.

Prior to the launch of its domestic brands, Polar Latex was manufacturing condoms which were sold under Government of India brands like Nirodh, Masti, Mithun, Tarang, *Sawan* and Bliss. Polar Latex manufactures 575 million pieces every year, of which around 240 million pieces are currently supplied\ to the Government of India. By adding two more lines to its existing five production lines, Polar Latex intends to expand capacity by another 120 million pieces.

PRODUCT DIFFERENTIATION

In order to create differentiation for its brands, Polar Latex Ltd. is launching a new brand of ice-cream flavoured condoms in the domestic market.

Premium Segment

Tonite, a brand popularised by Polar in the foreign market, will now be launched in India in seven different flavours–Vanilla, strawberry, butterscotch, chocolate, banana, orange and pineapple—for seven days of the week. The flavours are surprises which can be discovered only on opening the individual sachets, and are not mentioned on the pack.

Popular Segment

Polar has launched two other new brands recently, Adam Super (middle) and *Mard* (lower), to grab a bigger share of the 1,700 million-pieces condom market in India. The brands have already been launched in West Bengal and will be introduced in Mumbai soon.

Polar already has international brands like Senorita, Play Girl, Adam, and Love Me, for the export market. Globally, the company is present in 26 countries. It has recently introduced alcohol-flavoured-rum, whiskey and brandy-condoms in the Russian market. While Adam Super is priced at Rs. 7 for a pack of three, and *Mard* at Rs. 5, Tonite is priced at a premium Rs. 9. Polar Latex aims to sell 12 million pieces of Adam super, 52 million pieces of *Mard*, and 10–12 million pieces of the ice cream-flavored Tonite, in the first year. They are also hoping to sell another six million pieces of the super premium brand that they are planning to launch soon.

Positioning

Besides launching new brands, Polar Latex is also planning a major marketing initiative with twin objectives.

- One, to create a strong presence in the domestic market.
- Two, to contribute meaningfully towards the politically-correct (and strategically-prudent cause of AIDS.

Thus, while Polar is targeting the urban market with lifestyle, happiness, comfort and pleasure themes, in the rural market, the stress is on safety and security. Says Chief Executive and Director, Kalyan K Chattopadhyay: "The condom was seen with a stigma before. We are trying to present it as a pharmaceutical product". To drive home the point, Polar Latex changed its slogan four months ago from 'Protection with pleasure' to 'Turning a global concern into a business commitment'.

PROMOTION

For promoting the new brands, Polar Latex is looking at two distinct strategies: for the rural market, the focus is on creating pull through consumer awareness, while in urban centers it will push sales through incentives for wholesalers and dealers.

To target the rural market, Polar Latex is hiring *'Kripa'* vans which will travel from village to village promulgating sex education and awareness. An initial marketing spend of Rs. 1 crore has been budgeted for, for each state. In West Bengal alone, 17,000 villages are to be covered. Five vans have been hired, which will cover five villages each per day. While the rural marketing initiative has been rolled out in West Bengal and Andhra Pradesh, the company will target Bihar and Maharashtra in the next two months.

Polar Latex is also looking at indirect promotions through merchandising, price-offs and exchange offers, and network structuring. The marketing spend is estimated at Rs. 2 crore per metro. They are avoiding television ads although the competitors are doing it. Their logic: the subject is still a taboo in Indian homes and people do not feel comfortable with these ads. Also, advertising is an expensive affair. The focus instead is on packaging and distribution and point-of-purchase advertising. The company is preparing danglers, posters, show boards and window displays for advertising.

In addition, the company is open to sponsorships, events, workshops and direct marketing. For example, Polar plans to actively participate in condom *melas* organised by NGOs in states like Bihar. In fact, for the low-priced *Mard* brand, Polar is depending on the NGO channel to boost sales to truckers and sex workers.

DISTRIBUTION

For the urban market, the company is looking at 650 super distributors and C&F agents up from the existing 100 dealers. At the retail level, the company is trying hard to expand reach through *paan* shops, pharmacists and non-governmental organisations. Says Chattopadhyay "All this time the *paan* shops displayed porno stuff and made lots of money by selling any and every condom brand. But they always faced the risk of inadequate supply. Now, we want to offer the incentive of adequate supply and timely payment to them." In Calcutta, the company has already identified 720 such shops and 35 pharmacists, who will stock Polar Latex brands.

AIDING THE CAUSE

Apart from just manufacturing and marketing condoms, the company is also establishing AIDS forums across the country. It is setting up two research centers–one in Mumbai and Calcutta each—for which other corporates are also being towed in. the centre would contact schools and colleges and impart education on safe sex and ways to limit the spread of AIDS.

The centre would also deploy a team which would use the medium of humor/ laughter clubs/forums to bring AIDS-related issues in foucs. Once a month, mega-events will be organised which will bring in celebrities and important personalities to talk on the subject, along with an entertainment programme. The company is considering Wizcraft or Backstage as event managers for these events.

EXPORTS

Exports is another major thrust area. Polar Latex already exports about a dozen different brands to North America, South Africa, Russia, Sweden, Myanmar, etc. Next, Chattopadhyay is on his way to South Africa to strike "another relationship building exercise". Three months ago, Polar Latex went in for a marketing and manufacturing tie-up with a company in Vietnam. Says Chattopadhyay: "We want to have different strokes for different countries".

Source

Suman Layak and Anamika Rath, If it's Thursday, it Must be Butterscotch Tonite, *The Financial Express*, Thursday, July 8, 1999.

APPENDIX - II

CONSUMER PENETRATION LEVELS

Tea

Tea is by far the most popular beverage in India. Awareness about tea is close to universal in urban areas and 80 per cent in rural areas. Its penetration in urban areas is 89.3 per cent and 72.6 per cent in rural areas. At all India level, tea penetration averages 77.2 per cent.

Interestingly, tea penetration is higher in medium sized towns (0.5–1mn population) at 93.3 per cent compared to 90.5 per cent in metros (population above 1mn). This could be due to the fact that coffee penetration is significantly higher at 24.2 per cent in metros (above 1 mn population) compared to 16.7 per cent in medium sized towns with population between 0.5 and 1mn.

Coffee

In comparison to tea, penetration of coffee is significantly low at 8.8 per cent at all India level and coffee penetration is relatively high at 17.1 per cent in urban areas compared to only 5.6 per cent in rural areas. The rural penetration is represented by South India. In other parts of rural India, penetration is negligible.

Per capita consumption of coffee is 7 kg in Germany and 11 kg in Switzerland. Per capita consumption in North India is a mere 4 gm as compared to 240 gm in South India. Karnataka, Tamil Nadu, Kerala, and Andhra Pradesh are the major coffee consuming states in India. The present average per capita consumption is estimated to be 55 gm per annum.

Bakery

Bread and biscuits have been in the Indian market for a long time. The awareness is very high, close to 100 per cent in urban areas and around 90 per cent in rural areas. Penetration of bread is estimated to be close to 60 per cent in urban areas and around 15 per cent in rural areas. Biscuit penetration is about 60 per cent in urban areas and 20 per cent in rural areas. Penetration of cake and other products is insignificant and restricted only to large cities/ metros.

Tobacco

- Tobacco consumption habit is deep rooted. Almost 90 per cent of cigarette smokers are aware that it is harmful to health.
- There is an increasing social antipathy to smoking. Regulation regarding advertisement and smoking in public places are becoming stricter.
- If one or both parents smoke, the probability of their child picking up smoking is substantially higher.
- Other than parents, the most significant driver towards smoking habit is peer (friends) pressure. Advertisements rarely induce first smoking.
- India has the highest rate of excise duty, making cigarettes very expensive. This has helped boost other forms of tobacco consumption such as *bidis*, etc.

In India, there are about 200mn tobacco consumers. About 18 per cent of people in India smoke either *bidi* or cigarette. Among them 25mn smoke cigarettes. The relative share of smokers is higher in rural areas at 18.9 per cent, compared to 15.4 per cent in urban areas. However, penetration of cigarettes is extremely low in rural areas. Only 2.1 per cent of rural adults smoke cigarettes, compared to 6 per cent of urban adults in India. In contrast as high as 16.9 per cent of rural adults smoke *bidis* compared to 9.6 per cent of urban adult population. Overall penetration of *bidis* is 14.8 per cent and that of cigarette is 3.2 per cent. Awareness of these products among adult male population is over 90 per cent.

Paan products

Paan products refer to betel leaf that is chewed after meals as its juice is good for digestion. *Paan* and *paan* products are prepared and sold by tens of thousands of small roadside shops (called *paan* wallas) scattered all over the country.

Paan products

Tobacco based	Plain
Raw tobacco	Flavored *supari*
Paan	*Paan*
Gutkha	*Paan* masala

Paan products have a penetration of 16.8 per cent in India, almost equally distributed in rural and urban areas. *Paan masala* penetration is 7.2 per cent which is marginally higher in urban areas at 8.6 per cent as compared to 6.6 per cent in rural areas. *Supari* is reasonably popular, with a penetration of 14 per cent in urban as well as rural areas. The penetration is relatively higher in small towns. Penetration is higher in North India as compared to other parts of the country. The penetration of these products is significantly low amongst highly educated and upper class urban consumers.

The habit of eating *paan*/ *paan* products is more prevalent in Northern and Western states such as UP, Bihar, Rajasthan and Gujarat. *Paan* products are eaten either plain or with tobacco. Consumers who eat *paan* products with tobacco, are addicted and consume it several times a day. Plain *paan* products are consumed just for fun or occasionally after heavy dinner at parties, weddings, etc. Unbranded paan products like *supari, dhania dal,* etc. are also consumed at home in large quantities.

Paan shops are typically located outside restaurants and at key junctions in residential areas. These shops generally serve as meeting point for youngsters who spend spare time with their friends at such locations.

Kothari Products is the leading player with its Pan Parag brand name. Other players are Virat Crane Ltd. (Crane) and Raghunath International. Their annual sales are in the range of Rs. 1713mn, Rs. 103mn and Rs. 113mn respectively. There are a large number of regional brands also. Some of the well known *Gutkha* brands are Manikchand, Mahak, Vimal, Kuber, Tulsi, Badshan, etc. The *Gutkha* segment is growing at 25 per cent per annum.

Household Cleaning Products

Household cleaning products, penetration at all India level is a tiny 11.4 per cent represented predominantly by large metros, wherein the penetration is 47.2 per cent. In medium and small size towns, penetration varies between 25 per cent and 29 per cent. It averages at 30 per cent for all urban areas. Penetration of household cleaning products is very low in rural areas at 4.3 per cent. Most households use ordinary detergents for household cleaning also. Besides, floors are made of mud/ cow-dung and are not cleaned with disinfectants.

Insecticides/ Insect Repellents

Penetration of insecticides (cockroaches/ bed bugs) is a nominal 2.2 per cent at all India level represented largely by large metros wherein the penetration is 9.8%. in small and medium size towns, penetration of these products ranges at around 5–6 per cent, averaging 5.9 per cent for all urban areas. In rural areas, the penetration of these products is a negligible 0.8 per cent.

Mosquito Repellent

Mosquito repellent penetration is significantly higher in metros at 22.6 per cent compared to 16.4 per cent in all urban areas. Penetration in rural India is only 1.7 per cent. The same for all India averages at 5.7 per cent. Penetration is significantly higher in North and South due to climatic reasons. While rural penetration is growing slowly, power mats have relatively low demand, due to constant power disruptions. Coils have a larger market in the rural areas.

Edible oils

Among FMCG products, edible oil has one of the highest penetration of 98 per cent in urban as well as in rural areas. Other popular cooking mediums are Vanaspati (hydrogenated edible oil) and ghee (home made butter). Penetration of all of these three cooking medium is very high at 99.8 per cent in urban areas as well as rural areas. Vanaspati penetration averages 17.4 per cent at all India level, significantly higher at 28.8 per cent in urban areas and 13 per cent in rural areas. It is highest in medium size towns of 0.5–1mn population of 34.6 per cent compared to 32.3 per cent in metros and 26.6 per cent in small towns. In metros, refined edible oil is relatively a popular cooking medium.

Edible oil in one form or the other is consumed in almost every household. The peculiar Indian food habits prefer fried vegetables and several other fried snacks. Traditionally, North and West have been milk surplus regions in the country. This has led to surplus *ghee* (indigenous butter) production in these areas and higher *ghee* consumption. The lower end of the society which cannot afford *ghee,* consume *vanaspati* (hydrogenated oil which looks like *ghee*). Sweetmeat makers in the unorganised sector, particularly in the north represent one of the largest user segment for *vanaspati.*

In the South, there has been an abundant availability of edible oils, namely coconut oil, groundnut oil, sunflower oil, etc. This has led to different consumer habits. Southern consumers prefer refined oil cooking medium as compared to *ghee*/vanaspati. Similarly, the Eastern region which is milk deficient has preference for vegetable oil as cooking medium.

There are also regional and cultural differences in the type of edible oil used for cooking. South Indians use more of coconut oil for cooking their food, sesame oil is widely used in the north, mustard oil in the north and east, and there is an overwhelming preference for groundnut oil in the west.

Most consumers, specially in the rural areas buy edible oil in loose form. Whereas, in large metros, loose oil is scarcely available as retailers find it difficult to handle the same. In medium-sized towns, loose as well as branded oils are available.

In the last few years, popularity of branded oil has been increasing, particularly with low cost poly-packs. With the Government ordering compulsory packaging of edible oil in the wake of dropsy deaths in the country due to use of adulterated mustard oil, the usage of branded oils is expected to witness phenomenal growth.

Hair Oil

Hair oil is an everyday habit with about 50 per cent of the population. Hair oiling, a peculiarly Indian habit, is extremely popular in urban as well as rural India. Penetration of hair oil is 87 per cent at all India level and is almost evenly distributed in urban and rural areas. While penetration in urban areas is marginally higher at 90.2 per cent, the same closely follows at 85.5 per cent in rural areas. In urban areas, penetration is higher in small towns (0.1–0.5m population) at 91.8 per cent compared to medium and large town where it is 89.5–89.9 per cent. Awareness about hair oil is over 90 per cent in rural as well as urban areas.

Shampoos

Modern hair care products such as shampoos have yet not penetrated significantly. All India penetration of 12.9 per cent is largely due to 25 per cent penetration in urban areas. Also, there is a higher concentration in large metros where penetration is 30.5 per cent compared to 25–26 percent in small/ medium size towns. Shampoo penetration in rural areas is very low at 8.2 per cent largely represented by Southern India. Penetration in other parts of the country is still lower. Awareness about shampoo, however, is close to 90 per cent in urban areas and 80 per cent in rural areas. Urban markets account for 80 per cent of total shampoo market whereas rural market contributes only 20 per cent. Shampoo penetration in the North is concentrated in the upper class status conscious people, in contrast to the South where sachets have crack opened the market to include the lower income classes as well.

APPENDIX - III

Rural Facts

To get a feel of the Indian consumer market data is provided on population, villages, composition of economy, income levels, penetration, media reach and distribution channels.

Table 3.2 Indian States: Population (Rural and Urban)

State	*Population (mn)*	*Rural (mn)*	*Urban (mn)*	*Rural %*	*Urban %*
West					
Rajasthan	44.0	33.9	10.1	77.0	23.0
Goa	1.2	0.7	0.5	59.0	41.0
Maharashtra	78.9	48.4	30.5	61.3	38.7
Gujarat	41.3	27.1	14.2	65.6	34.4
Total West	165.4	110.1	55.3	66.6	33.4
West (%)	19.7				
East					
Manipur	1.84	1.33	0.5	72.3	27.7
Nagaland	1.21	1	0.21	82.6	21.0
Bihar	86.4	75	11.40	86.8	15.2
West Bengal	68.1	49.4	18.7	72.5	37.9
Arunachal Pradesh	0.9	0.8	0.1	88.9	12.5
Sikkim	0.41	0.37	0.04	90.2	10.8
Assam	22.4	19.9	2.5	88.8	12.6
Meghalaya	1.8	1.4	0.3	77.8	21.4
Orissa	31.6	27.4	4.2	86.7	15.3
Total East	214.7	176.6	37.95	82.3	21.5
East (%)	25.5				
North					
Delhi	9.4	0.9	8.4	10.1	89.9
Chandigarh	0.6	0.1	0.6	10.3	89.7
Madhya Pradesh	66.2	50.8	15.3	76.8	23.2
Punjab	20.3	14.3	6.0	70.5	29.5
Haryana	16.5	12.4	4.1	75.3	24.7
Uttar Pradesh	139.1	111.5	27.6	80.2	19.8
Himachal Pradesh	5.2	4.7	0.4	90.9	9.1
Jammu & Kashmir	7.7	5.9	1.8	76.4	23.6
Total North	265.0	200.5	63.6	75.7	24.3
North (%)	31.5				
South					
Tamil Nadu	55.9	36.8	19.1	65.9	34.1
Andhra Pradesh	66.5	48.6	17.9	73.1	26.9
Kerala	29.1	21.4	7.7	73.5	26.5
Karnataka	45.0	31.1	13.9	69.2	30.8
Total South	196.4	137.9	58.6	70.2	29.8
South (%)	23.3				

Union Territories					
Andaman Nicobar	0.3	0.21	0.07	73.3	26.7
Dadra & Nagar Haveli	0.1	0.13	0.01	91.5	8.5
Daman & Diu	0.1	0.05	0.05	53.2	46.8
Lakshadweep	0.1	0.02	0.03	43.7	56.3
Pondicherry	0.8	0.3	0.52	36.0	64.0
Total UT	1.4	0.7	0.7	50.7	49.3
Other states	3.4	2.7	0.7	78.5	21.5
All India	**846.3**	**628.5**	**216.9**	**74.3**	**25.7**

Population is as per 1991 Census

Table 3.3 Indian States: Number of Villages

State/ Union Territory	*No.*
All India	580781
Andhra Pradesh	26586
Arunachal Pradesh	3649
Assam	24685
Bihar	67513
Goa	360
Gujarat	18028
Haryana	6759
Himachal Pradesh	16997
Karnataka	27066
Kerala	1384
Madhya Pradesh	71526
Maharashtra	40412
Manipur	2182
Meghalaya	5484
Mizoram	698
Nagaland	1216
Orissa	46989
Punjab	12428
Rajasthan	37889
Sikkim	447
Tamil Nadu	15822
Tripura	855
Uttar Pradesh	112803
West Bengal	37910
Andaman & Nicobar	504
Chandigarh	25
Dadra & Nagar Haveli	71
Daman & Diu	24
Delhi	199
Lakshadweep	7
Pondicherry	263

Source: IRS 99

Table 3.4 Composition of Rural Economy

Component	*1993–94*	*1970–71*
Agriculture	5.3	6.8
Trade, hotels and restaurants	7.8	2.7
Transport and communication	3.4	1.3
Social community services	9.6	6.4

Table 3.5 Share in National Income (2000–01)

Sector	Rural	Urban
Agricultural (%)	94	6
Industrial (%)	43	57
Services (%)	54	46
Overall (%)	61	39
Per Capita Income (Rs)	12,700	29,100

Source: NCAER and CSO estimates in *Economic Times*, July 2, 2001, p.5.

Between '93–94 and '99–00, the share of FMCG products in the per capita consumption expenditure has dropped by 5.7 per cent in urban India (in a basket of 89 goods), and by 2 per cent in the rural areas (in a basket of 85 goods). Per capita total expenditure on these basket of goods has gone up by 15.34 per cent in urban India and 5.2 per cent in rural areas, according to the National Sample Survey Organisation. The results of NSSO's 55th and 50th rounds have been compared to obtain these results. As per the analysis of the primary data of '99–00 over '93–94 consumption patterns, the FMCG basket (comprising 14 items) did show some laggards and fast runners.

Table 3.6 Real Growth in Per Capita Expenditure '99–00 over '93–94

Products	*Rural*	*Urban*
Tea Leaf	37.0	27.4
Tea Cups	12.3	15.7
Biscuits	7.6	5.4
Salted Refreshments	27.9	38.4
Bidi	33.0	54.1
Cigarettes	29.0	15.7
Matches	5.1	14.2
Soaps	5.5	13.8
Hair Oil/Shampoo	26.9	38.5
Toothpaste	67.0	29.0
Powder/Cream	52.1	62.8
Shaving Blade	26.7	12.1
Washing Soap	36.3	34.1

Table 3.7 Media Reach–Urban & Rural Reach

Demographic	*TV (%)*	*Press (%)*	*Radio (%)*	*Cinema (%)*	*Internet (%)*
Sex					
Male	47.0	45.0	16.0	16.0	0.1
Female	42.0	21.0	12.0	7.0	–
Age (Years)					
12–14	57.0	34.0	11.0	11.0	–
15–19	57.0	44.0	15.0	20.0	0.1
20–24	51.0	42.0	17.0	21.0	0.1
25–34	44.0	35.0	15.0	14.0	0.1
35–44	41.0	32.0	15.0	8.0	0.1
45–44	38.0	27.0	14.0	5.0	0.1
55+	29.0	19.0	11.0	2.0	–
Education					
Illiterate	19.0	–	7.0	5.0	–
Below SSC	54.0	42.0	17.0	13.0	–
SSC and above	75.0	82.0	23.0	21.0	0.1
Graduate and above	87.0	96.0	26.0	22.0	1.4
Occupation					
Industry/Businessmen	92.0	90.0	15.0	21.0	2.0
Prof/Senior Execs.	93.0	97.0	21.0	18.0	5.0
Trader/Shop owner	70.0	63.0	15.0	22.0	0.1
Junior Execs.	95.0	98.0	21.0	20.0	4.0
Clerk / Salesman / Sup	90.0	94.0	22.0	21.0	1.0
Skilled Worker	72.0	64.0	17.0	26.0	0.2
Unskilled Worker	53.0	35.0	14.0	23.0	–
Non-Working / Retd. / House wife	79.0	54.0	13.0	15.0	0.2
Farmers	27.0	25.0	13.0	7.0	–
Fish/ Poultry	25.0	21.0	13.0	10.0	–
Shop Owners / Traders	43.0	47.0	23.0	16.0	–
Service	58.0	69.0	26.0	15.0	–
Artisans	35.0	36.0	23.0	19.0	–
Labourers	24.0	15.0	13.0	12.0	–
Others	–	–	–	–	–
Not Working	37.0	22.0	13.0	7.0	–
SEC					
A1	94.0	87.0	16.0	21.0	21.0
A2	91.0	77.0	16.0	23.0	23.0
B1	90.0	76.0	18.0	23.0	23.0
B2	87.0	67.0	15.0	22.0	22.0
C	84.0	59.0	16.0	24.0	24.0
D	72.0	41.0	15.0	24.0	24.0
E	54.0	21.0	16.0	23.0	23.0
Not Ascertained	70.0	45.0	7.0	23.0	23.0
R1	76.0	74.0	30.0	15.0	–
R2	64.0	58.0	22.0	10.0	–

R3	48.0	41.0	19.0	12.0	–
R4	22.0	12.0	10.0	8.0	–
Population Strata					
10 lakh +	84.0	65.0	16.0	16.0	1.0
5–10 lakh	80.0	61.0	14.0	18.0	0.2
1–5 lakh	77.0	57.0	14.0	18.0	0.1
50,000–1 lakh	71.0	54.0	14.0	21.0	0.2
< 50,000	61.0	47.0	14.0	17.0	–
>= 5000	44.0	37.0	23.0	15.0	–
1000–4999	31.0	22.0	13.0	9.0	–
< 1000	27.0	18.0	11.0	6.0	–
Income (MHI Rs)					
Up to 1000	24.0	16.0	12.0	10.0	–
1001–2000	40.0	28.0	14.0	11.0	–
2001–3000	59.0	45.0	16.0	12.0	–
3001–5000	76.0	62.0	18.0	15.0	0.1
5001–8000	88.0	79.0	19.0	18.0	0.7
8000=	93.0	86.0	18.0	21.0	2.1
Not disclosed	49.0	40.0	14.0	9.0	0.3

Source: IRS 98

Table 3.8 Media Reach—Rural 1998

Demographic	TV (%)	Press (%)	Radio (%)	Cinema (%)
Sex				
Male	35.0	35.0	16.0	13.0
Female	30.0	12.0	11.0	5.0
Age (Years)				
12–24	47.0	26.0	11.0	8.0
15–19	45.0	35.0	16.0	17.0
20–24	39.0	33.0	17.0	16.0
25–34	31.0	25.0	15.0	11.0
35–44	28.0	22.0	14.0	7.0
45–54	26.0	18.0	10.0	4.0
55+	19.0	12.0	13.0	1.0
Education				
Illiterate	15.0	–	7.0	5.0
Below SSC	45.0	35.0	18.0	11.0
SSC + but not graduate	62.0	76.0	28.0	19.0
Graduate and above	73.0	92.0	23.0	23.0
Occupation				
Farmers	27.0	25.0	13.0	7.0
Fish/Poultry	25.0	21.0	13.0	10.0
Shop Owners / Traders	43.0	47.0	23.0	16.0
Service	58.0	69.0	26.0	15.0
Artisans	35.0	35.0	23.0	19.0
Labourers	24.0	15.0	13.0	12.0

Others				
Not Working	37.0	22.0	13.0	7.0
SEC				
R1	76.0	74.0	30.0	15.0
R2	64.0	58.0	22.0	10.0
R3	48.0	41.0	19.0	12.0
R4	22.0	12.0	10.0	8.0
Income (MHI Rs)				
< 1000	22.0	15.0	11.0	9.0
1001–2000	33.0	24.0	14.0	9.0
2001–3000	46.0	36.0	17.0	9.0
3001–5000	60.0	48.0	22.0	12.0
5000–8000	75.0	65.0	25.0	14.0
8000	82.0	68.0	22.0	18.0
Not disclosed	37.0	29.0	13.0	6.0

Source: IRS 98

Table 3.9 Media Reach State-Wise 1999 (Urban & Rural)

Zone		*Region*	*Total (mn)*	*Press (%)*	*TV (%)*	*Satellite (%)*	*Radio (%)*	*Cinema (%)*
West	Goa	All	1.0	48.0	72.0	11.0	10.0	25.0
		Rural	1.0	41.0	67.0	8.0	11.0	21.0
		Urban	0.4	59.0	79.0	16.0	9.0	30.0
	Gujarat	All	34.0	25.0	41.0	24.0	4.0	11.0
		Rural	21.0	13.0	24.0	9.0	3.0	5.0
		Urban	13.0	45.0	70.0	50.	5.0	22.0
	Madhya Pradesh	All	54.0	17.0	54.0	14.0	11.0	12.0
		Rural	41.0	8.0	44.0	5.0	11.0	7.0
		Urban	13.0	42.0	84.0	41.0	11.0	27.0
	Maharashtra	All	69.0	33.0	60.0	17.0	10.0	19.0
		Rural	42.0	18.0	45.0	4.0	7.0	13.0
		Urban	27.0	57.0	83.0	52.0	16.0	24.0
East	Assam	All	18.0	11.0	34.0	4.0	25.0	12.0
		Rural	16.0	6.0	26.0	0.8	26.0	9.0
		Urban	2.0	42.0	87.0	27.0	18.0	34.0
	Bihar	All	66.0	13.0	23.0	3.0	17.0	13.0
		Rural	57.0	9.0	17.0	1.0	17.0	11.0
		Urban	9.0	36.0	61.0	18.0	15.0	31.0
	Orissa	All	25.0	14.0	39.0	4.0	19.0	13.0
		Rural	22.0	11.0	34.0	0.9	20.0	11.0
		Urban	3.0	31.0	68.0	22.0	15.0	30.0
	West Bengal	All	57.0	19.0	55.0	12.0	30.0	20.0
		Rural	40.0	10.0	44.0	5.0	32.0	17.0
		Urban	17.0	40.0	80.0	27.0	26.0	27.0

North	Delhi	All	8.0	53.0	85.0	39.0	28.0	16.0
		Urban	8.0	53.0	85.0	39.0	28.0	16.0
	Haryana &	All	14.0	18.0	54.0	16.0	13.0	7.0
	Chandigarh	Rural	10.0	7.0	42.0	5.0	13.0	4.0
		Urban	4.0	44.0	84.0	42.0	16.0	14.0
	Himachal	All	4.0	27.0	68.0	9.0	24.0	10.0
	Pradesh	Rural	4.0	13.0	58.0	10.0	22.0	3.0
		Urban	0.4	48.0	91.0	64.0	20.0	16.0
	Punjab	All	17.7	20.0	59.0	14.0	11.0	10.0
		Rural	12.0	10.0	48.0	5.0	8.0	4.0
		Urban	6.0	40.0	84.0	32.0	17.0	20.0
	Rajasthan	All	34.0	21.0	27.0	7.0	10.0	9.0
		Rural	27.0	13.0	14.0	1.0	10.0	5.0
		Urban	9.0	53.0	74.0	27.0	10.0	24.0
	Uttar	All	110.0	14.0	32.0	4.0	7.0	8.0
	Pradesh	Rural	86.0	7.0	22.0	0.2	7.0	5.0
		Urban	24.0	39.0	67.0	18.0	9.0	19.0
South	Andhra	All	57.0	22.0	51.0	24.0	12.0	46.0
	Pradesh	Rural	41.0	15.0	41.0	15.0	12.0	43.0
		Urban	16.0	39.0	78.0	45.0	12.0	55.0
	Karnataka	All	37.0	28.0	61.0	24.0	30.0	41.0
		Rural	25.0	19.0	51.0	13.0	32.0	40.0
		Urban	12.0	48.0	83.0	47.0	24.0	42.0
	Kerala	All	24.0	68.0	68.0	9.0	60.0	33.0
		Rural	17.0	65.0	63.0	6.0	62.0	31.0
		Urban	7.0	76.0	81.0	17.0	54.0	38.0
	Tamil Nadu	All	49.0	33.0	63.0	25.0	35.0	43.0
		Rural	32.0	24.0	54.0	13.0	35.0	41.0
		Urban	17.0	51.0	80.0	48.0	35.0	47.0
All India		All	681.0	23.0	47.0	13.0	18.0	20.0
		Rural	494.0	14.0	36.0	5.0	18.0	16.0
		Urban	187.0	46.0	78.0	35.0	18.0	31.0

Source: IRS 99

Table 3.10 Media Reach—Age Group (Urban + Rural)

Age Group	*Size (mn)*	*Distribution %*	*Press %*	*TV %*	*Satellite %*	*Radio %*	*Cinema %*
12–14	67.0	10.0	19.0	62.0	12.0	15.0	20.0
15–19	93.0	14.0	30.0	60.0	15.0	20.0	33.0
20–24	88.0	13.0	29.0	53.0	15.0	21.0	34.0
25–34	150.0	22.0	24.0	46.0	14.0	19.0	24.0
35–44	112.0	16.0	22.0	43.0	13.0	18.0	15.0
45–54	79.0	12.0	19.0	40.0	14.0	17.0	8.0
55+	92.0	14.0	14.0	30.0	11.0	13.0	3.0
Total	681.0	100.0	23.0	47.0	13.0	18.0	20.0

Source: IRS 99

Table 3.11 Media Reach—Education Wise (Urban + Rural)

Education	*Size (mn)*	*Distribution %*	*Press %*	*TV %*	*Satellite %*	*Radio %*	*Cinema %*
Illiterate	278.0	41.0	0.0	22.0	4.0	8.0	10.0
Literate but no formal education	13.0	2.0	6.0	37.0	8.0	15.0	11.0
Schooling upto 4 years	58.0	8.0	10.0	44.0	8.0	19.0	15.0
Schooling upto 5–9 years	199.0	29.0	29.0	63.0	15.0	23.0	25.0
SSC–HSC	89.0	13.0	59.20	76.0	28.0	28.0	35.0
College not completed	14.0	2.0	81.0	85.0	37.0	34.0	50.0
Graduate–PG: General	26.0	4.0	86.0	88.0	47.0	33.0	38.0
Graduate–PG : Prof	3.0	1.0	95.0	94.0	59.0	29.0	39.0
Total	681.0	100.0	23.0	47.0	13.0		

Table 3.12 Penetration Rates—Rural & Urban

	1985–86 (%)	*1995–96 (%)*	*Increase*
Personal Products			
Washing Cake	89.32	93.28	3.96
Washing Power	44.14	61.19	17.05
Toilet Soap	26.7	98.47	71.77
Toothpaste	26.7	43.8	17.1
Tooth Powder	34.59	38.52	3.93
Talcum Powder	39.6	45.12	5.52
Face Cream	9.25	20.22	10.97
Lipstick*	3.67	5.23	1.56
Nail Polish*	4.43	6.6	2.17
Hair Oil/Cream	57.25	77.3	20.05
Shampoo*	10.3	15.39	5.09
Food & Beverages			
Cooking Medium Oil	84.85	91.27	6.42
Cooking Medium Vanaspati	33.88	40.95	7.07
Package Biscuits	18.37	31.67	13.3
Tea	75.65	85.99	10.34
Health Beverages	4.59	10.37	5.78
Cigarettes	16.49	21.47	4.98

* The penetration rates of lipstick, shampoo and nailpolish are available from 1992–93 onwards only. Therefore 85–86 numbers refer to penetration in 1992–93.

Source : NCAER

Table 3.13 Penetration Rates - Rural

	1985–86 (%)	*1995–96 (%)*	*Increase*
Personal Products			
Washing Cake	83.92	91.82	7.9
Washing Powder	37.37	55.37	18
Toilet Soap	18.46	97.92	79.46
Toothpaste	18.46	32.97	14.51
Tooth Powder	31.59	37.03	5.44
Talcum Powder	35.16	36.85	1.69
Face Cream	6.98	14.82	7.84
Lipstick*	0.56	1.18	0.62
Nail Polish*	2.34	3.14	0.8
Hair Oil/Cream	52.97	73.14	20.17
Shampoo*	5.40	8.10	2.70
Food & Beverages			
Cooking Medium Oil	83.93	89.82	5.89
Cooking Medium Vanaspati	31.15	36.55	5.40
Packaged Biscuits	14.52	23.11	8.59
Tea	72.56	83.58	11.02
Health Beverages	2.35	5.16	2.81
Cigarettes	13.65	18.68	5.03

* The penetration rates of lipstick, shampoo and nailpolish are available from 1992–93 onwards only. Therefore, 85–86 numbers refer to penetration in 1992–93.

Source: NCAER

The relative share of grocers dropped from over 50 per cent in the early 90's to 35 per cent in the late 90's. Chemist outlets on the other hand, have been expanding their product range to include high margin FMCG products from shampoos to ketchup. *Paanwallas* are also emerging as full fledged consumer product outlets.

Table 3.14 Growth in Retail Outlets (m nos)

Year	*Urban*	*Rural*	*Total*
1978	0.58	1.76	2.35
1984	0.75	2.02	2.77
1990	0.94	2.42	3.36
1996	1.80	3.33	5.13

Table 3.15 Composition of Urban Outlets

Grocers	34.7%
Cosmetic Stores	4.0%
Chemist	6.3%
Food Stores	6.6%
General Stores	14.4%
Paan + Stores	17.0%
Others	17.0%

Table 3.16 Composition of Rural Outlets

Grocers	55.6%
General Stores	13.5%
Chemist	3.3%
Others	27.6%

CHAPTER 4

Model Case Analysis

A STITCH IN TIME SAVES NINE

CASE 1

Satyam founded Sasi Beverages in 1991. Located in Tirupati, a town in Andhra Pradesh, a semi-urban area, he established a successful family operation fostering friendly relationships with trade and local customers. The major bread winner of the firm is its coffee blended with chicory in different proportions. Priced reasonably, the *'Bharat'* brand attracted the lower and middle income groups in the towns and rural areas of Rayalseema region.

Satyam decided to have a relook at the firm's operations and prospects. "This has become necessary" he says "because times have changed. We have been doing the same things over the years profitably. But now, many things look different even in the rural areas. The boiling point is reached". He sat with Sasi, his wife and business partner to discuss the measures to be taken. They together examined the 10-year sales data given in Table 4.1.

Table 4.1 Sales History of Bharat

Year	*Sales value (Rs lakhs)*
1992	25
1993	30
1994	36
1995	43
1996	49
1997	58
1998	68
1999	78
2000	84
2001	85

Sasi : The figures show that the sales have stagnated last year. Even in the first quarter of this year the movement of the product is not satisfactory compared to the previous year. This is no good against the said market growth rate of 15 per cent in the trade journals.

Satyam : Well! The reason may be the marketing agency. I doubt their commitment. I think we have to go on our own.

Sasi : May be it is the consumer. Now there is more money, more products and more information. Their preferences might have changed.

Satyam : It may be another reason because we have never advertised our product. We do not have any direct relationships with our consumers.

Sasi : I think we need a sort of market survey to finalise our plans.

They hired Sundar and Padma, two MBA students from Sri Venkateswara University to carry out research. The two students surveyed the rural areas for one month and came up with the following findings.

1. Almost all the households are aware of the brand.
2. Image of the brand is good (Table 4.3).
3. The preferences for the brand are high (Table 4.2).
4. Retailers prefer to stock the brand. According to them the brand movement has slowed recently.
5. The main threat is from a new local brand, *'Suraj'*. It is being pushed with high retailer discounts and price-off coupons. It is priced Rs. 2 above *'Bharat'* with a claim of latest technology used in processing for better quality.
6. Health consciousness is growing. The social workers and primary health centres (PHCs) are advocating against coffee drinking.
7. The brand has a traditional name. On the package, the picture of *'Bharat'* with Sri Rama's *paduka* (footwear of Lord Sri Rama) with the description 'trustworthy companion' is outdated. Values have changed. *Suraj* advertised it as a natural and energetic coffee with the pictures of coffee beans, rising sun and a well dressed young lady sipping the coffee.

Table 4.2 Images of Bharat (% ages)

Groups	*Descriptors*				
	Strong	*Tasty*	*Attractive Colour*	*Good Fragrance*	*Economy*
Sex					
Men (N=150)	70	65	60	70	80
Women (N=180)	80	70	70	70	90
Income					
Middle (N=200)	50	55	60	70	80
Lower (N=130)	80	85	85	85	90

Table 4.3 Preferences for Bharat (% ages)

Groups	*Yes*	*No*
Sex		
Men (N=150)	80	20
Women (N=180)	90	10
Income		
Middle (N=200)	60	40
Low (N=130)	90	10

The discussion between the partners went on like this:

Sasi : Let us go in a phased manner. First, we will distribute in towns leaving rural areas to our agency. It helps us to learn. Also, we do not anger the agency by terminating it abruptly. After all, they are with us for the last three years. The most important thing is promotion. Let us reinforce identity and push sales through advertising and consumer incentives.

Satyam : Why should we go slowly? I think a stitch in time saves nine!

QUESTIONS

1. **Analyze the situation faced by Sasi Beverages.**
2. **Develop a plan of action.**

CASE ANALYSIS
A STITCH IN TIME SAVES NINE

Brief of the Case

Sasi Beverages, is a well established 11 year old partnership firm. Its major brand, *'Bharat'* coffee, which had so far good sales in the Rayalseema region of Andhra Pradesh, has showed a declining trend. The partners, Satyam and Sasi have decided to evolve a new strategy for reviving the brand. To this end, a market survey was conducted and interesting findings were obtained.

Q (1) Analyze the situation faced by Sasi Beverages.

Organisation	:	Sasi Beverages & Co.
Partners	:	Satyam and Sasi
Line of Business	:	Coffee products
Major Brand	:	Bharat—coffee with chicory
Market	:	Low and middle income groups in the towns and rural areas of Rayalseema region
Events	:	Started the firm in 1991 Marketing agency is hired to sell products Sales are growing slowly Satyam and Sasi worried about poor sales had a discussion Got a market survey done; results ready Discussing marketing strategy for Bharat

Sales Facts	Assumptions/Predictions
• Low sales growth of around 1–2 per cent (Table 1) • Sales in first quarter of this year is also low	Market growth rate is 15 per cent

Reasons

The performance of marketing agency is not good (compared to sales before it was hired).	* Low commitment of the agency * Competition from Suraj * Changed preferences of consumers * Lack of promotion; competitors are doing good promotion * Health consciousness is growing Anti-coffee campaigns are on the rise * Traditional brand name * Middle income groups are relatively less favourable to the brand (Table 4.2 & 4.3)

Favourable Points

- Awareness is total
- High brand preferences
- Good image
- Retailer preferences are positive
- Low income groups are highly favourable (Table 4.2 & 4.3)

The Present Situation

- The marketing environment of Bharat is less favourable only in two aspects.
    1. Competition from Suraj
    2. Less strong preferences of middle income groups
- Performance—Sales are declining.

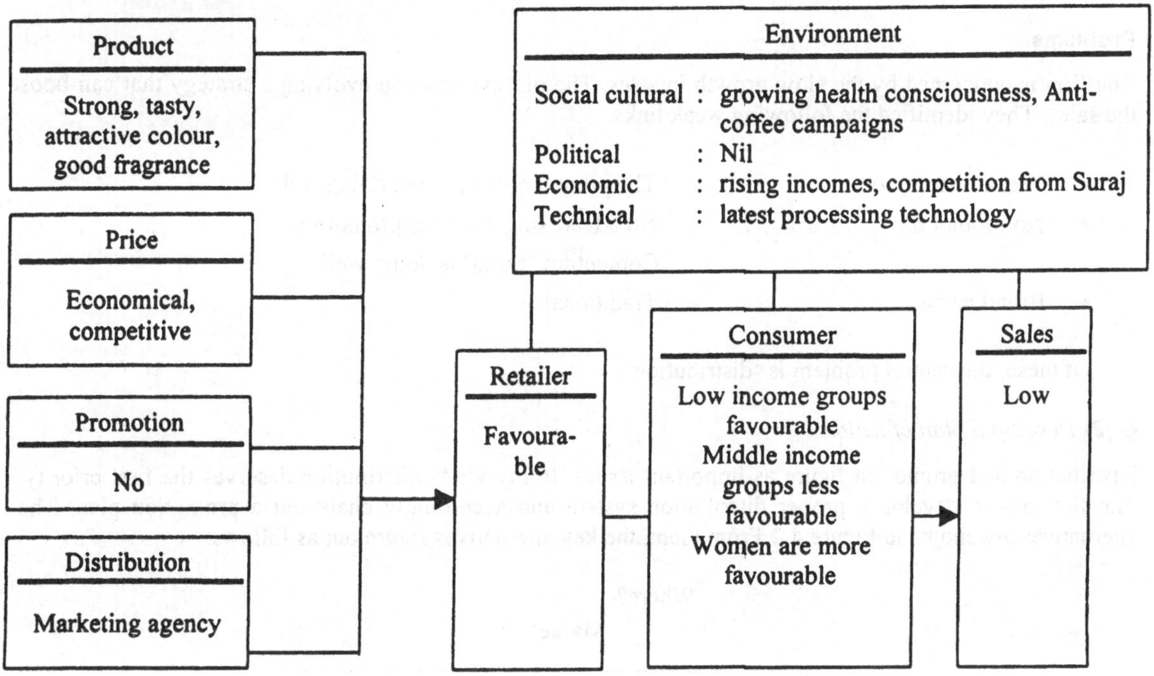

Fig. 4.1 Analytical Marketing Model

Objectives and Constraints

The market is growing at a rate of 15 per cent (supposedly). The annual growth rates of the firm are:

Year	Growth rates (%) (Over previous years)
1993	20.0
1994	20.0
1995	19.4
1996	14.0
1997	15.5
1998	14.7
1999	12.8
2000	7.1
2001	1.1

Growth rate before the agency was hired was in the range of 14 per cent. It declined to 1.1 per cent from 12.8 per cent during the three years.

The firm has to achieve a growth rate of 15 per cent. This looks formidable in view of the low sales during the last two years. The hurdles on the way are:

—Competition
—Changing preferences of middle income group people

Problems

The firm is concerned by the slow growth in sales. The discussion is on evolving a strategy that can boost the sales. They identified the following weak links:

- Weak distribution : The present agency is not doing well
- No promotion : No advertising, no sales promotion
  Competitor 'Suraj' is doing well
- Brand name : Traditional

Of these, the central problem is 'distribution'.

Q (2) Develop a plan of action.

Distribution and promotion figure as important issues. In my view, distribution deserves the first priority. The firm has to develop a proper distribution system and accordingly chalk out a promotion plan. The alternatives are shown in Figure 4.2 From them, the key alternatives figure out as follows.

Where? Market / Who?	Rural Only	Urban Only	Total
Present agency			
New agency			
Firm			

Fig. 4.2 Distribution Alternatives

1. Marketing on our own. Terminate services of the agency (Satyam's proposal).
2. Marketing on our own in urban areas while the present agency markets in rural areas. (Sasi's proposal).
3. Appoint a new agency for rural or urban or for the whole market.
4. Continue with the existing set up.

The last alternative is ruled out is it was proved incapable of even maintaining the earlier growth in sales. Now the first three alternatives are analysed.

Factor Analysis

Alternative 1 Marketing on our own in the entire market.

For	*Against*
1. The marketing agency has failed totally. We have to be on our own as agencies cannot be trusted. 2. Eleven years of standing in the business equipped us with enough knowledge base to start marketing operations. 3. Market is receptive. Competition can be thwarted by promotion. Most important task is making the product available. Transporters will help us in this regard. 4. Economics of own sales force will be favourable when sales go up.	1. We do not have any previous experience of managing sales force. Supervising sales force will be difficult. Handling an agency is easier than managing a sales team. Besides selling there will be human relations problems. 2. Awarness is not sufficient. Expertise is needed particularly, when the going is tough. The situation is very bad. Experiments may cost the firm heavily. 3. The selling costs may be more with our sales force.

Conclusion.

The arguments on both sides merit equal attention. However, going on own, needs confidence, aggressiveness (risk-taking attitude) and managing competencies.

Alternative 2 The firm markets in urban areas and present marketing agency in rural areas.

For	*Against*
1. By choosing urban areas, the risk of firm's marketing operations will be lowered. Urban agreas are easy to reach and understand.	1. The agency may not prefer rural areas. In such a case, they have to appoint a new agency. 2. The porportion of rural sales in the total sales is not definityely known. So bargaining with an agency may be difficult.

Conclusion

The alternative sounds good. The only problem seems to be how to work out terms of agreement with the agency.

Alternative 3 Appoint a new agency.

For	*Against*
1. Marketing on our own is a difficult and expensive propostion. 2. The present agency had showed poor performance. So, replacing it is necessary. 3. Agencies do good job as they are specialized in that activity.	1. Agencies will be dealing with serveral items. They promote items which are easy to sell. They do not pay required attention to our product unless we give attractive disocunts. 2. When we market on our own, we have control on operations and feed back. More of market information will be available to formulate

4. New agency can be made to achieve targets if properly chosen and monitored.	marketing strategies. Unless incentives are given, agencies do not supply us with information that can be used in product development, pricing, promotions, planning, etc. Information will become expensive.

Conclusion

Marketing through agencies will be less cumbersome and beneficial if relationships are handled properly and performance is monitored on a continuous basis.

Evaluation

The criteria for evaluation are:

(i) Sales accomplishment
(ii) Cost effectiveness
(iii) Information availability
(iv) Ease in management

The three alternatives can be evaluated as follows:

S.No	*Alternative*	*Criteria*			
		Sales	*Cost*	*Information*	*Ease*
1.	On our own	Moderate	High	Fully	Less
2.	Agency + own	Good	Moderate	Partly	Moderate
3.	New agency	Moderate to poor	Less	Marginal	High

From the above, it is abvious that Alternative 2 is the most desirable one as it can provide the required sales growth. Also, it is a middle of the road choice between the 'depend on agency' and desired 'be on our own' operations. It takes time and requires experience for a producing firm to become a marketing firm. As such, the movement should be gradual and well planned. It is better if a new agency is hired to undertake sales in rural areas.

Promotion

Hitherto, the firm has not undertaken any promotion campaign. It should consider the following questions.

(i) Why do we need promotion?
(ii) What should be its objectives?
(iii) What should be the media-mix?
(iv) What should be the message?

Promotion has become necessary because:

1. Competitor 'Suraj' is advertised and promoted with retailer discounts, price-off coupons.
2. Middle income groups are less favourable than lower income groups. Perceived image of the brand and preferences are on the lower side.
3. Promotion is regarded as an effective marketing element in boosting the sales.

Objecties of promotion may include:

-
- To improve the image of the brand
- To increase the preference level
- To generate sales of the product

The brand name, and package, the only communication elements so far, are out dated. should it be changed?

This is a difficult question. The arguments against such a change are:

1. The brand has rural sales. Rural markets are growing. So preferences of these consumers is important.
2. Low income groups are part of the target market. They like the brand.
3. Even in urban areas, with *'Ramayan'* as TV serial, the present package may go well. The main problem may be absence of advertisements.

In conclusion, the firm should continue with the present brand name and package. Instead of going for several changes at a time they are supposed to go for gradual changes. The issue may be considered next year if sales are found to be influenced by this factor.

The preference levels are to be raised in the case of middle income groups. The ratings are low for the brand in respect of three attributes: strong, tasty ad attractive colour. The strong points are: economy and good fragrance. The effective ways of creating preference levels are:

— Advertising
—Door-to-door selling

The media-mix, therefore, should comprise of advertising and sales promotion. Of these two, advertising is more effective as the same message reaches effectively to a larger people with less expenditure. Door-to-door selling can be effective as an on and off promotool. It will be effective when a price-off is given.

The message that is used to promote 'Bharat' is traditional whereas that of 'Suraj' is contemporary. A mix of contemporary values with the tradition is desirable. While the package remains traditional, advertisements may harp on modern values. The brand is to be positioned with reference to economy and good fragrance. It may be advertised through local TV channels and vernacular magazines.

WHERE EAGLES DARE

CASE 2

Seven Star Food Products is a member of Pasuparthy group of companies. It was established in collaboration with DOTT.INGG.M.G. BRAI BANTI & Co. Italy, in 1993 and started production in 1994. The plant is located in Tirupati. It produces vermicelli for the consumer market and various items of pasta (noodles, macaroni and spaghetti) catering to the needs of restaurants and hotels. The output of vermicelli varies between 200 to 300 tonnes per month. It is marketed under the brand name 7-Star in different pack sizes as shown below.

Pack size	Price (Rs.)
5 kg	190
1 kg	39
400 gm	15.50
200 gm	8

The major competitors are Bambino, True and Savorit. The product is distributed in three southern states—Aandhra Pradesh, Karnataka and Tamil Nadu. Three area sales managers having ten sales persons each monitor the distribution and retail promotion. The product is advertised in vernacular newspapers and magazines having the largest circulation. Point-of purchase advertising is also employed.

As the company has been facing stiff competition, the Managing Director Mr. Dwaraka Nath felt the need to take a fresh look at the markets and make some key decisions about markets, products and promotion. Accordingly, a consumer survey was conducted and opinions of sales personnel and retailers were pooled. The Marketing Manager Ms. Lalitha prepared a brief summary of the findings and presented them to the managing director.

ABOUT PASTA FOODS

Pasta is a dough of wheat flour and water. It is made into several shapes and forms and there are more than twenty types of pasta in the world. Pasta is a traditional food of the Italians. The Australians and Americans consume pasta in the form of macaroni. Indians use pasta in four forms—the noodles, macoroni, spaghetti and vermicelli, of which, the last is the most popular one.

Pasta is a good nourishing food, high in vegetable protein, carbohydrate, vitamin-B and iron. It is low in fat, easily digested and satisfying with a flavour that tends to enhance the food with which it is combined. Pasta is easy to prepare and lends itself to much variation, adaptation and imagination. Being easy to digest, it is particularly suitable for babies, school going children and men and women of different ages and occupations.

FINDINGS

The findings of the consumer survey are enumerated under two heads, viz., heavy users and light users in Table 4.4.

Table 4.4 Summary of Findings

Aspects	*Heavy Users*	*Non-Heavy Users*
Socio-economic characteristics	Highly educated, employed, large incomes, large or small families.	Less educated, medium or low income, medium size families, both working and non-working.
Awareness	Awareness very high and complete. A few of them do not know wheat base of vermicelli.	Some are not aware of short and thin types. Roasted type is very less known. *Maida* content is known. But *maida, sooji* combination is less known. Base is less known.
Use	Breakfast and supper are occasions to use. *Pulav* and Kesari are popular dishes. Regular users. Festivals push up consumption.	Breakfast and lunch are occasions to use and *uppuma* and *payasam* are the popular dishes. Occasional users. All occasions influence purchases.
Evaluation	Branded vermicelli with flavour, short in size and white in colour is preferred. Long vermicelli with other colours is preferred by a few. Bambino is more tasty, thin in size, takes less preparation time. 7-star, True and Savorit are tasty to a few. 7-Star is considered medium and thick in size and reported to take more time than Bambino in looking.	--do--
Price	Price is slightly higher.	O.K
Purchase influencers	Housewife	Children
Trial	Bambino and True are often tried. 7-Star and Savorit are seldom tried. In second preference, True is bought. Next, 7-Star and Savorit.	--do--
Place of purchase	Purchased at supermarkets and provision stores. 400 gm packs are frequently bought. Consumption is 1 kg or more.	Supermarkets or near by *kirana* shops. 200 gm packs are frequently bought. Consumption is 400–800gm.
Post-purchase attitude	Strong first preferences for Bambino. Next come True, Savorit and 7-Star.	--do--

The findings obtained by way of observation and discussions with sales personnel and retailers are given below:

1. Weak packaging The 8 kg cases containing 20 packets of 400 gm of long vermicelli is heavy compared to the short vermicelli cases and is not packed properly. It is leading to breakages when lifted and additional repacking costs.

2. Inadequate transport Transport of 7-Star is less adequate than Bambino who supply by company vans to every retailer.

3. Slow stock movement At times, retailers are finding supplies in excess of demand and returning stock after expiry date. The primary cause behind this slow stock movement is the divided attention of retailer which is less favourable to 7-Star. The retailers are retained by premier companies like Parry & Co., Hindustan Lever, MTR Condiments, and Burroughs Welcome, etc.

4. Less emphasis on sales force motivation Performance of sales personnel needs improvement. While there is enough encouragement to good performers, management of mediocre is less effective.

5. Less effective promotion The advertisements are in black and white and less attractive. Pop material needs improvement. Consumer incentives are attractive. However, unique and striking features are not found as in the case of competitors—Auro foods in 1993 promoted sales by its 'True' queen who distributed prizes. Recently, it struck deals with Food Specialities Ltd., and Godrej soaps to give vermicelli packs as incentives along with their products.

Mr. Dwaraka Nath has gone through the summary report and asked Ms. Lalitha to develop an appropriate strategy. He said: "In my view we have to spread our sales to rural markets. In cities and large towns, we have competitive disadvantage. Therefore, I want you to come up with improvements in our strategy keeping an eye on rural penetration." Assume the role of Ms. Lalitha and advise Mr. Dwaraka Nath.

CASE ANALYSIS
WHERE EAGLES DARE

Background

Seven Star Food Products markets vermicelli and pasta items. In view of stiff competition, the managing director ordered for a study of the marketing problems. The study revealed that the consumers are aware of its Vermicelli product but their brand preferences are less favourable to 7-Star. The price is considered reasonable but quality is rated poor in comparison with the competitive brands. There are then minor problems in distribution and sales force management. In view of this, the Managing Director, Mr. Dwaraka Nath asked Ms. Lalitha, the Marketing Manager, to evolve a competitive strategy to improve urban sales and initiate rural penetration.

Situation analysis

Seven Star is in a difficult competitive situation. It is facing stiff competition from Bambino, which is strong in distribution and promotion. Consumer preferences indicate that 7-Star is the least preferred product. Bambino, True and Savorit are rated better in taste and quality.

Problems

The central problem is: How to increase the sales of 7-Star against a tough competition?
The other problems which are part of this are:

- Weak packaging
- Inadequate transport
- Slow stock movement
- Less emphasis on sales force motivation
- Less effective promotion

Objectives

The company needs a marketing strategy to serve the following objectives:

- Increase penetration in the current markets.
- To expand to new markets–urban as well as rural.

Plan of Action

The action plan considers feasibility of rural penetration and improved marketing mix for current urban markets.

Entering Rural Markets

Though the managing director is preferring rural markets, it would be wise to consider the pros and cons of going rural.

The rural market has two strata.

- One which emulates urbans in tastes and preferences. This segment prefers good quality products. The consumers are mobile and buy goods from feeder towns. They can be reached in a way similar to the existing urban markets. The present strategy may be given some rural bias to reach them effectively.
- One which aspires to emulate urbans. This prefers low-quality and low-price products. Reaching them involves some consideration. The pros and cons are:

Pros

- Rural incomes are rising. The average monthly income per household has risen to Rs. 2,000. Britannia and Colgate-Palmolive have been able to derive more than 30 per cent of their revenues from the rural markets.
- Most FMCG players who do not have the critical size for going all out for rural marketing concentrated both on rural and urban marketing: focus on urban markets for value and focus on rural markets for volumes. Seven Star may follow them.
- Rural tastes have changed. They are comparable to urban counterparts. Good quality products offer the best price and aspirational values to the rural consumer who has a peculiar tendency to mimic his urban counterpart.
- Selling in rural areas is not difficult now a days as connectivity by roads has improved. To make cost-effective distribution, Nirma relies on the wholesale network. Nirma's competitor, HLL, is trying to get around this problem by giving credit to the distributors. There are other initiatives too. The FMCG stalwart Hindustan lever has started its ambitious project "Project Shakti", marketing initiative involving women belonging to micro-credit self-help groups (SHGs) in the Nalgonda district of Andhra Pradesh, similar to the highly successful experiment like Bangladesh's Grameen Bank used in rural areas of the country.
- The major competitors—Bambino, True and Savorit have not entered rural markets. It is a virgin market for branded vermicelli.
- A successful brand commands premium over non-branded products. According to a recent A&M-ORG-MARG study, the share of branded goods is high for a number of daily used products. Branded goods comprise of 65 per cent of sales in villages. Brands are the key determinants of success in the market place.
- In rural market, the battle is between fewer brands because retailers feel shy of stocking too many brands of a product category. Obviously one brand tends to dominate. The first entrant will have the obvious advantage.
- Products can be promoted by the media like propaganda stalls in fairs /*haats*, mobile vans, wall paintings, etc.
- Customer-centric and market-savvy FMCG companies have always chased prospects when they perceive there is a latent demand. For instance, Hindustan Lever's Rin, Surf and Lux are available even in India's most obscure villages.

Cons

- Rural income-levels are largely determined by the vagaries of monsoon and thus rural demand is not a steady horse to ride on. This makes rural marketing a gamble.

- Converting rural consumers from loose vermicelli to branded vermicelli is as difficult as converting urban consumers from Bambino to 7-Star.
- Seven Star is not sure of its sales volumes in the rural area. To make rural marketing profitable a critical size in necessary.
- The cost of marketing in rural areas has seen many causalities, the notable being the P&G which abandoned its plan to fight the likes of Lever in the rural segment on its own. The only way out of 7-Star is to put in place an aggressive cost structure, which would enable it to offer low-price and value-for-money products. But then, food products is generally a low-margin business with a high cost of raw materials.
- Our logic is that if we are well distributed in the urban areas, where there is a lot of untapped potential for our products, the products will find their way into the rural areas also through the rural retailers. There is no need for separate rural focus.
- Competition from unorganized sector is heavy. The unorganized segment plays spoilsport and benefits mainly due to their strategy of "low price, high volumes". They benefit without spending even a single penny on advertising and brand building.
- Rural market is at once a challenge and an opportunity as it calls for a substantial allocation for distribution. This, is turn, affects product pricing, making it either more expensive or less profitable. Distribution may be sluggish for reasons like:

  —Difficulty in reaching the small towns which act as feeder towns in villages.

  —Costs of operating mobile vans, propaganda stalls, etc.

Conclusion

Having identified that 7-Star is a low quality product, Dwaraka Nath has set his sights on the rural market considering it a low-quality market with good potential. Sure, there is a lot of money in rural India. Rural marketing could open the doors of opportunities, but the path is paved with thorns. That is why a few FMCG companies are not putting in concerted efforts to tap the rural market. Consider the case of Cadbury. The company has clarified that the rural market is not for it, at least for now. Only FMCGs with deeper pockets, unflinching rural commitment and staying power can play this rural game.

In this market, 7-Star may have to fight on price front by reducing its price. This may not pay off until volumes are achieved as distribution costs will go up. In view of this, it is better for the company to go for product improvements and put up a fight in the urban markets. At the same time, instead of viewing rural sales as a bonus, it would be wise to make some conscious efforts in a phased manner to woo the rural consumers. Gradually, the product may wear a rural look and capture the rural markets.

Improved Marketing Mix

The proposed marketing mix with modifications, required for 7-Star to promote its sales in the current market with rural bias is briefly described here.

Product.

The company should focus on short vermicelli with flavour and white colour. Packaging for distribution should be made strong and protective to avoid damage in transportation.

Price

To increase heavy use of the product, price may be reduced or incentives may be offered to consumers. The later step is preferred as price reduction is not desirable unless there is a cost advantage either by improved technology or efficient administration.

Distribution

The present distribution set-up which envisages the company selling stocks to wholesalers and retailers can be continued. To eliminate physical distribution problems, company may consider owning a few vans and reduce dependence on hired transportation. To promote sales in small towns, marketing agencies may be hired. Another alternative is mobile traders. Mobile traders score over the conventional wholesale channel on both counts of cost and reach. They travel either on foot or on cycles. That means transportation costs are virtually non-existent. Besides, these traders can target smaller villages, which conventional distribution channels often do not touch. Mobile traders, therefore, are a smart way of reaching women in their home environment. The women rely on these mobile traders to sell them goods in the security of their home.

Rural markets have the practice of fixing specific days in a week as market days when exchange of goods and services are carried out. This is another potential low cost distribution channel available to the marketers. *Haats* serve a good opportunity for promotion after brand building has been done at the *Mela*. In rural India, annual *melas* organized with a religious or festive significance are quite popular and provide a very good platform for distribution. Rural markets come alive at these *melas* and people visit them to make several purchases. The average daily sale at a h*aat* is about Rs. 2.25 lakh while the annual sales at *melas* amount to Rs. 3,500 crore.

Promotion

Promotion should aim at:

1. Improving the performance of the sales personnel.
2. Motivating retailers to give more attention and push the product.
3. Increasing the consumer pull of 7-Star brand.

Sales force effectiveness

The major supplemental incentives listed below may be considered for adoption.

- Contests
- Recognition
- Reports
- Meetings
- Promotion Opportunities

Seven Star should consider holding at least a few contests in a year for the sales force. Meetings, conferences, conventions and the like inspire and encourage sales force. Recognition awards can take many forms—some tangible and others more intangible. Table- 1 shows the use of various recognition awards. The costs of such recognition awards are less, while the benefits can be significant. 'Star Salesman' recognition may be given. The winner may be given a Silver Star, a briefcase, and a tie in addition to monetary incentives.

A sound promotion policy ensuring job advancement is highly essential. It is time for the company to re-examine its policy to achieve high commitment.

Reports should not be seen as control devices but as information sources and means for incentives. Daily sales reports are to be obtained and strict review should be made by the concerned sales officer.

Personal selling is to be supported by 'Door-to-Door Campaign' particularly in areas where sales are either slow in pick-up or in the initial stages. The door-to-door campaign can be organized, hiring young students of both sexes as a novel feature.

Retailer promotion effectiveness

Retailer promotion schemes should be strengthened with a view to attaining the following objectives.

- To carry higher levels of stock
- Off-setting competitive promotions
- Building brand loyalty of retailers

1. A display allowance for carrying display of Seven Star vermicelli should be given to those retailers strategically located.
2. Free goods which are extra cases of merchandise should be offered to retailers selling above a fixed sales level.
3. Contests for retailers may be organized for display as well as sales level achievements at least once in a year.
4. Retailer promotion schemes should be held round the year with a variety of incentives and care should be taken for proper implementation.

Consumer Motivation

Consumer motivation needs a two-pronged approach involving sales promotion and advertising.

(1) Sales promotion It should be carefully worked out and implemented to meet the objectives given below:

- Encouraging more usage and purchase of larger size units among light users.
- Building trial among non-users.
- Attracting competitors' brand users.

1. The point of purchase (POP) materials being made available are not satisfactory. They are to be improved. The POP material includes danglers, posters, and stickers, etc. Seven Star should bring in changes in the POP material in line with the suggested ad campaign.
2. Attractive offers to housewives and children should be considered. Some schemes for consideration are:

   For Children: Masks, time-table cards, labels, book marks, pencils, erasers, pencil boxes, sketch pens, etc.

For Housewives: Spoons, cups (*Katoris*), recipe books, *garam masala* packs, small mirrors, hand purses, key chains, calendars, etc.

3. Tie-ups with the manufacturers of convenience products like—soaps, processed foods like edible oils, beverages, etc., in case of which women have major influence in buying should be envisaged. One of the major competitors, True is benefited by its tie-up with Godrej Soaps Pvt. Ltd. and Food Specialities Ltd., which offered its vermicelli packs to those who bought their products.
4. Seven Star should consider conducting contests for housewives and children. Some contests for favourable consideration of the company are:

- 'Delicious Pasta Contest' inviting housewives to send new recipes for dishes that can be prepared with vermicelli.
- A simple 'Nutritive Value Quiz Contest' for both housewives and children.
- Vermicelli's children's day contests in schools of major cities with competitions like—quiz, essay writing and debates which are less expensive and easy to arrange may be held.

(2) Advertising Advertising should be made more competitive with well defined purposes and additional outlay. Seven Star needs the following promotional objectives:

- To generate brand awareness among non-heavy users and unawares.
- To influence the perceptions of users of competitors' brands to increase triers.
- To effect sales in the existing and new markets to increase users.

The first objective needs informative approach and the latter one requires persuasive approach to advertising.

The target audience is moderately educated, working or non-working housewife who is health conscious, variety seeking and an economizer. Another important group is the children. The theme should be both rational and emotional. Ads should be positioned on health, variety of life and occasions. They should furnish details of nutritive values and also arise a sense of joy in cooking, love in serving and pride in satisfying the needs of the family. The nutritive values that can be highlighted are: protein (8.7%), energy (352 calories), minerals (0.7%) and vitamins like Thiamin, Riboflamin and Niacin.

Some slogans which may be considered for use in this context are:

1. Seven Star Vermicelli—A 100% value added wheat product. An excellent vitaminised food.
2. Seven Star Vermicelli—A pasta for all ages. A promise for good health and taste.
3. Seven Star Vermicelli—A gift to mothers. A boon for working women.

Ads should present in detail in a colourful way the various dishes of vermicelli. The dishes described in any ad should be not more than three and should be changed form ad to ad. The occasions on which vermicelli could be used should also be highlighted. The occasions are to be chosen keeping in mind the different religions.

*Birthdays *Marriages *Weekends
*Festivals like *Sankranti*, *Ugadi*, *Dussehra* and *Deepavali* for Hindus,
Christmas for Christians and *Ramjan* for Muslims.

The media of advertising should be chosen keeping in mind the rural markets.

- Daily newspapers and weekly magazines in regional languages (Table- 1).
- TV advertisements in local channels.
- Cinema slides in semi-urban towns and villages.
- Bill boards in select urban towns.
- Wall paintings in villages.
- Closed circuit TVs at railway stations and bus stations in principal towns.

Table 4.5 List of Print Media Recommended for Advertising

Periodicity	*States*		
	Tamil Nadu	*Karnataka*	*Andhra Pradesh*
Dailies	*Dina Thanthi*	*Prajavani*	*Eanadu*
	Dinamani	*Kannada Prabha*	*Vaartha*
Weeklies	*Kumudam*	*Sudha*	*Andhra Bhoomi*
	Ananda Vikatan	*Prajamatha*	*Swathi*
Monthlies	*Mangai*	*Vanitha*	*Vanitha*
	Ambulimama	*Chandamama*	*Chandamama*

Utilizing the various rural folk media may be considered to reach them in their own language and in large numbers so that the brand can be associated with the myriad rituals, celebrations, festivals, *melas* and other activities where they assemble. The traditional media like folk/street plays, wall signs/shop painting product demonstrations can be effectively used for this purpose.

PART

2

Rural Marketing Perspectives

- New Marketing Opportunities
- Customization
- Promotion of Solar Energy Use

CASE

1 New Marketing Opportunities

New population figures have become available which estimate that India will cross China by 2050 with a population of 1.55 billion. What does this mean to marketers?

MARKET CHARACTERISTICS

With this population, there will be a tremendous spurt in the economically active portions of the population aged between 50 and 59, which between 1996 and 2016 is expected to grow from 54.2 per cent to 63.4 per cent. The population of the aged, above the age of 60 will also grow from 7.4 per cent to 8.7 per cent.

Table 1 Income Distribution in Rural and Urban Areas

Annual Income Group (Rs)	*Rural*		*Urban*	
	Hhds	*Share in Income*	*Hhds*	*Share in Income*
Up to 12,000	16.21	5.28	2.33	0.37
12,000–18,000	25.71	14.20	7.74	2.12
18,000–24,000	17.92	13.67	9.61	3.50
24,000–48,000	29.91	36.47	35.83	22.20
48,000–72,000	5.86	12.58	19.80	20.07
72,000–96,000	2.10	6.33	11.32	16.30
Above 96,000	2.29	11.47	13.47	35.43
Total	100.00	100.00	100.00	100.00
Avg. income per household (Rs.)	27411.00		57675.00	

The sharp decline will be in the age group below 15 from 38.2 to 28.7 per cent. The major chunk of population continues to be in the rural areas. Of the total estimated gross income generated in the house hold sector, the share of rural income accounted for 55.6 per cent with 74.6 per cent of the country's population. The income distribution is as given in Table 1.

Financing in rural India, between 1971 and 1991 has moved dramatically from money lenders to banks. Agricultural and professional money lenders accounted for 17.2 per cent of borrowings by rural households in 1971; in 1991 this was down to 5 per cent. Commercial banks which were at 0.4 per cent in 1971 rose to 7.5 per cent in 1991. The availability of banking, the dominance of road transport accounting for 71 per cent of all freight in India, the penetration by television and the private operators providing interesting programmes in regional languages, now create a climate which will enable further dramatic increases in the rural consumer markets.

THE SUCCESSES

ORG-MARG in their survey of rural markets have reported that between 1995 and 1999, the penetration of sophisticated FMCG's has grown faster in rural than in urban markets—for products such as scourers (19.2%), mosquito repellants (22.5%), sanitary napkins (9.2%), skin creams (8.1%), twin blades (19.5%), shampoos (12.4%), hair dyes (26%), biscuits (14.4%), squashes/cordials (19.3%), jams/jellies (35.9%) and confectionery (35.4%).

Some outstanding successes are:

- Ruf & Tuf Jean kits of Arvind Mills crossed 1 million pieces;
- The launch of the Tiger brand glucose biscuits by Britannia raised their rural market share in glucose biscuits from 7 to 15 per cent;
- HLL's A1 tea became a Rs. 100 crore brand within less than a year of being introduced in the rural markets;
- While HLL's Operation Bharat which offered for Rs. 15 composite pack (soap, toothpaste and fairness cream) achieved 30 per cent conversion;

STRATEGY

Products designed for the rural consumers and taking account of their cultural diversity, lifestyle, standard of living, disposable income, consumption pattern, and communication facilities appear to be the key elements in a rural marketing strategy.

Product

ORG-MARG data shows that the so-called "necessity" products (like popular soaps, detergent cakes, premium soaps) show signs of saturation in both urban and rural markets, but "the growth of emerging products" (like toothpaste, toffee, chewing gum") and "lifestyle" products (like chocolate, coffee) is fuelled by the rural market. Rural markets have shown fast growth when special small pack sizes are available, and more so in the case of "necessity" and "emerging" products, while lifestyle products show good growth even in standard packs.

At the same time they find that rural markets are dominated by local brands and unpackaged loose purchases. This may not indicate a lower preference for brands but only low purchasing power. A NCAER study on advertising has shown that brand awareness and association of established brands with quality, is as high in rural as in urban markets.

The developed states with good infrastructure (Gujarat, Haryana, Karnataka, Kerala, Maharashtra, Punjab, Tamil Nadu) show faster penetration growth than the developing states, and even more so for lifestyle products. Similarly, relatively large pack sizes are bought in developed than in developing states, as also a larger proportion of premium products.

Price

The players obviously believe that the key obstacle to recruiting new users lies in the high price of a product. Therefore, marketers have been working at scaling down prices further.

CavinKare made the first such attempt last year. It introduced a smaller 50 paise sachet of Chik, when most other sachets retailed at Rs. 2. The effort appears to have been an unqualified success, with the Chik brands expanding by 40 per cent after the launch. A new 50 ml bottle Chik priced at Rs. 6 (when most other brand were available in 100 ml bottles and above) has also expanded the brand.

HLL has responded with its own 50 paise version of Lux shampoo. The company claims the recently launched 30 ml bubble pack for Clinic Plus (Rs. 8), is an innovative and cost-effective alternative for sachet users. While sachets are difficult to store and re-use, the bubble pack allows the user to extract just the right quantity for a single wash.

The scaled down versions could help pep up volume growth rates for major players. But they have also had the effect of lowering margin expansion for the players.

Promotion

Regional television has become a vast and growing area, with penetration in the rural areas at 26 per cent and urban at 35 per cent. It will be a major means for opening rural consumption of consumer goods. Sun TV in Tamil Nadu last year raised Rs. 110 crore in advertising revenues against Rs. 15 crore by DD, and out of a total of Rs. 159 crore from the state, in Andhra, Enadu raised Rs. 60 crore out of a total of Rs. 130 crore, with DD way behind at Rs. 30 crore. In Karnataka, Udaya raised Rs. 60 crore in ad revenues against DD's Rs. 25 crore, while in Kerala, Asianet raised Rs. 35 crore out of a total of Rs. 70 crore with DD at Rs. 22 crore.

There is a transformation taking place in the television industry in India as private operators go after mass markets through cable, and move away from the Westernised and English focused programming of the past. DD has been unable to keep pace and is not using its huge land based transmission capacity effectively. This is one segment (regional TV), where domestic players for the present appear to be holding foreign entrants at bay, as Zee is doing at the national level. The aggression of private entrants in understandable given the numbers of growth in rural markets.

Distribution

There is a revolution taking place in distribution with the entry in the metros as well as smaller cities and towns, of self service stores, super markets, shopping malls, departmental stores, chain stores, and information technology. At the same time, direct selling by mail order, and door-to-door, will see a tremendous growth. Already, a recent entrant like Amway has crossed Rs. 100 crore in turn over and is expecting much faster growth, especially as they prepare to tap rural and mass markets. An ORG-MARG in house survey shows that 75 per cent of the Indian and multi-national companies are taking the help of rural marketing organisations to establish distribution links in rural markets.

Competition

Foreign brands will dominate most Indian consumer products. Indian brands that are in niche markets have

a better chance of surviving and growing. So do those that have already reached, a large size. Indian businesses have to overcome their history of past short term thinking.

QUESTIONS

1. **Crystallize the trends in the markets and marketing.**
2. **Analyze the prospects for the following products and outline suitable marketing strategies.**
   (a) Detergents
   (b) Chocolates

Source

Prof. S.L.Rao, Consumer Markets In India: The Second Phase of Consumer Demand. (Internet) and *MIMAP Study*

CASE

2 Customization

India's large gross cropped area (GCA), next only to USA and Rùssia along with fragmented land holdings has helped India to become the largest tractor market in the world. But it drops to eight position, in terms of total tractors in use in the country. (Table 1)

Table 1 Tractors in Use: India Vs World

Description	*Units*	*World Total/Avg*	*India*	*India's Rank*
Available Land	Million hectares	1,444	170	2
Irrigated Area	Million hectares	249.6	45.8	2
Tractors in Use	tractors/'000 hectares	28	10.5	8

Market Shares

The industry is segmented on the basis of the power of the tractor engine expressed in terms of horse power (HP). The HP-wise composition of tractor industry sales as shown in Table-2 reveals that 31–40 HP tractors constitute the largest segment with 54.7 per cent of the total tractor sales in FY2000. It can also be seen that the demand for less than 30 HP segment, which used to be the largest in FY94, has been pushed back by the 31–40 HP segment.

Table 2 Segment-Wise Market Shares

Segment	*FY94 Market Share*	*FY99 Market Share*	*FY2000 Market Share*
< 30 HP	36%	22.5%	26.1%
31–40 HP	46%	57.8%	54.7%
41–50 HP	15%	15.9%	14.7%
> 51 HP	3%	3.8%	4.4%

Source: SIAM/TMA

Table 3 Major Markets for Tractors

Tractor Power (HP)	*Major Markets*
Less than 30 HP	UP, MP, Rajasthan, Haryana and Bihar
31-40 HP	MP, Rajasthan, Punjab, UP, Haryana, Gujarat and Bihar
41-50 HP	Punjab, MP and Rajasthan
More than 51 HP	Punjab and also some volumes in Kerala and Maharashtra

Source: SIAM/TMA

Table 4 Region-Wise Market Shares

Region	*FY94 Market Share*	*FY99 Market Share*
North	54%	41%
Central	18%	27%
Western	12%	15%
South	16%	17%

This graduation to a higher HP segment can be easily explained if one considers the fact that region-wise share of tractor sales has also shifted from the northern states to other parts of the country. North India constituting UP, Punjab and Haryana leads among the regions, by contributing 44 per cent of tractor sales in FY99, but its contribution has come down in the last five years from a peak level of 53.3 per cent in FY94. Among the states, UP stands first with a contribution of 23 per cent of the country's tractor sales. MP and Punjab stand next with around 12–13% contribution each. Initially, the population of tractors was concentrated in states like Punjab and Haryana which received the benefits of the so-called 'Green Revolution'. The soil in these states are alluvial in nature and thus require a low powered tractor for tilling it.

However, over the years, with an increase in irrigated cropped area, the population of tractors began to increase in other states as well. These included states located in the western and southern parts of the country where the soil—laterite soil, black soil etc—is harder and needed high powered tractors. In the future, new tractor sales are expected to take place mainly in the western and southern regions of the country while the mature markets of the north will mainly see higher replacement sales.

In FY2000, the share of the less than 30 HP segment improved by around 3.5 per cent while that of the next higher segment fell by 3 per cent. This could be attributed to the fact that in the 1999–2000 budget, the excise duty for the plus 1800cc tractors (above 30 HP) was increased from 13 per cent to 16 per cent while that of the less than 1800cc segment remained at 8 per cent.

Demand Determinants

During the last 20 years from FY78 to FY98, the tractor industry has performed substantially better in comparison to the growth in Indian agriculture production and GDP. As given in Table-5, the CAGR of tractor sales was almost four times the growth of agriculture production.

Table 5 Tractor Sales Vs GDP Growth

Particulars	*CAGR Growth from FY78 to FY98 in (%)*
Agriculture Production	2.2
GDP	5.15
Tractor Sales	8.31

Government Policies

All the agriculture related industries in India have been highly controlled by the government and tractors are not an exception to this. The important government policies affecting the tractor industry are excise duty and licensing.

(1) Excise Duty In the past, government has used excise duty as an effective tool for controlling the demand for various types of tractors. The main objective has been to keep the price of small tractors purchased by marginal/small farmers, at affordable level. But this seems to have changed now. However, the 2000–2001 budget has raised the excise duty on the less than 1800cc tractors from 8 per cent to 16 per cent. This is expected to affect a drop in the segment demand during FY2001.

(2) Licensing The liberalization process that started in 1991 has brought relief to the tractor industry, by providing free hand in setting up of additional capacities to the existing players and allowing new players to set up plants. The tractor implements sector, which is very important for the effective usage of tractors, was now de-reserved from the SSI list in 1998–99 budget so that the implements can be produced with better design and technology that can help in farm mechanization.

Usage of Tractors

In India, tractors are mainly used for three basic purposes, viz, farming operations, transportation and as a power source. In farming operations, the tractors are used for seedbed preparation, irrigation and harvesting. Tractors help in reducing the time required for these operations. It is also used as a power source in farms for harvesting, pumping of water, etc.

Tractors are also used in the transportation of people, fodder, food grains, etc. from rural area to the nearest market place and in earth-moving and forest clearing operations.

Tractors also have a number of industrial applications, like loaders, fork lifts road rollers and baggage haulers at airports. But because of the availability of cheap labour in the country, industrial usage is limited only to large firms. Therefore, the usage in these areas is very small compared to total industry size.

The use of tractors in operations other than farming is sizable and as per industry estimates, it ranges from 40 to 50 per cent of the total tractor utility in the country.

Tractors used in different parts of the country are adapted to the local conditions. For instance, a tractor model in the south is adopted to harder soil and wet cultivation of the principal crop paddy. A tractor is normally equipped with power takeoff shafts, which drive auxiliary equipment such as pumps and compressors. They are also equipped with high power air cleaners, that ensure smooth operations even in the dusty conditions.

Technology

In India, all the tractor manufacturers indigenised the models. Punjab Tractors is the first company to start with indigenously developed tractor model in the country. All the leading companies in the country have very strong in-house R&D capabilities, which has resulted in the development of tractors suitable to different soil conditions and crop. The Indian tractor market is characterized with low price, no frills, rugged, versatile and low to medium power tractors. The farmer, key user of tractors, is unwilling to pay a premium for sophisticated modern technology, which can reduce fatigue, emission and noise levels.

Land Holding Pattern

The optimal land holding required for different hp tractors is approximately 8 to 10 hectares for 1800 cc or 25 HP tractors, 25 to 30 hectares for 35 HP and beyond that, it is higher HP tractors. But the actual relationship between different land holdings and the power of tractors is dependent on earning stability, type of soil, type of operation and affordability by farmers.

Nearly 78.2 per cent of India's agricultural land is held by small and marginal farmers having less than the prescribed land holding. For these small and marginal farmers there is very little potential for economic use of tractors by outright purchases.

The change in the number of farmers with minimum economic land size (due to a variety of reasons including split in family, etc.), over the decades will have an impact on the demand pattern for tractors.

Irrigation Potential

HP per hectare of mechanized power in India varies between 0.32 to 2.88 averaging 1.14 as compared to 2 to 5 HP per hectare for developed countries. Punjab (2.88) and Haryana (2.55) are ahead of other states.

As of now, about 65 per cent of the total irrigation potential has been achieved in India. Thus, there is still some way to go before making Indian agriculture free from the vagaries of monsoons. It remains to be seen how much the government gives priority to irrigation on which would depend tractor sales.

Monsoons

Indian agriculture is still subject to the vagaries of monsoon as the gross irrigated area constitutes only 37.5 per cent of the gross cropped area. Monsoon has a dual impact on demand. While on the one hand, poor monsoon causes hardening of soil and weakening of farm animals, it calls for a greater need of tractors. On the other hand, a poor monsoon also leaves the farmer with low purchasing power not even able to pay 15 per cent down payment, thus affecting the demand adversely. But the actual demand during monsoon failure would depend on state support in terms of subsidies, concessions, etc.

Availability of Credit

Nearly 95 per cent of the purchases of tractors is through loans taken from banks and agricultural institutions. Bank lending for acquiring tractors is part of the priority sector lending. Any change in limits for priority sector lending from the current minimum requirement of 40 per cent and 32 per cent of the net bank credit for domestic and foreign banks respectively will affect the demand for tractors as nearly 95 per cent of the tractor sales is through credit taken from banks. The loans given for tractors, by banks is refinanced by NABARD under the head "farm mechanization", which includes power tillers, harvesters, engines, pumps, etc., besides tractors.

Growth in Income of Farmers

The improvement in procurement prices of controlled agricultural product leads to increase in disposable income of farmers and in turn their purchasing power. The farmer would then be in a position to increase his share of the initial investment in the tractor. In the 80s, procurement prices of paddy and wheat (the two staple crops) increased by CAGR of 7 per cent and 5.6 per cent respectively. In the 90s, it has been higher being 10 per cent and 11 per cent respectively. Liberalisation in exports of cash crops has helped increase their prices. This will have a major impact on the tractor demand in future also.

Implementation of Scientific Farming Practices

A package of scientific farming practices is a pre-requisite for the use of tractors. The tractor is the heart of farm mechanisation. However, farm mechanisation would not be feasible without a complete package of scientific farming, which would include irrigation, use of high yielding variety seeds, fertilizers and modern farming practices such as intensive cultivation, multi-cropping, etc. Due to high capital cost, acquisition of a tractor would not be feasible unless it is used optimally with these compliments.

Increase in Multiple Cropping

Multiple cropping requires repeated tilling of the land. This, along with increased cropping intensity has resulted in the need for deeper tilling for the same effect, thereby leading to increased need for tractors. Though latest figures for cropping intensity is not available, a rough estimate is that it would have gone up to 1.34 crops a year in FY99 and around 70 per cent of the total tractor population is used in multiple cropping assuming that all area under multiple cropping use tractors.

Increase in Literacy

Increase in education level will help understand and implement farm mechanisation in India. This will in turn lead to better utilisation of tractors.

Supply

The capacity of tractor industry has increased from 150,300 tractors in FY92 to 418,000 tractors in FY01. The increase in capacity will be from expansion projects of existing players and entry of three new players in the segment.

Market Dynamics

In the past few years, the tractor market has moved from a sellers market to a buyers market as competition, from both the existing and new manufacturers, intensified and fresh capacity was created. This has created a scenario where dealers have been maintaining higher inventories so as to provide wider choice and immediate delivery to the farmer. Tractor prices in India are about a quarter, of the similar powered tractors, in international markets.

Market Players

The industry is controlled by six major players contributing 99 per cent of the industry's total sales. The major players are M&M, TAFE, Punjab Tractors, Escorts, Eicher and HMT. In FY2000, M&M led the table with a market share of 27 per cent. The challengers for M&M are Punjab Tractors, with a market share of 19.4 per cent as against 18.9 per cent recorded in FY99, and Escorts with market share of 19.9 per cent as against 19.2 per cent in FY99. Table 6 shows the market shares of major players. Eicher and M&M are leaders in the less than 30 HP and 31–40 HP segment respectively. In the 41–50 HP and above 51 HP segment, Escorts and Punjab Tractors lead with above 50 per cent market shares respectively.

Table 6 Company-Wise Share in Different Power Segments

Market Share (%)	*<30 HP*	*31–40 HP*	*41–50 HP*	*>51 HP*
Eicher	27.6	2.7	-	-
Escorts	16.5	15.6	50.2	-
Gujarat Tractors	0.37	0.06	1.3	1.1
VST	1.2	-	-	-
HMT	8.0	5.6	3.7	25.4
Mahindra & Mahindra	26.0	26.2	34.9	-
Punjab Tractors	8.4	25.0	0	73.6
TAFE	7.7	25.0	9.8	-
Total	100	100	100	100

Sales Performance

After exhibiting a compound annual growth rate (CAGR) of 16 per cent in the period FY94 to FY98, demand for tractors have since remained stagnant. FY02 also turned out to be a bad year for the industry (Table 7). The tractor sales fell 9.47 per cent to 236,076 units in this year from 260,773 units in the previous year.

The process of reducing retail inventory (estimated to be nearly 100,000 units at the beginning of FY02) continued throughout the year. This had a direct effect on production and costs of operation.

Company	*Year of Establishment*	*FY 2000*	*FY 2001*	*FY 2002*
Mahindra & Mahindra	1965	70,595	79,595	58,073
Punjab Tractors	1974	50,705	45,688	40,100
Escorts	1964	47,697	44,954	38,034
Eicher Tractors	1977	22,629	18,613	19,026
TAFE	1961	45,432	33,296	28,759
HMT	1971	15,775	13,327	11,051
Bajaj Tempo	1977	1,324	1,674	1,100
VST	1983	736	927	323
Gujarat Tractors	1963	859	369	521
Total Market		225,752	260,773	236,076

At the retail level, sales failed to pick up, as rural income remained affected by the surplus stock situation in the country. Except for the states of Gujarat, Rajasthan, and Madhya Pradesh (recovering from a drought year in FY01), all the other states posted a decline in sales. The largest consumer state of Uttar Pradesh recorded a sharp 35 per cent year-on-year fall in sales while it was 23.8 per cent for Haryana.

All the companies except Eicher, suffered during the year. The market leader Mahindra & Mahindra posted the sharpest decline in sales. Although, its presence throughout the country helped it post higher sales in Gujarat and Madhya Pradesh, it lost heavily in states like Uttar Pradesh, Maharashtra, Andhra

Pradesh, and Orissa where sales fell in excess of 40 per cent. The second largest manufacturer, Punjab Tractors, was affected by a 26 per cent fall in sales in Uttar Pradesh. It managed to do well in Rajasthan and Madhya Pradesh. Higher sales in the states of Madhya Pradesh, Punjab, and Rajasthan helped Eicher Tractors post a small growth.

Segment Sales Performance

In terms of sub-segments, tractors of all power configurations showed a fall in sales during the period April to December 2001. The 0 to 30 HP segment recorded the highest fall at 23.7 per cent with Mahindra & Mahindra posting a drop of 37.5 per cent. Mahindra & Mahindra managed to do better high power sub-segments due to higher sales of its 60 HP 'Arjun' model. Punjab Tractors has done relatively well in this segment with sales of its 48 HP model falling by just 4 per cent during the fiscal year.

The sales of 41 HP and above models have risen to constitute 21.2 per cent of the total sales in 2001 due to the lower price differential between a 20–30 HP tractor and a higher-powered tractor. This has been brought about by the removal of the concessionary rate of excise duty (8 per cent) on less than 1,800 cc tractors two years ago. Another reason could be the fact that increasingly, farmers in Punjab, Haryana, and some parts of Gujarat, Andhra Pradesh, and Tamil Nadu are replacing their existing tractors with higher-powered models. The margin money required for getting a loan for the high-end tractors is obtained by selling the used tractor. The utility of a higher-powered tractor is more than a small tractor. Apart from farming, the tractor can be used to transport people, construction materials, and haul water from wells. Moreover, a large tractor is also a status symbol in large parts of rural India. It is estimated that replacement sales are currently around 40 to 45 per cent of total sales and if this trend continues it will ultimately affect sales of low powered tractors.

Outlook for M&M

Though M&M has succeeded in increasing its market share (which is currently over 33 per cent) its margins have come under pressure. The company has reported a 60.5 per cent decline in net profit for the quarter ended March 31, 2001—to Rs. 29.3 crore against Rs. 74.1 crore during the corresponding quarter last year. To tackle over capacity problem and to keep the pace of growth, major players are implementing key management and marketing strategies. Mahindra & Mahindra (M&M) is also looking at ways to bring down costs and increasing market share in the face of demand slump. M&M is implementing BPR to control processes and cost of production, PTL is expanding into South India by appointing new dealers, Eicher is entering higher HP segment through a collaboration strategy.

Some companies are looking at the export market to boost their top line. Among the potential foreign market is the USA. There, the market for garden tractors (40–70 HP) is estimated to be 60,000 to 80,000 per annum and is growing at 10 per cent annually. In FY02, Mahindra & Mahindra posted a 53 per cent growth in sales to around 5,000 units. Its 'Arjun' model (60HP) has received a good response. Others like Punjab Tractors and TAFE are also exploring opportunities to increase sales in this market.

M&M is also considering plans to further sharpen the competitive edge. The plans are based on the following assumptions.

- Demand for tractors in heterogeneous. Success in tractor business would, to a large extent, be determined by promptness with which manufacturers respond to the heterogeneous demand.
- In the longer run, fresh demand will be driven by states in the west and south and high powered segments of the country, while Punjab and Haryana will witness more replacement demand. Demand is also expected to arise out of the increase in irrigated crop area which has stagnated of late.

- With the hike in the excise duty for the less than 1,800 cc tractors, demand will again concentrate on the medium and high powered segments.
- Customization alone meets crop specific requirements and caters to the diverse farming belts.

In a bid to promote customization of tractors, M&M is setting up a string of satellite units which would take up "distributed manufacturing" in line with local demand. Having built its first satellite factory at Rudrapur in Uttar Pradesh, the company is now setting up the second assembling unit near Jaipur which is expected to be completed in the next few months.

The satellite units, which would eventually cover the major farming belts, are being set up with an investment of Rs. 4–6 crore each and would be able to roll out around 500 tractors a month. They would enable farmers to get factory-fresh tractors, which would be customized in line with the local requirements.

With the satellite units, the target is to be present in at least 10 agricultural belts in the near future. Eventually, M&M plans to convert its main tractor facility at Kandivli into a product development centre, while the product assembly will be shared between the Nagpur factory and the satellite units. M&M is the biggest investor in product development in tractors. Over the years, it proposes to have different types of tractors to suit cultivation of all major crops.

While the 'pudding special' is being launched for catering to paddy belts, the company is also planning to roll out tractors with specific application for other crops, such as ground nut, potatoes and sugar cane.

QUESTIONS

1. Identify the factors which determine the demand for tractors.
2. Evaluate the customization strategy of M&M.
3. Can M&M retain its leadership position? To retain, what should it do?

Source

The Economic Times, July 10, 2001, p.10.
www.Indiainfoline.com, Report on Automotive-Tractor.

CASE

3 Promotion of Solar Energy Use

Renewable energy programme is now considered very important. Apart from environmental aspect, by using renewable energy systems basic energy services can be provided economically allowing improvements in the quality of life and economic productivity for the people of remote isolated backward areas. Hence,*Lokasiksha Parishad* started motivating the people long back to adopt renewable energy systems such as fuel saving improved *chullah*, biogas plant, etc.

THE CRUSADER

Ramakrishna Mission Ashrama, Narendrapur, is a branch centre of Ramakrishna Mission having its headquarters at Belur Math,in Howrah, West Bengal. Through its integrated development wing, i.e., the Ramakrishna Mission *Lokasiksha Parishad*, this Ashrama is actively engaged in various rural as well as urban development programmes for the last few decades. Presently, Ramakrishna Mission *Lokasiksha Parishad* is working, with about 40 affiliated cluster organisations and 1,500 youth clubs spread over 4,000 villages in 12 districts of West Bengal.

THE PROJECT

The Indo-US Renewable Energy Project in the Sundarbans is being implemented in collaboration with the Ministry of Non-Conventional Energy Sources (MNES), Government of India, West Bengal Renewable Energy Development Agency (WBREDA), Government of West Bengal and National Renewable Energy Laboratory (NREL), Government of USA, for providing some basic energy services through solar photovoltaic systems to some isolated remote villages of Sundarbans where grid connection is a distant possibility.

The project will install domestic lights in 300 homes spread over 3 villages of 3 different islands @100 per village. Each home will have two 9W compact fluorescent lights (CFLs) and one wall socket. Besides three hundred homes, solar photovoltaic systems will also be installed in some of the village institutions like health centre, women training-cum-production centres, youth clubs etc. There is also provision for installation of vaccine preservator, street lights, institutional lighting facilities, fan, surface pump and battery charging unit.

IMPLEMENTATION

The implementation involves two major activities.

- Training and placement of field staff
- Sales-cum-service network formation

Training and Placement of Field Staff

Availability of trained maintenance staff at the grass-root level in rural areas is one of the most important aspects for successful implementation of non-conventional energy projects in India. Well before the launching of the project, 13 village and cluster level personnel have been trained on the maintenance of solar thermal and solar PV systems, taking resource persons from Jadavpur University and other institutions and placed in the respective rural areas. Besides this pre-service training, a higher level training on installation and maintenance of solar thermal and solar PV systems had also been organised for supervisory staff to be posted at both cluster unit and project headquarters taking resource persons from U.S.A. Apart from these trainings, in-service trainings will be organised at regular intervals.

Sales-cum-service Network

An extensive sales-cum-service network is set up in the un-and under electrified villages. *Lokasiksha Parishad* has set up a solar sales-cum-service-cum-exhibition centre entitled ADITYA (THE SOLAR SHOP) at Narendrapur with the following objectives:

- Sale of solar energy systems according to customers' choice.
- Direct disbursement of subsidy for the Government approved items.
- Extension of maintenance and repair facilities to the buyer.
- Sale of other fuel saving and non-conventional energy using items such as improved *chullahs*, biogas oven and lamps, highly efficient electric lamps etc.
- Permanent display on the use of Solar systems and related information.

From The Solar Shop 'Aditya' solar lanterns, solar PV modules, solar energy operated fan, battery for solar energy storage, solar pumps, solar cooker, solar water heater, solar water distillator and various other allied products will be sold to the prospective customers coming here regularly from different parts of West Bengal. This centre will also sell spare-parts and attend to the after sale services. All these envisaged functions of the centre will be performed by a team of well qualified and experienced technical staff through its three-tier network i.e., sales-cum-service centre at Narendrapur, sub-centres at cluster level organisations and the village level youth clubs. The cluster level sub-centre headed by a well trained technician will:

1. Act as a bridge between the youth clubs and village workers on one end and the sales-cum-service centre on the other end.
2. Sell system components like batteries, CF lamps, electronic circuits, etc., and
3. Undertake repair works passed on by the village workers.

One trained village worker will be engaged at each and every youth club. He will be a resident of that particular village. Already 13 such village workers have been trained and placed in the respective villages. The main functions of village workers will be:

1. creation of demand through motivation and awareness generation,
2. helping in installation of the systems,
3. collection of service charges and loan instalments from the beneficiaries,
4. arranging hiring of solar lanterns given to them under Entrepreneurship Development Programme,
5. attending to minor repairing works,
6. sending the defective equipments requiring complicated repairs to the cluster-level sub-centres and
7. keeping constant contact with the sub-centres.

COST RECOVERY AND SUSTAINABILITY

Ramakrishna Mission *Lokasiksha Parishad* had already thought of a methodology for making the sales-cum-service centre and its constituent tyres self-reliant. The maintenance and personnel cost of the centre at Narendrapur will be met from the income of

1. Sales margins and
2. Service charge for repairing works at 'Aditya'.

The personnel and other costs of sub-centres will be given from the share of

1. Service charges (maintenance charges on contract basis),
2. Part of interest on loan to the beneficiaries and
3. Incentives on sales promotion (pro-rata basis) to be provided by 'Aditya'.

Remuneration on commission basis will be provided to the village workers from the income of

1. Incentive on sales promotion to be provided by 'Aditya'
2. Share of service charges,
3. Share of interest on loan to the beneficiaries and
4. Hiring charges of solar lanterns.

The project will financially and otherwise support the installation of various PV systems in the village institutions, but in case of domestic units it envisages partial cost recovery—partly as down payment and the rest through easy installments spread over 5 years. The fund thus created will be utilised for the upkeep of the systems as well as replicating the same even after the end of the project tenure. Nominal service charge will also be collected from the end users which will be equally shared among the village worker, the youth club, and the cluster organisation.

FUTURE PLAN

Ramakrishna Mission *Lokasiksha Parishad* is negotiating with various other organisations for soft loans to be provided to the people towards different solar thermal, solar PV and other renewable energy systems. If materialized, the present operational area may be expanded to other areas of Sundarbans as well as a number of backward villages of other districts.

QUESTIONS

1. 'Successful implementation of projects of this kind need marketing approach'—Examine whether such approach is followed in case of this project?
2. 'The key success factors are cost recovery and sustainability'—Appraise the project based on the two criteria.

PART
3

Market Analysis and Information Systems

- Rural Search
- Measuring MKTORIENT
- Segmentation Dilemma
- Success Needs System
- Testing Innovation

CASE

4 Rural Search

When Nitya, an MBA project student from Sri Padmavathi Mahila University, met Manoj, General Manager (Marketing) of Subhasri Cosmetics Pvt. Ltd., he was delighted as he had a research project in mind. The company launched last year a new brand of ayurvedic soap 'Fresh' in Andhra Pradesh. The soap was positioned as family health soap with 24-hour fragrance. Made available in two pack sizes—75g and 100g, it was priced at Rs. 6 and Rs. 8 respectively.

THE PROBLEM

Though sales of the brand were initially encouraging, they did not reach the expected level by the end of the year. This raised the basic question: "Why are sales picking up slowly and what can be done to improve the situation?" Manoj explained his concern to Nitya and further said: "Let us examine the problem in detail.

- First, the distribution: It does not seem to be the bottleneck. We have an extensive distribution network of wholesalers, semi-wholesalers and retailers. Also, we hire vans to reach rural interiors.
- Second, price cannot be a barrier but the perception that it is a cheap quality product might have hampered the sales. You know, rural people are also now looking for value products.
- Third, promotion effectiveness is one difficult aspect, we have only used radio ads, cinema slides, wall paintings and point of purchase displays.

I think we need information on consumer awareness levels, brand preferences and media habits to devise our future promotion strategies, what do you say?"

Nitya replied: "Sir, besides consumer information, we need retailer information too. It helps us to know how good the supply was."

Manoj agreed with her and asked her to undertake a survey.

RESEARCH PLAN

Nitya developed a research plan in consultation with Manoj.

Objectives

- To determine the brand awareness, usage and preference levels of toilet soaps among consumers.
- To know the media habits of and social influences on consumers.
- To understand retailer views on distribution of the toilet soap.

Data Sources

The secondary data sources include census reports of Andhra Pradesh and Thompson Rural Index. They are useful in identifying districts and villages. Primary data sources consist of consumers and retailers.

Data Collection

The primary data collection instrument is questionnaire. Two different questionnaires are designed, one for the consumers and the other for the retailers. (Appendices I & II)

Sample

It is decided to select one district from each of the three regions of Andhra Pradesh viz., Andhra, Rayalaseema and Telengana. To select the districts, Thompson's Rural Index was consulted. The index developed by Hindusthan Thompson Associates provides an assessment in quantitative terms the rural market potential for a district as compared to other districts in the country. Exhibit -1 provides the indices for the districts in Andhra Pradesh.

Exhibit 1 Districts of Andhra Pradesh in Descending Order of Market Index Numbers

State Rank	*All-India Rank*	*District*	*Rural Population (Lakhs)*	*Population Index*	*Market Index Number*	*Class of Market*
1	9	West Godavari	22.8	64.28	73.68	A
2	32	Chittoor	22.7	64.23	52.63	B
3	37	Krishna	20.6	58.05	50.44	B
4	41	Guntur	24.9	70.27	47.81	B
5	51	Nalgonda	20.2	57.03	43.42	B
6	59	East Godavari	28.8	81.27	41.23	B
7	78	Nizamabad	13.6	38.31	36.84	C
8	100	Kurnool	18.2	51.31	32.89	C
9	113	Mahbubnagar	21.8	61.47	30.26	C
10	118	Karimnagar	20.5	57.92	29.39	D
11	142	Nellore	15.9	45.07	26.32	D
12	144	Prakasam	19.8	55.91	25.44	D
13	163	Srikakulam	17.5	49.29	23.68	D
14	164	Visakhapatnam	17.7	49.98	23.68	D
15	165	Warangal	19.0	53.75	23.68	D
16	173	Medak	15.9	44.90	22.37	D
17	195	Cuddapah	15.6	44.01	20.18	D
18	202	Anantapur	20.2	56.94	19.74	E
19	209	Adilabad	13.2	37.32	18.86	E
20	227	Rangareddi	12.1	34.02	17.11	E
21	237	Khamamam	14.5	41.05	15.79	E
22	326	Vizanagaram	15.2	42.82	4.82	E

Based on the indices, Nellore from coastal Andhra, Warangal from Telengana and Cuddapah from Rayalaseema ,categorised as 'D' class markets are chosen. In the next step, 6 villages from each district are chosen based on population size as shown in Exhibit-2.

Exhibit 2

Population	*Andhra*	*Telengana*	*Rayalaseema*	*Total*
	Nellore	*Warangal*	*Cuddapah*	
Less than 2000	2	2	2	6
2000–500	2	2	2	6
More than 5000	2	2	2	6
Total	6	6	6	18

It decided to cover at least 100 consumers and 50 retailers in each district as the project was to be completed during the 8 weeks internship of Nitya. Anything over and above that would be a happy addition to improve accuracy of the study.

CONSUMER SURVEY FINDINGS

Nitya collected data from 391 consumers. The data are presented in the following tables.

Table 1 Brand Awareness Levels

Brand	*Nellore (N=136)*	*Warangal (N=119)*	*Cuddapah (N=136)*	*All (N=391)*
Lifebuoy	126(92.6)	119(100)	133(97.8)	378(96.7)
Hamam	123(90.4)	108(90.8)	136(100)	367(93.9)
Lux	113(83.1)	112(94.1)	136(100)	361(92.3)
Rexona	104(70.5)	95(77.8)	136(100)	335(85.1)
Cinthol	82(60.3)	92(77.3)	114(83.8)	288(73.7)
Liril	72(62.9)	27(22.7)	69(50.7)	168(43.0)
Chandrika	48(35.3)	43(36.1)	75(55.1)	166(42.5)
Fresh	87(63.9)	62(52.1)	125(91.9)	274(70.1)

Figures in parentheses are percentages

Table 2 Brand Usage*

Brand	*Nellore (N=136)*	*Warangal (N=119)*	*Cuddapah (N=136)*	*All (N=391)*
Lifebuoy	45(33.1)	39(35.3)	45(33.1)	129(32.9)
Hamam	25(18.4)	11(9.2)	14(10.3)	50(12.8)
Rexona	35(25.7)	31(26.1)	28(20.6)	94(24.8)
Cinthol	18(13.2)	21(17.6)	24(17.6)	63(16.1)
Liril	3(2.2)	8(6.7)	6(4.4)	17(4.3)
Chandrika	0(0)	7(5.9)	0(0)	7(1.8)
Fresh	10(7.4)	8(9.2)	17(12.5)	35(8.9)

*Multiple responses allowed   Figures in parentheses are percentages

Table 3 Brand Switching Patterns

Time frame	*Nellore (N=136)*	*Warangal (N=119)*	*Cuddapah (N=136)*	*All (N=391)*
Last 1–3 months	20	10	16	46
Last 3–6 months	08	72	82	262
Last 6–12 months	179	115	154	448

Table 4 Attributes Preferred

Attributes	*Nellore (N=136)*	*Warangal (N=119)*	*Cuddapah (N=136)*	*All (N=391)*
Price	110(80.9)	71(59.7)	105(77.2)	286(73.1)
Perfume	88(64.1)	67(56.3)	86(68.2)	241(61.6)
Long lasting	62(45.6)	39(32.8)	63(47.1)	165(42.2)
Lather	58(42.6)	33(27.7)	73(53.7)	164(41.9)

Figures in parentheses are percentages

Table 5 Toilet Soap Consumption Per Month

No. of Soaps	*Family size*			*All*
(75g)	*1-3*	*4-6*	*7-9*	
4–6	55	14	--	69
7–9	17	212	--	229
10–12	8	21	64	93
Total households	80	27	64	391

Table 6 Source of Awareness of Toilet Soaps

Media	*Nellore (N=136)*	*Warangal (N=119)*	*Cuddapah (N=136)*	*All (N=319)*
POP	127(93.4)	95(77.8)	128(94.1)	350(89.5)
Wall Paints	124(91.2)	96(80.7)	116(85.3)	336(85.9)
Radio	96(70.6)	88(73.9)	136(100)	320(81.8)
Print	105(77.2)	73(61.3)	116(85.3)	294(75.2)
Television	104(76.5)	68(57.9)	68(50.0)	240(64.2)

Table 7 TV and Radio Ownership Consumers

	Nellore (N=136)	*Warangal (N=119)*	*Cuddapah (N=136)*	*All (N=319)*
Radio/Transistors	93(68.4)	82(68.9)	136(100)	311(79.5)
TV	47(34.6)	32(26.9)	33(24.3)	112(28.6)

Table 8 Media Habits of Consumers

	Nellore (N=136)	*Warangal (N=119)*	*Cuddapah (N=136)*	*All (N=319)*
Radio listeners	116(85.3)	103(86.6)	136(100)	355(90.8)
TV viewers	122(89.7)	73(61.3)	66(48.5)	261(66.1)
Cinegoers	136(100)	119(100.0)	136(100)	391(100)
Newspaper readers				
Telugu	71(52.2)	55(46.2)	3(46.3)	189(59.4)
English	14(10.3)	--	5(3.7)	19(5.8)

Some Observations:

1. Head of the household or male earning member is mostly the decider of the purchase.
2. 45.7 percent of the consumers reported that they bought their monthly toilet soap requirements in the first week of every month.
3. Around 71 percent of the consumers purchase their requirements from local village shop.
4. The feeder towns for the villages surveyed are:

Nellore—Nellore, Kavali
Warangal—Warangal, Huzurabad, Hasanparthi
Cuddapah—Cuddapah, Rajampet

All the feeder towns are well connected by pucca roads with the surrounding villages.

RETAIL SURVEY

The retailer survey was undertaken in Kurnool district only. The distribution of retail out lets in the areas surveyed is given in Table 9.

Table 9 Distribution of Outlets

Population	*Villages*		*Outlets*				
	No	*Survey*	*K*	*M*	*F*	*P*	*Total*
Less than 2000	560	3	17	7	2	1	27
2000–5000	284	1	6	2	1	1	10
More than 5000	48	2	19	11	3	2	35
Total	892	6	42	20	6	4	72

K—Kirana, M—Medical, F—Fancy, P—Paan shop.

The survey found that

- All the retail outlets are serviced by distributors' vans.

- *Paan* shop would obtain their stocks from the local retailers. However, in Rajampet area retail outlets are not serviced by vans. They buy from the feeder towns.

Credit Pattern

Except HLL, all other companies supply stocks on a cash-down payment basis. HLL services retailers twice in a month, whereas others service once in a month. As such, HLL could extend 15-day credit to the retailers.

Sales

The sales are more in the first week of every month. The fast moving soaps are Lux, Lifebuoy, Rexona and Hamam.

Questions

1. Critically evaluate the research plan of Nitya.
2. Analyze the findings and draw conclusions.
3. What suggestions do you offer to Manoj to improve the sales of Fresh?

Credits

S.M Chakrapani Raju, Branch Manager, Birla Yamaha Limited, Coimbatore.

APPENDIX-I

Questionnaire for Consumers

1. Do you use toilet soap?
   – Yes – No
   (If No, go to question 7 and then to 13)

2. Which brand of toilet soap are you currently using?
   ____

3. For how long have you been using this soap?
   – less than one month
   – One to three months
   – Three to six months
   – Six months to one year
   – More than one year

4. Which brand of toilet soap were you using before this?
   ____

5. How did you first come to know about the soap you are using now?
   – Television
   – Radio
   – Point-of-purchase material
   – Wall paintings
   – Hoardings
   – Newspapers

6. Do the village *panchayat* leaders in any way try to influence your toilet soap purchase decision?
   —Yes
   —No

7. What do you like about the soap you are using now?
   (Check as many responses as obtained).
   – Price – Perfume – Lather giving ability – Long lasting.

8. What brands of toilet soaps are you aware of?
   (Open ended—record response)

9. Who in your family decides which soap to buy?
   (Open ended)

10. How many persons are there in your household?
    – 1 to 3 – 4 to 6 – 7 to 9 – more than 9.

11. How many soaps does your household use per month?
    – Less than 3 – 4 to 6 – 7 to 9 – more than 9.

12. Which part of the month do you buy the soaps?
    – 1st week – 2nd week – 3rd week – 4th week.

13. Where do you buy your soaps from?
    – Village shop – Go to nearest town.

14. Do you read newspapers?
    – Yes – No
    (If No, go to 19)

15. Which newspapers do you read?

English		Telugu	
	__________		__________
	__________		__________
	__________		__________

16. Do you own a TV set?
    – Yes – No

17. Do you watch programmes on TV?
    – Yes – No
    (If No, go to 18)

18. Do you own a radio set?
    – Yes – No

19. Do you listen to radio?
    – Yes – No
    (If No, go to 21)

    ____

20. Do you watch movies in theatres (in your village or in neighbouring village)?
    Yes
    No
    (If No, terminate).

21. How often do you go to the movies?

    ____

    Terminate.

Consumer's Classificatory Data:

1. Name : ______________________________
2. Age : ______________________________
3. Sex : ______________________________

4. Address : ______________________________

____

____

5. Educational Qualifications: ________________

6. Occupation : ______________________________

APPENDIX-II

Retailers' Questionnaire

1. Which brands of toilet soap do you sell?

   ____

   ____

2. Which brand of soap sells the most on a weekly basis?

   ____

3. How do you obtain your stock?
   – Local distributor
   – Company/distributor van
   – Go to nearest town to make purchases
   (Which town? ________)

4. What is your current level of stocks of various soaps?

   ____

   ____

5. Which part of the month sees more sales?
   – 1st week – 2nd week – 3rd week – 4th week.

6. What are the credit terms offered by different companies?

   ____

   ____

   Terminate.

Retailers' Classificatory Data:

1. Name : ____________________

2. Type of Outlet : – *Kirana*
   – Medical
   – Fancy
   – *Paan*/cold drinks

3. Address : ____________________
   ____
   ____

CASE

5 Measuring MKTORIENT

At present there are 196 Regional Rural Banks (RRBs) in India and most of them are sick. However, lots of efforts have been made to revitalize them (the latest being the Bhandari Committee, 1994) but these efforts were invariably outside the frame work of marketing orientation. Hence, there is a need to measure the level of marketing orientation of the RRBs and suggest measures to improve their performance. Sharma, Desh Bandhu and Gurjeet Kaur undertook a study to measure marketing orientation of rural banks. The study is divided into two phases: in phase- I, marketing orientation instrument was developed. In phase- II, marketing orientation in RRBs is measured.

PHASE-I *INSTRUMENT DESIGN*

A schedule for the data from bank customers was developed within the framework of marketing orientation after several exercises of testing and refinements. Besides demographic profile, the schedule consisted of 7 queries on general information, 60 items on marketing orientation pertaining to different mix in rural banks and 15 suggestions from the customers. Items covering all the six Ps (Kotler 1996) of bank marketing mix were generated from the literature and through discussions with experts. Some items were kept in negative form for internal cross checking. A five point Likert scale (5<------>1) has been used for the schedule. The scale values of negatively worded items were reversed before data processing.

Pretesting

The aforesaid schedule used in the study has passed through four stages of frequent testing and refinements as discussed below:

Stage 1 The Original two point scale (Yes/No) draft schedule for the collection of data from bank customers was tested by administering it to 25 randomly (first at random and subsequently every 5th house) chosen respondents out of 150 households from a small village, viz., *Basti* Govindpura of Jammu district. The schedule consisted of four items of demographic profile and 25 queries relating to four Ps of bank marketing.

Stage 2 After making necessary alterations, the schedule was transformed into 5-point scale and it was again tested by administering it to 300 randomly selected (first at random and subsequently every 3rd house) customers out of approximately 950 households from a comparatively larger village, viz., Gho Manhasan of Jammu district.

Stage 3 The schedule was again modified and tested by administering it to 300 randomly selected (first such a house which was not selected at stage 2 and subsequently every 3rd household) respondents of the same village, viz., Gho Manhasan. Besides the number of items in the schedule at the 2nd stage, the present schedule incorporated 10 more items relating to customer awareness about newly added banking product and services.

Stage 4 The original draft schedule after the aforesaid three stages was finally tested by administering it to 60 randomly selected (first at random and subsequently every 2nd house) customers residing in Dablehar village of Jammu district. The schedule comprised of 7 items of demographic profile, 15 queries of general nature, 40 queries of MKTORIENT in RRBs and 10 items of similar nature relating to commercial/ cooperative/money lenders pertaining to six Ps of marketing-mix.

Sample Design

A sample of 500 respondents for the collection of needed information was drawn from three separate villages of Jammu district which were purposely selected on the basis of available data under three self-developed groups, viz., highly developed, developing and under-developed with the draw of chits. The villages of Jammu were divided into above-mentioned three groups on the basis of literacy rate, poverty level, per hectare yield and infrastructural facilities such as roads, electricity and schools, etc, and having a branch of RRB.

Accordingly, Simbal Camp (developed),Sarore (developing) and Jakh (under-developed) got selected in the areas under reference (Exhibit-1). The list of customers (depositors and loanees) of JRB branches operating in these was obtained from its head office. The number of customers of Simbal Camp, Sarore and Jakh branches of JRB figured out to be 4645, 3310 and 220 respectively. The approximate proportion of JRB customers of every selected branch to total number of customers of these branches taken together came out to be 9:7:5 and accordingly the schedule was properly filled in by 215, 170 and 114 customers. The respondents in the areas were selected through systematic random sampling, i.e., after selecting first household at random and subsequently every 4th house in case of Simbal Camp and Sarore and every 3rd house in case of Jakh were contacted. For the selection of the first respondent, names of all the household heads were procured from the concerned village *Sarpanch*. Chits of all households in a village were prepared and shuffled. The first chit thus picked up was the first respondent.

The research findings have been drawn from the data so collected with as many as 60 statements within the domain of MKTORIENT purified through factor analysis, which finally resulted into 41 statements, grouped under 12 dimensions (6 product, 1 place and 3 promotion) of MKTORIENT (Exhibit-2).

Scale Purification

For determining the bank marketing mix ingredient-wise dimensionality of items of scale, the principal axis procedure of factor analysis was used along with varimax rotation. After a series of several iterations, finally 12 factors got selected and items with high loadings on more than one factor were discarded. After recognizing the relative importance of each and every item, the factor loadings with less than 0.5 were also ignored.

Items of schedule were designed in such a manner so as, to cover six Ps of bank marketing mix (Kotler 1996) but while analyzing the factors it was observed that some factors of six Ps contain one or two statements only. Thus, in order to get more reasonable composition of various dimensions having strong perceptual loadings, 6 Ps were converted into McCarthy's four Ps, because people and process are an extension of main four Ps only (Kotler 1996). All the statements in the schedule pertaining to rural banks were segregated and factors were computed separately for each P.

Validation

Extensive testing and refinement of the schedule led to the determination of independent variable extracted from six Ps with considerable face validity. Thereafter, two marketing experts and three specialists in rural banking undertook a careful analysis of the objectives and actual subject matter covered in the schedule which provided sufficient grounds for determining content validity. After the systematic evaluation of the contents of data collection forms, SPSS was used with the help of computer to simplify the data by reducing a large number of variables to a smaller manageable number through interdependent statistical technique, viz., factor analysis.

The factors finally emerged were put under screen test so as to know which of them are contributing significantly to the total variance in the results obtained. This test examines the graph of Eigen values which stop factoring at the point where these values begin to form a straight line with an almost horizontal slope . The marketing orientation within its domain determined through the aforesaid procedure for RRBs has, thus, been measured for each group, every MKTORIENT element taken and also for whole of the domain separately in terms of arithmetic mean which varies from the lowest of one point to the maximum of five points.

Thus, the factors which finally emerged as the most important for the study were used to establish a relationship between MKTORIENT (dependent variable) and four Ps of marketing mix (independent variables) with the help of multiple regression and subsequently the strength of association between dependent and independent variables was worked out through coefficient of determination. Reliability and validity of the findings were statistically tested with the help of t-test, F-test and convergent validity. A measure of a theoretical concept has convergent validity when it is highly correlated with different measures of *similar construct.* Convergent validity has been worked out by examining the nature of association between MKTORIENT scores and responses to two statements regarding 'overall performance' and 'service quality'.

PHASE-II *MEASURING MARKETING ORIENTATION*

Objectives

The objectives of the study were:

- To determine the degree of marketing orientation at different management levels.
- To measure the degree of marketing orientation judged by the bank customers.
- To work out a strategy for marketing orientation in RRBs.

Hypotheses

The hypotheses emerging from the review of literature and pilot survey conducted for the present study were:

- Moderate level of marketing orientation prevails in Jammu Rural Bank.
- Assessment of marketing orientation of consumers vary with level of satisfaction and literacy level.

Methodology

It was decided to adopt case study method to have complete understanding of the issue.

Research Site:

Selection of the bank for carrying out research was made based on the following criteria:

- It should have environment similar to a majority of RRBs.
- It should be a bank with long experience.
- It should be offering wide range of services.
- It should be without a marketing department.

Jammu Rural Bank (JRB) was selected because its profile matches closely with that of RRBs in other states. It has similar problems with regard to political, social, cultural and economic conditions facing most other RRBs in the country. Moreover, the jurisdiction of JRB's business also resembles very closely with other RRBs as it deals with all the categories of farmers, agriculturists, small businessmen and dependents. Therefore, it has been selected as a representative of RRBs.

Jammu Rural Bank was the first RRB in Jammu and Kashmir State, established in March, 1976, with its head office at Jammu and has been sponsored by Jammu and Kashmir Bank Ltd. (a leading private sector bank in the country). JRB has completed 22 years of its services in the field of rural development through a network of 94 branches in Jammu, Kathua, Rajouri and Poonch districts.

Jammu Rural Bank has been extending financial support to the people of the area for the following loan schemes:

1. Carpets
2. Bakers
3. Hand printing
4. Pashmina shawls
5. Dhaba units
6. Bamboo furniture
7. Denting and painting
8. Winding of electric motors
9. Electrostat machine
10. Pottery
11. Wheat grinding and cotton carding
12. Two buffaloes schemes in district Rajouri
13. Dairy scheme for 3 animals in Jammu district
14. Mushroom scheme (200 and 400 trays)
15. Fishery scheme for Jammu and Kathua districts

Like other RRBs, JRB has no formal marketing department for the promotion of banking business in a rural setting, on social marketing lines. Whatever marketing orientation exists, it is the outgrowth of the traditional rural banking objective and policies. However, over a period of about 22 years of its operation, the nature of work culture has undergone a change and it is in this context that the effectiveness of the on-going work culture was examined within the parameters of marketing orientation in a social banking mechanism for rural development.

Data Sources The study was primarily based on the information collected from managers and customers of the bank.

Data Collection Data were collected with the help of a schedule from a sample of managers of JRB's branches and customers. The ratings obtained on 5-point scale about these two aspects were converted to three points, viz., Below Average (>3), Average (=3) and Above Average (<3) to make interpretation more meaningful.

Sampling A village Gho Manhasan with about 950 houses, having about 60 per cent literacy rate, and every household having atleast one bank account in JRB, has been selected for the study. Data was collected from 600 bank customers (about 60 per cent of total households) by personally contacting every third house of the village, after selecting the first at random. As per the research plan, the customers have been classified into six groups such as: (a) literate, (b) illiterate, (c) target group (below Rs. 11,000 p.a.), (d) non-target group (above Rs. 11,000 p.a.), (e) small farmers (upto 2.5 Acres), and (f) medium farmers (2.5 to 5 Acres). The needed information for counter checking the extent of marketing orientation was also obtained through a similar questionnaire from the officials of the bank.

Findings

The major findings of the study are given as under.

Marketing-mix variables of bank as assessed by customers and shown in Table 1 reveal that a majority of JRB customers have given "above average" rating of satisfaction to almost all the aspects of 'product mix' except loan formalities which enjoys just average satisfaction. 'Price mix' variable has generated "below average" (interest rates on advances), "average" (interest calculations) satisfaction in all of its aspects. 'Promotion mix' variable has secured "below average" satisfaction in almost all the aspects of marketing communication. Majority of the customers have given "above average" score in 'customer awareness efforts' and 'employees competence'.

Management judgment about the culture of marketing in the bank's operation, worked out through 5-point Likert scale revealed positive orientation towards marketing mix. When compared with the score obtained through customer judgement, the management's perception about marketing orientation in the bank is higher but the customer satisfaction index is a widely acceptable measure than that of management judgment as there is a possibility of defensive attitude in the perception of management about bank's performance even if sufficient precaution might have been exercised while collecting the attitudinal information about marketing orientation.

STRATEGIC ACTION

Respective mean values revealing extent of MKTORIENT facilitate five strategies to maintain and enhance the present level of marketing orientation in rural banks.

(a) Effective Communication System The present communication system has to be made effective by making "frequent and educative advertisements" on TV, radio, newspapers, and magazines particularly regarding new schemes and interest rates. Further, 'attractive posters revealing current changes in the services', frequent customer-banker meets' and 'more efficient and effective fieldworkers in communicating rural banking services' will not only make the marginal communities aware about the banking facilities but also motivate them for undertaking income and employment generating projects.

(b) Rationalization of Interest Rates Thus keeping in mind the prime objective behind their establishment, rural banks should try to increase present deposits so as to motivate rural masses for deposit and decrease loan interest rates, so as to motivate rural masses for obtaining loans through suitable advance schemes.

(c) Simplification of Procedures Simplify the banking procedure keeping in view the literacy level in rural areas and their hesitation in approaching the banks even for routine deposit and/or loan services.

Further, efforts should be made to cooperate with the customers in the completion of various banking formalities particularly with regard to new cases.

(d) Awareness Campaign Educate rural masses about various existing advance schemes and the present interest rate structure so that they can avail loan facility from rural banks and obtain self-employment and self-sufficiency at the village level itself.

(e) Rural Development-Oriented Recruitment and Training Specialized training programmes for rural bank staff to inculcate the desire to serve the rural borrowers effectively need to be carried on regular basis through the institutes exclusively established for the integrated development of rural sector in the country.

Table 1 Marketing Orientation: Management's Assessment

Variables *Management*	*Product*	*Price*	*Promotion*	*Distribution*	*Overall Mean*
Top	3.93	3.75	4.00	3.00	3.67
Middle	3.07	3.50	3.63	3.40	3.40
Lower	4.43	4.25	3.75	3.67	4.03
Overall	3.81	3.83	3.79	3.36	3.70

Table 2 Marketing Orientation: Assessment by Small Farmers

Groups	*Illiterate*	*Literate*
Target	3.4	3.3
Non-target	3.2	3.4

Table 3 Marketing- Mix Variables as Perceived by Customers Across Satisfaction Levels

Below Average *(Below 3 points)*	*Average* *(3 Points)*	*Above Average* *(Above 3 points)*
Incentives to customers (100%)	Attractive and convincing interest rates on deposit (57%)	Accurate interest calculations (86%)
Dissemination of information by employees (65%)	Unnecessary loan formalities (67%)	Suitability of banking schemes (62%)
Promotion of banking schemes by field workers (95%)	--	Existing range of schemes (70%)
Field workers advice to avail banking services (92%)	--	Convenient bank branch location (100%)
Advertisement of banking schemes (87%)	--	Prompt and accurate banking services (98%)

Reasonable and motivation interest charges on loan (72%)	--	Competent and efficient bank staff (97%)
	--	Cooperative and friendly employees (95%)

Exhibit-1 Brief Profile of the Villages, viz., Jakh, Sarore and Simbal Camp of Jammu District as on 31–3–1997

S. No		*Jakh*	*Sarore*	*Simbal Camp*
1.	Total Population	1506	3472	6697
2.	Male : Female	57:43	51:50	59:41
3.	Total Households	341	604	880
4.	Poverty	64%	33%	30%
5.	Literacy	58%	72%	72%
6.	Infrastructural Facilities			
	(a) Roads	Broken	*Pucca*	Good condition
	(b) Electricity	Frequent Cuts	Rare Power cuts	Regular Supply
	(c) Government School	Two	Two	Two
	(d) Private School	Three	Three	Five
7.	Per Hectare Yield			
	(a) Irrigated			
	Wheat	32 qtl/hec.	30 qtl/hec.	40 qtl/hec.
	Maize	--	--	--
	Paddy	--	46 qtl/hec.	42 qtl/hec.
	(b) Non-Irrigated			
	Wheat	18 qtl/hec.	20 qtl/hec.	20 qtl/hec.
	Maize	18 qtl/hec.	--	--
	Paddy	--	19 qtl/hec.	--

Exhibit-2 Summary of Results from Scale Purification: Loading and Variance Explained

Bank Marketing Mix	*Factor-wise Dimension*	*Factor Loading*	*% of Variance explained*
Product	Factor First:		29.7
	Comfortable loan security and guarantee	0.95	
	Easy loan recovery policy	0.95	
	Comfortable repayment instalments	0.94	
	Convenient purchase of assets through bank finance	0.94	
	Sufficient number of loan schemes	0.90	

Need meeting loan schemes	0.90	
Standard product purchase through Bank finance	0.88	
Factor Second:		18.0
Simple loan formalities	0.85	
Loan procedure easy even to a layman	0.84	
No switching intentions for loans	0.79	
Timely purchase through bank	0.52	
Factor Third:		8.9
Need meeting deposit schemes	0.89	
Sufficient number of deposit schemes	0.83	
Bank proves to be a good prime bank	0.72	
Factor Fourth:		6.7
Quick withdrawal facilities	0.83	
No delay in depositing money	0.82	
Factor Fifth:		6.1
Accurate pass book entries	0.88	
Timely updating of passbooks	0.80	
Factor Sixth:		5.4
Easy procedure for fixed deposit schemes	0.76	
Simple account opening formalities	0.70	
Immediate issuance of new cheque/passbook	-0.52	
Total Variance Explained=74.8%		

QUESTIONS:

1. Critically evaluate the research methodology and procedure adopted for the development of instrument.
2. Comment on the strategic actions suggested in the study.

Source

1. R.D.Sharma, Desh Bandhu and Gurjeet Kaur, 'Marketing Orientation Strategy for Rural Banks: A Case Study '*Prajnan,* Vol.XXVII, No.1.1998–99.pp.47–56.

2. R.D. Sharma, Gurjeet Kaur and Mahesh Gupta, Measuring of Market Orientation in Rural Banks Through a Customer Judgement Multi-item Scale: A Case Study of Jammu Rural Bank, *Prajnan,* Vol XIX, No. 1, 2001-02, pp. 31-58.

CASE

6 Segmentation Dilemma

"Selling consumer durables in rural areas is not a piece of cake. It requires understanding of the revolution taking place in the rural areas. The contribution of rural market is growing. But penetration rates for big ticket items are still abysmally low" said Mr. Sekhar, Vice-President (Marketing) of Sonica Televisions. He was making a presentation to his management team on how to segment market with focus on rural markets. He proceeded: "I have statistics to substantiate this point".

Table 1 Penetration of Products (%)

Product	*1985–86*	*2000–01*
Toilet Soaps	18.4	97.92
CTVS	1.1	4.5

DURABLES VS FMCG's MARKETING

Marketing durables is different from the marketing of FMCG's for the following reasons.

- Consumer durables are priced rather high when viewed in relation to the rural disposable income. This is especially true, when looked at from an international perspective.
- In the case of FMCG's, it is easier to create products for the rural market through differentiation. However, this is not very easy to achieve with durables.
- Setting up a distribution network in areas with a population lower than 1 lakh is challenging because the volumes are unviable.
- Few retailers have ventured into rural India. This imposes restrictions on the display and selection of durables.
- Creating an after-sales support structure in rural areas is still very expensive and often pushes up the price of the product.

- Developing communication strategies that appeal to rural India as a whole is rather difficult given the diversity of languages and cultures.
- Demand in rural India is highly dependent on the vagaries of agriculture.
- Availability of finance is limited as most finance companies have a limited presence in rural areas.
- Measuring sales and capturing sales data is a problem as most of the sales is through dealers and agents who buy from urban stockists.

THE REVOLUTION

However, if we understand the nature of transformation on the way in rural areas, we can simplify our marketing approaches. The drivers of the change in villages are education, reservation policy and government programmes. The implications of the change in marketing terms are:

- The young and the educated in the villages are already large in number and their number is increasing. Already 40 per cent of all those graduating from colleges are rural youth.
- They are the decision-makers.
- They are very different in education, exposure, attitudes and aspirations from their counterparts, at least in smaller cities and towns.

Given the above, we can as well hypothesise that the educated youth will encompass most of the households which are significant consumers of branded goods. Since the argument is that educated youth in the villages are urbanized, it follows that almost all the households of relevance to the marketer are urbanized or have a strong urban influence within. In other words, we can see such households as representing the urbanized staying in the suburbs of districts called villages!

SEGMENTATION

Since marketing is to target the growing segments, we can see the urban-like village dweller as an urbanized person from the districts. The point of such a perspective is that we are reducing complexity and making targeting more feasible by looking at the market as comprising just two segments—the cosmopolitan city dwellers and the urbanized people from the districts. The village then becomes a location or a suburb of a district. And the district becomes the basic geographical entity.

If we take the above logic forward, we can look at India as comprising of large cities, meaning those with a population of over 500,000 and other urban areas. The cut-off at one to five lakh cities is not arbitrary. One to five lakh cities are the primary feeder markets for small towns and rural areas in logistic terms. And because, individually, they are not big enough and their economies are closely linked to the economies of villages, they are unlikely to dominate the attention as the large cities do.

The next move will be to see districts as those with a large city and those without a large city. And, we can call those with a large city simply as 'city markets' and those without a large city as 'district markets'. If we then aggregate them along the respective lines, we have two entities which are sizeable and reasonably homogeneous among themselves and therefore become viable segments requiring focused attention.

The benefits of this type of segmentation are obvious.

- When city is separated, the districts get proper attention. In the district segment, rural areas are dominant. As such, they receive due attention.

- A district perspective removes the cobwebs of complexities, heterogeneity, access, target ability and so on which have hindered rural marketing initiatives.
- Marketing-mix suitable for rural areas can be developed.

QUESTIONS

1. Examine the differences between marketing of durables and FMCG's in the rural market.
2. Do you agree with the segmentation approach proposed by Sekhar? If yes, why? If no, why?

Source

Business Line Catalyst, Thursday, October 11, 2001.

CASE

7 Success Needs System

KCL company was a large manufacturer of cosmetics, detergents and scourers with sales of over Rs. 152 crore in the year 2000–01. It had manufacturing plants in five locations to provide effective coverage of market divided into five zones viz, Central, Western, Eastern, Northern and Southern. It had an extensive line of 20 products sold for use in business organizations and households. Its sales force was organized geographically into three to four areas, and each area comprised four to six districts. The Area Manager supervised the team at district level which comprises mainly sales force. The Area Manager was assisted by product managers whose chief responsibility was to report to and advise the company on product movement.

The projected sales of KCL for the year 2001–02 was Rs. 160 crore. It reflected the conservative annual growth rate of the company at 5 per cent for the past three years. However, the reports by the end of the third quarter showed that the sales would reach at the most Rs. 153 crore by the end of the year. The report perturbed Mrs. Radhika, the General Manager. She called Mr. Venkatesh, the Chief Manager (Marketing) to discuss the reasons for the stagnation. She also enquired about the information system he mentioned to her about four months back. Mr. Venkatesh seemed quite surprised at the General Manager's memory and interest. He could not clearly answer her queries.

Her questions were:-

(i) What were the sales of different brands district-wise, area-wise and region-wise?

(ii) What was the rise or fall of the above sales over the previous year sales?

(iii) Which of the products were doing better? Which need more attention? Which might be considered for termination?

(iv) Which brands of competitors were faring better? Why?

(v) What were our sales in rural areas? What was the potential there?

She gave him two days time to answer the questions with supporting data.

Mr. Venkatesh, the fifty year old executive, came in as Chief Manager (Marketing) after extensive experience with several other companies. When he joined this company, he found that information available to him was not adequate. Particularly, information on key result areas (KRAs) was not properly available. He had been highly displeased and brought this information gap to the attention of the General Manager. At that time, she was too busy forging alliances with a multi-national company and had asked him to prepare a report.

Sensing her genuine interest in his problem, Mr. Venkatesh called in Manager (Marketing Research) Susila Ram, to discuss a marketing information system. Susila, though surprised by the idea, endorsed it enthusiastically. They sat together, reviewed the existing system and figured out the current and prospective information needs. Then they prepared a draft of what the system should look like.

"The time had come" thought Mr. Venkatesh. After two days, he presented to the General Manager the answers with some data, which was not satisfactory even to himself. He then explained to her how the present reporting system failed in supplying her the necessary information in detail. He presented his draft proposal to her with a request to consider it immediately. The proposal is reproduced in Exhibit-I.

Exhibit-I Proposed Marketing Information System

Subject	Frequency	Type of Data
Sales Value	Monthly	• Current sales • Cumulative for the period vs Quarterly and annual budgeted sales. • % age of achievement in the quarter - by product - by geography (Zone, Area, District and Rural Vs Urban) - by branch - by sales person
Sales Achievement Reports	Quarterly	Quarterly sales in units and amounts against budgeted. (same break down as above) Gross margin on sales
New Markets	Quarterly	Distribution net work New customers
Credit Sales	Quarterly	Accounts receivables - Length of delinquency by customer by district

Advice Mrs. Radhika of KCL Company.

CASE

8 Testing Innovation

Sri Harsha & Sri Teja Research Associates (SSRA) is a successful marketing research agency operating in several cities of South India. A soft drink company has approached them to undertake a study in rural markets. The client organization, after prolonged, careful deliberations concluded:

(i) The company should introduce 125 ml and 200 ml bottles in rural areas for a price of Rs. 4 and Rs. 7.

(ii) Advertising, not mere availability, is necessary to promote sales.

Sri Harsha told the marketing manager of the company:

> *"The marketing executive who relies on information derived from his own life experiences is usually handicapped when faced with the problem of marketing to low-income groups and ruralites because their lifestyle is quite different from their higher-income and urban counter parts". "As such let us go for experimental study. Besides giving reliable behavioural information, it helps to promote your product. In expenditure, it is obviously rupee effective".*

Convinced with the argument, the company gave SSRA green signal to organize experiments in three different rural markets, with and without localized outdoor advertising (ad).

Table 1 Experiment Results Soft Drink Sales (Rs. 000)

Weekly Markets	150 ml		300 ml	
	Without ad	With ad	Without ad	With ad
Ballipadu	24	30	20	25
Sanivarapeta	28	35	22	31
Polagam	32	40	9	34

Based on the results, what advice should SSRA give to the client?

PART
4

Product Strategies

- Brand Reengineering
- Rural Financing Strategy
- Silky Routes
- Launching the Killer
- Devil or Angel?

CASE

9 Brand Reengineering

Ever since, Hindustan Lever Ltd. (HLL) announced its decision to focus on 30 power brands in January 2001, it has taken a series of initiatives ranging from refurbishing Fair & Lovely to pulling on AIM, its tooth paste targeted at the rural market. Now the focus is on Lifebuoy. The decision is to replace it with an entirely new product.

THE HERITAGE BRAND

Launched in 1895, Lifebuoy for over 100 years has been synonymous with health and value. The brick red carbolic soap, with its cresylic perfume and *"tandurusti ki raksha"* (safeguard to health) jingle have carried the Lifebuoy message of health across the length and breadth of the country, making it the largest selling soap brand in the world. With Rs. 500 crore plus sales, the brand has 18 per cent volume share in the toilet soaps market and contributes as much as 25 per cent to HLL's profits.

COMPULSIONS TO CHANGE:

Sanjay Dube, who now heads the mass market business cell, which has been carved out to specially manage brands like Breeze, Wheel and Lifebuoy says: "We have tried doing things incrementally on the brand, but that did not work. So we have to try big things". For the past five years, Lifebuoy had willy-nilly fallen into a trap. Across the rural heartland, where 75 per cent of Lifebuoy's sales come from, the emergence of television had begun to substantially influence buying decisions. Increasingly, women and children in the household had begun influencing brand choices, yet Lifebuoy's communication remained locked in on the male consumer. Lifebuoy's product form, with its cresylic perfume, tended to keep the new consumers away.

To contemporize the brand, Lever made the wrapper more attractive. The advertising was targeted at a younger male consumer and the association with sports like football was widened to include other events as well. This helped arrest the brand decline. However, the last nail was hit when the prices of vegetable oil–a key ingredient in the manufacture of soaps, touched a new low. Acting swiftly, competitors like Nirma offered better quality soaps at lower prices and unleashed a massive promotion drive, namely, two soaps for the price of one. Coupled with that, they upped trade margins from 8 per cent to as high as 20 per cent in some cases. As a result, Lifebuoy's volume declined for five consecutive quarters.

REALISATIONS

On introspection and analysis of the changing scenario, HLL has its own realizations.

- Business has to now stand on their own feet to give a competitive edge to the company.
- It is unwise to blame the weak demand from rural markets any more for poor sales. The responsibility of growing the market lies with manufacturers.
- The onus of expanding the market could not be left to brands like Breeze. A heritage brand like Lifebuoy has to be revitalized and used to expand usage. Every product has to be a growth driver.
- A new 'Lifebuoy' is necessary as a part of the overall game plan to shake up the Rs. 10,972 crore FMCG giant and make it less risk averse.
- Lifebuoy needs revitalization not mere tinkering. If Lifebuoy is left locked into male-macho victory kind of syndrome, it will remain locked there; and largely remain irrelevant to other family members, who may want a soap which is more cosmetic.

THE NEW BORN

But how do you transform a brand as old as lifebuoy and make it relevant to the changing consumer need and profile? A task of this kind requires top management support, project management and market research. The decision to radically alter Lifebuoy's brand DNA had HLL Chairman, Vindi Banga's personal backing. He oversaw many of the changes in the product-mix. This greatly helped to cut out the bureaucracy in the system and made the transition smoother.

The reinventing of lifebuoy, code named as '*Project Butterfly*' was entrusted to Sanjay Dube. Under his leadership, the well-knit five-member team–where everyone strongly believed in these changes–was able to take decisions quickly. The team had an unenviable task of modernizing a heritage product. The team worked with the following premises:

- Rural market has new decision makers in children and women.
- Rural consumers are adaptive. They do not buy brands based on sheer habit; like urban folks they too try new products and enjoy advertising much the same.
- The loyalty to Lifebuoy is strong at emotional level. Its share in the mind market is large and significant.

Accordingly, the following decisions were taken.

- Widen the health promise – Health and hygiene for the whole family in the place of hard working victorious male. Now the target audience is family.
- Maintain association with the core brand–Lever retained the brick shape of the soap, the red colour, the jingle as well as the plus symbol. The product form (carbolic to milled, and the perfume (cresylic to a health fragrance) were new. The weight of the soap was reduced from 150 to 125 grams and the price was increased by 50 paise to be Rs. 9 per cake.

The new formulation has an ingredient, Active-B, which offers protection against germs, which can cause stomach infection, eye infection and infections in cuts and bruises. The new health perfume has been selected after one of the most extensive perfume hunts in the industry. The new milled formulation offers a significantly superior bathing experience and skin feel.

The new Lifebuoy range now includes Lifebuoy Active Red (125 gm,100gm and 60gm) and Lifebuoy Active Orange(100gm). Lifebuoy Active Orange offers the consumer a differentiated health perfume while offering the health benefit of Lifebuoy.

The new Lifebuoy is targeted at today's discerning housewife with a more inclusive "family health protection for my family and me" positioning. Lifebuoy has made a deliberate shift from the male, victorious concept of health to a warmer, more versatile, more responsible benefit of health for the entire family.

The Lifebuoy Active was launched in January 2001. It stemmed Lifebuoy's decline, increasing volumes by 3 per cent in the first quarter, even as the soap market shrunk by 9 per cent in 2001. Buoyed by the success, Lever refined the same mix and tested it among its core users–the 45 year old male was neither excited nor alienated by the new concept, and rated it on par. On the other hand, the lady of the house seemed enthused by the change over. Given that the Lifebuoy franchise cut across population and income strata, the research had to be carefully mounted to ensure that the sample was representative.

Lifebuoy's new communication tack centred around health and hygiene. While the first set of ads targeted the core consumer and told him about the switch, the next sets of ads were pitched at the mother and talk about how Lifebuoy prevents kids from picking up germs.The new formulation, new health perfume and superior skin feel, along with the popular red colour, have registered conclusive and clear preference among existing and new users.

Lifebuoy offers ample scope for upgradation. At the upper end of the market, Lifebuoy offers specific health benefits through Lifebuoy International (Plus and Gold). Lifebuoy International Plus offers protection against germs which cause body odour, while Lifebuoy International Gold helps protect against germs which cause skin blemishes.

The promotion of Lifebuoy is going to be backed by one of the largest ever direct contact programmes launched across rural India to drive the consumption of soaps starting in April 2000. HLL expects to cover more than 10,000 villages in nine to ten states.

VARIED OPINIONS

There is a mixed reaction among observers. The strategic management guru at Sri Venkateswara University, Prof. Chandrasekhar, commending the act of HLL maintained "The Lifebuoy makeover is the best example of HLL's ability to tune to the markets". However, some have opined that Lever has swung to the extreme. "They run the risk of alienating their core consumer" said Jagadesh Kapoor, CEO of Samsika Marketing.

"It is a wise as well as a foolish decision. Wise because it brings back switchers to HLL's fold. Foolish because Lifebuoy has a sizeable market loyal to it. The burial will disappoint many consumers" opined Ms. Padmini, who teaches marketing at Sri Padmavathi Mahila University."I think Levers, missed out a chance by going for better product at a slightly higher price. If they lowered the price of old Lifebuoy slightly, they could have favourably changed usage patterns of those who sparingly use the soap and those who do not use the soaps" observed Ashok, a retailer.

QUESTIONS

1. What is your reaction to HLL's decision to reengineer the heritage brand?
2. Evaluate the brand reengineering approach of HLL?
3. Analyzing the market situation, what proactive measures do you recommend to HLL?

Source

Ranju Sarkar, Throwing a Life Line, *Business World* March 14, 2002, pp.16–18.

CASE

10 Rural Financing Strategy

The demand for rural credit is estimated at Rs. 143,000 crore. For banks, the challenge is not in disbursement but in loan recoveries. Some of the reasons for poor loan recoveries are:

- Farmers are risk averse and do not shift from established farming practices.
- The agri services provided by government and private agencies are intermittent and less intensive.
- The agri input sellers are only sales oriented. The dealers are prone to give incorrect information that sometimes ruins the crop.
- At *mandi*, the farmer is exploited. He is not able to realise the profitable price. Unfair practices, shabby treatment and inconvenience adversely affect the psychology of a farmer.
- Farmers are unable to invest in capital assets. As a result, the yields are very low.

The recent RBI report on currency and finance concluded that one of the main reasons for the low levels of yield is the unsatisfactory spread of technology due to the lack of capital assets. So, though India leads the world on total area of cultivation for paddy and wheat, its productivity is way below that of other countries. For instance, in 1998, China's yield per hectare of paddy was 6,059 kg compared to India's 2,890 kg. The government's 10th working group report on agricultural finance says the sector will need funds to the tune of Rs. 750,000 crore in the next five years. In the last year of the 9th plan, only Rs. 60,000 crore was disbursed to the sector. Says an ICICI executive; "Now that margins in corporate lending are falling, the farm sector is suddenly more appealing".

ICICI

Two years ago, when asked to set up an agribusiness group at ICICI, Zarin Daruwala realized she had a big task on her hands. No one in ICICI had any clue about the business. Sure, it had financed food processing, but this was different. So Daruwala began talking to input firms and output buyers. In the last two years, ICICI has disbursed Rs. 60 crore.

ICICI aligns itself with either NGOs or agri-ventures like Rallis to route rural credit. "We tend to extend credit only where there is a package of inputs and services being offered by an agri-services company. Wherever there is a package, we will supplement it", says Brahmanand Hegde, Chief Manager (Agri Business Group). ICICI pays off the input companies to that extent. ICICI has also tried to arrange marketing for the farmer so that he doesn't have to market his produce. For instance, it roped in HLL and Food World for the Rallis project. In this case, Rallis would pay the farmers for their produce after deducting the loans, "so, I trap my receivables through a marketing company and I channelise my credit through wholesale means", explains Daruwala, Deputy General Manager of the Agri Business Group. The other sensible way to mitigate risk, says Daruwala, is to target those areas, either with fewer *mandis* (so that the produce can be bought out directly),or those that are well irrigated (risks of crop failure are lower).

So far, the strategy is paying off. In Piparlya, where ICICI collaborated with Rallis to provide loans to farmers, it found there were no defaulters. So it is extending the relationship to Chitradurga in Karnataka. It is also riding on the Mahindra *Krishi Vihar*. "We are continuously forming new alliances; every time we spot a marketing company or an input company, we try to bring them to the table. If these alliances keep fructifying, then we can keep scaling it up", adds Daruwala. ICICI's end game is interesting: once it sells a farmer a crop loan, it could try to sell him a two-wheeler loan or a car loan, even a housing loan.

SBI MODEL

SBI's new initiative has its moorings in the Kisan Credit Card (KCC) scheme announced by the Union Finance Minister in 1998. So far banks have issued 21.5 million cards with a total credit of Rs. 45,543 crore. SBI, too, joined the fray by issuing a total of 1.7 million cards. But now, SBI is moving one step forward, it introduced Kisan Gold Card (KGC).

1. The Reserve Bank of India had stipulated that banks would have to lend at least 18 per cent of their net banking credit to agriculture. SBI's Chief General Manager M.A. Kishnan says: "We had to come up with a new idea to drive up credit to farmers. Investment credit was the way to go".
2. By studying the credit history of borrowers under the KCC scheme, it found that large farmers, who were less risky to lend to, needed money for investing in long-term capital assets rather than merely for working capital. SBI's think-tank also noticed that over the years, investment credit to farmers was slipping, even as crop credit was rising. The writing on the wall was clear; if farmers did not invest in increasing farm productivity, ultimately crop credit levels would tend to plateau.
3. Under KCC scheme, farmers had to repay the amount borrowed on the card within one year. For example, the card wasn't a relevant instrument for a farmer, who wanted to add a processing unit to his tomato farm because the pay-offs would invariably take more than a year.

That's when managers at SBI discovered a new opportunity: Why not tweak the KCC and come up with a concept that would allow farmers access to long-term capital? It also had to be careful that recovery rates did not spin out of control. For KCC, SBI's recovery rates were close to 90 per cent, so there were few worries on that score. Unlike the KCC, the farmer will have considerable discretion in using the money in case of the Gold Card. He can decide on the purpose of the loan and repayment programme under certain guidelines. In fact, even though farmers are expected to buy farm equipment, SBI will theoretically allow them to use the money on consumer durables like refrigerators as well.

But how does SBI manage the risk inherent in microcredit? For starters, only farmers with a sound record of repaying loans are eligible. For loans above Rs. 25,000, the farmer has to pledge his land or issue a third-person guarantee. The local branch manager, through his network of field officers, personally examines the standing of the farmer in the community. The local *patwari* has to certify that the farmer uses his land for agricultural purposes. Says SBI's Deputy General Manager, E.S. Balasubramaniam: "These days, there is a lot of community pressure on the farmer to pay up so the recovery rates are moving up".

SBI's next step is to scale up operations. Next year, it's target is to give away Rs. 1,000 crore on 100,000 Gold Cards. Says Vijay Mahajan, director , Basixindia, an NGO specializing in giving microcredit to farmers: "The crux of the issue lies in product delivery. SBI's long experience with farmers should help it to do that better".

The story doesn't end there. SBI eventually plans to issue a plastic card, which will act as a debit card in the hands of the farmer, who can use it freely in specially marked outlets to buy agricultural inputs. SBI is now tracking purchase patterns at local co-operative stores so that it can build a relevant "member establishment" network in rural India, replete with swipe machines. Then, farmers will no longer need to get each purchase cleared by bank officials. Krishnan says this will automatically lower administrative costs for SBI. And, hopefully, earn higher profits.

QUESTIONS

1. Evolve a rural credit financing strategy based on ICICI and SBI models.
2. Will the debit card scheme of SBI be successful?

Source

1. T. Surendar, "SBI plays Its cards", *Business World,* April 15, 2002, pp. 24–25.
2. Ranju Sarkar, "The Roots of Success", *Business World*, February 4, 2002, p. 26.

CASE

11 Silky Routes

CavinKare Ltd., an unlisted company from Chennai has joyous moments as it has become a distinct player in the shampoo market. What started in 1983 as Beauty Cosmetics with a meager investment by first generation entrepreneur, C. K. Ranganathan is now a 170 crore personal products player with a new face–CavinKare. To all those befuddled by the name, Cavin denotes beauty and fairness in literary Tamil. This firm has been steadily establishing itself in the FMCG segment, eating into the market shares of multinationals like HLL and P&G. In absolute volumes and market shares, CavinKare may not be comparable to the biggies but growth-wise it has been scoring. Just take the shampoo market. CavinKare's shampoo business has grown 34 per cent in 2000, faster than the overall market.

CavinKare can no longer be dubbed the 'Chik' company, catering only to the lower segments with an economy shampoo pack. Today, CavinKare has quite an array of brands. While Chik, Nyle, (haircare), FairEver (skincare) and Spinz deodorant and Talc have been rolled out nationally, the others–Meera, Indica hair dye–are still regional. Chik and Nyle together have been giving a run to Hindustan Lever's Sunsilk and Clinic as well as P&G's Pantene and Head & Shoulders, while FairEver has been gaining on HLL's Fair & Lovely. It is now crossing the consolidation stage and is expected to become aggressive in the future. Ranganathan doesn't rule out an entry into new categories and even acquisitions. With all this and more, the company is looking at a Rs. 5000 crore turnover in 10 years. Small now, but not for ever.

MARKET AND BARRIERS

The current size of the shampoo market, according to ORG-MARG is Rs. 850 crore, equivalent to 30,000 tonnes in volume terms. At present, the penetration is around only 18 per cent . The share of CavinKare is 19.8 per cent against 65 per cent of HLL. P & G is the only other large player in this category. The product range is quite baffling to the consumers. The brands of the major players are:

HLL	– Sunsilk, Clinic Plus, Clinic All Clear
CavinKare	– Chik, Nyle
P & G	– Pantene Pro-V, Head & Shoulders

New entrants are probably discouraged by the formidable task of establishing a distribution network from scratch. HLL's long established ties with retailers and its extensive distribution reach probably acts as an entry barrier for new entrants.

Mr. D. Shivakumar, General Manager Marketing, Personal Products, Hindustan Lever has identified three major barriers to shampoo use in India.

- The perception that shampoos contain harsh chemicals that could damage hair,
- The view that shampoo is more of a glamour product rather than a hygiene product, and
- The high price.

SUCCESS ROUTES

CavinKare has managed to garner a significant share of the shampoo market . It has rightly focused on scaled-down versions of its brands and herbal shampoos, the two segments where the market leader did not have a presence.

Scaled-down Versions

Roughly a fourth of the shampoo market is in rural India. But the rural market is the key driver for sachets, which make up for 70 per cent of the total shampoo sales. HLL has higher stakes in the rural market with an 80 per cent share. Unlike other FMCG categories, where marketers are experimenting with low unit packs, as a concept, the low unit shampoo packs have been around for over a decade. Therefore, marketers have been working at scaling down prices further.

CavinKare made the first such attempt last year. It introduced a smaller sachet of Chik, at 50 paise when most other sachets retailed at Rs. 2. The Chik brand expanded by 40 per cent after its launch. A new 50 ml bottle of Chik priced at Rs. 6 (when most other brands were available in 100 ml bottles and above) has also helped expand the brand. HLL acknowledges that the Chik innovations have expanded the overall market, trimming HLL's volume shares by 2-3 per centage points. "CavinKare has expanded the market itself. Though our volume shares are down, our brands have not lost volume. They continue to sustain their earlier growth rates,'' says Mr Shivakumar.

HLL has responded with its own 50 paise version of Lux shampoo. The company claims the recently launched 30 ml bubble pack for Clinic Plus (Rs. 8), is an innovative and cost-effective alternative for sachet users. While sachets are difficult to store and re-use, the bubble pack allows the user to extract just the right quantity for a single wash.

Herbal Products

One of the key barriers to shampoo usage lies in the reluctance to use a synthetic product on hair. Worldwide, therefore, herbal shampoos or botanicals, are a fast growing category. Ayur from RDM Traders Private Limited and Nyle Herbal, a herbal shampoo launched by CavinKare, have been some of the early entrants in the Indian herbal shampoo market.

These products claim to use traditional Indian herbs such as *shikakai*, soap nuts and *amla* as ingredients and have been a success. Nyle Herbal is among the top five shampoo brands in the country and herbal shampoos today account for 10 per cent of the market size. Surprisingly, the industry leader, Hindustan Lever, does not as yet have a presence in this segment.

STRATEGIC PERSPECTIVES

The growth of the company is dependent on how the company builds its marketing muscle and evolves share gaining strategies.

Distribution

According to analysts tracking the sector, even as CavinKare has scored on pricing and pack sizes, it is still to work on the distribution network. Today, CavinKare has 2,200 stockists and retail presence in around six lakh outlets including some *kiranas* in the smallest of villages. Currently, the company has been concentrating on a few pockets in the South and North across Class 1 and 2 towns.

It's now looking at beefing up its distribution network in the metros on the one hand and the rural areas on the other. To cater to the growing distribution needs, it's strengthening its back-end structure with a SAP R/3 package focusing on distribution management, at a total cost of Rs. 2.5 crore. The company has also undertaken a special rural drive with exclusive stockists for rural areas.

Promotion

"We undertake separate promotional schemes for rural areas including free screening of films," says Ranganathan. "With just 50 per cent of the rural masses exposed to TV, we have to reach out through other methods". For example, in Tamil Nadu, its "video-on-wheels" screen films–predominantly, MGR films–for the public. During the free screenings, it does some brand publicity activity, and distributes samples.

Expanding Shampoo Market

The expansion routes have to take into cognizance the problems in the existing product strategies as well as the trends in the market.

- Problems

The scaled-down versions could help pep up volume growth rates for major players. But they have also had the effect of lowering the per ml cost of the major brands retailed through sachets. Till the time the players upgrade users to the larger pack sizes, the sachet revolution could restrict margin expansion for the players. High price could be a key barrier when it comes to herbal shampoos. The key challenge in manufacturing herbals lies in efficacy. Users typically require larger quantities or higher concentrations, of herbal shampoos to replicate the results of synthetic shampoos. Bringing down prices can, therefore, be quite difficult in this case. This is probably why 90 per cent of the herbal shampoos still sell only in the urban markets.

- Other Routes

(1) Not Glamour Products Players have also tried other routes to expand the shampoo market. Fighting the perception that shampoos are essentially glamour products, marketers have tried to add a utility value to shampoos by offering functional benefits. Anti-dandruff shampoos represent this attempt. Clinic Plus, one of the first anti-dandruff brands, is the largest shampoo brand today, with a market share of 31 per cent. Clinic All Clear, an anti-dandruff extension targeted at the youth has also managed to garner a 13 per cent share. Due to its low pricing (Rs. 71 for a 160 ml bottle against Rs. 68 for a 100 ml bottle of Head & Shoulders, an anti-dandruff shampoo), the brand also has a significant rural market share of 44 per cent.

(2) Premium Products HLL has experimented with different versions of Sunsilk for dry, normal and oily hair. Procter & Gamble's Head & Shoulders, Menthol and Pantene Lively Clean offered functional benefits to users. Since these add-ons enable brands to command a price premium over the plain shampoos, this strategy could aid both volume and margin expansion.

(3) Moving Across Category Barriers Meanwhile, the value-added shampoo segment is getting quite crowded, with a range of pharmaceutical and cosmetics companies launching specialised products. While Dabur has leveraged Vatika's brand equity to launch Vatika Herbal shampoo, Godrej Soaps has leveraged its dominance of the hair colour market to launch Godrej Colourgloss shampoo, for users with coloured hair. This apart, several Pharma companies (including Johnson & Johnson), have launched medicated anti-dandruff shampoos (which will probably carry higher credibility with buyers), while cosmetic companies such as Biotique and Lotus Herbals also have herbal shampoos on the shelves.

Diversification

The company is now looking at new categories of soaps and perfumes. At present it is test-marketing Chik bath soap in Andhra Pradesh. "The test market results showed us that modifications had to be done. Hence, we have gone back to incorporate these changes" said Ranganathan.

Philosophy

C. K. Ranganathan, MD, CavinKare attributes the success of his brands to one philosophy—"It's not good enough to know to play the game properly. Sometimes a win is possible only if you change the rules of the game."

- With Chik, the company scored on its low-unit packs.
- "The saffron and milk combination in FairEver clicked with the people because they were familiar with the goodness of the products. And we changed the rules by introducing saffron which had never been used in fairness creams in the past."
- Our brand extensions are research based. "If the brand does not add significant improvement in market-share, then there is no use in introducing the product. FairEver was a hit the first time but then the company went back to the drawing board. We do not want to be just another player," Ranganathan asserts. The same pattern has occurred with most of its products: launch, withdraw to incorporate new findings and then a re-launch. Another example is Nyle: "Consumers felt that the conditioning was less than expected. Hence, both communication and the formulations were changed and it became a hit," Ranganathan says. That brand's success, he feels, is mainly due to the quality of the product, communication, and packaging. But mostly, it was able to plug the gap that existed in the market for herbal shampoos.

CavinKare's corporate strategy revolves around three cardinal rules that Ranganathan has imposed.

- First, CavinKare will never venture into marketing and will only focus on brand building, R&D and distribution management. The company has a line of third party manufactures including exclusive producers mostly in the tax haven of Pondicherry. "When we refrain and outsource products, we are able to maintain a clear focus on brand building. There is no desperate working capital requirements and above all, we are able to maintain flexibility in juggling with products," he says.

- Secondly, CavinKare will never undertake to distribute products of other manufactures. "We have been receiving offers from both Indian and multinational FMCG companies to distribute their products. But we are firm that we will never do that," says Ranganathan.
- "Thirdly, we will not let our products be distributed by other people," he adds.

QUESTIONS

1. In the shampoo market crowded with varieties, how could CavinKare make its mark?
2. Outline its overall strategy to reach its ambitious targets. Within that how can CavinKare gain larger share in the shampoo market in the future?

Source

1. Aarati Krishnan, Shampoos: Putting money where it is. *Business Line*, Sunday, January 21, 2001.
2. One Size Beats All, *Brand Equity, The Economic Times* , January 10, 2001.

CASE

12 Launching the Killer

The marketing team at Agri Friend Pvt. Ltd., was busy during the last fortnight working on the launch strategy for its new 'Killer' brand. Since Andhra Pradesh (AP) and Karnataka are the major consumption states of pesticides, they have preferred AP as their launch pad and conducted a quick market survey to have a fresh look at the market. The company has good market standing and financial soundness, to fight with biggies like Rallis, Nagarjuna Fertilisers, Coromandel Fertlisers, and EID Parry in Andhra Pradesh.

INDUSTRY PROFILE

Domestic agro chemical industry has about 80 players in the organized sector and more than 600 in the small-scale sector. More than 60 technical grade pesticides are manufactured indigenously by 125 producers. Others are engaged in making pesticide formulations. There are a large number of subsidiaries of MNCs like Monsanto Chemicals, Bayer (India), Novartis (India) and Cyanmide Agro. Many Indian companies invest little in R&D. Consequently, very few proprietary molecules and product patents are owned by them.

The industry is affected by seasonal demand, (monsoon dependant), small scale operations (landholdings are small), strong competition (entry of foreign companies) and environmental regulations. Most of the companies have achieved only an average capacity utilisation of 65-70 per cent which has affected their profit margins. The pointers to growth in demand include:

- Growing rural incomes, rising education levels and innovative farming practices together will improve insecticide resistance and control management.
- Corporate assisted farming in place of individual farming. Already, EID Parry, Rallis, and Mahindra & Mahindra have started *Kisan Kendras* to guide farmers.
- Growing awareness to global practices. India has the lowest spend at US $ 3 per hectare (Table 1).

Table 1 Expenditures on Crop Protection

Country	Expenditure (US $ Per Hectare)
Japan	1113
USA	43
Brazil	26
China	6
India	3

- Growing market. The size of the global agro chemical market for the year 2000 was about US $ 34.4 bn and is expected to grow at 5 per cent per annum. With this, the generics market is worth US $ 24 bn (about 72 per cent of the total). It is expected that generics market will be US $ 30 bn by 2002. Growth in India is relatively less (Table 2).

Table 2 Production and Consumption of Pesticides

(000 tonnes)

Year	Production	Consumption
1990–91	74	53
1991–92	72	58
1992–93	76	63
1993–94	83	68
1994–95	90	75
1995–96	96	89
1996–97	102	72
1997–98	96	83
1998–99	98	86
1999–00	100	89
2000–01	102	91
2001–02	105	93

Given the scenario, the Indian companies can respond to the global competition and slow growing markets in many ways.

- Set up manufacturing base for global players.
- Exploit the generic business (as 70 per cent of molecules are off patent) before MNCs launch their patented products.
- Increase pest consumption by introducing cost-effective pests and educating farmers.
- Develop niche markets and low dosage molecules in future.

PRODUCT

Cartap is a new pesticide far different from the normally used pesticides to control the pest of crops. It contains cartap Hydrochloride, an insecticide that is analogous to insecticidal natural product 'Nereistoxin'. This analogue has more insecticide toxicity and less mammalion toxicity compared to naturally occurring 'Nereistoxin'. The main reasons for considering its introduction are:

- Though it is advocated for paddy , it is officially recommended in more than 16 countries for a variety of crops like ginger, potato, cabbage, cotton, maize and tomato. It is used against paddy stem borer, diamond back moth, cabbage worm, potato beetles, etc.
- Highly soluble than other granules used in paddy crop. Hence, enables the plant to take higher quantities to kill the pest. Lower doses develop pest resistance; such an adverse affect is inhibited by this.

Granules used in paddy	Amount soluble at 25°C (mg per litre of water)
Phorate	25
Corbofuran	320
Fipronil	2
Cartap Hydrochloride	200,000

- It does not cause any harm to the nature as it dissociates into non-toxic compounds.
- It gives long term control, sometimes even upto 15 days. Thus, the applications of insecticides come down reducing the cost of pest control. Also, it does not give succulence to the crop, but improves plant resistance to the pest. Hence, there will be no secondary infestation of other pests like leaf folder, if applied for stem borer.
- It gives immediate and comprehensive protection. It is a contact poison. The pest becomes paralyzed when it comes into contact with the chemical. The chemical is taken up by the plant through the root system and translocated to the entire plant system. This makes all the plant cells poisonous including the cell sap.

SURVEY RESULTS

A preliminary survey of granular pesticides market in AP gave the following results.

- The market is dominated by Phorate followed by Carbofuran and Cartap. Reagent has less demand.
- Among the three pack sizes available, 1 kg and 5 kg pack are widely purchased. The 25 kg is preferred only in case of Carbofuran.
- The reasons for buying granular pesticides as cited by farmers are: to control pest, for greenness, more yields, succulence and ease of application.
- Factors influencing purchase decisions are varied—previous experience, dealer's advice, post quality attributes, export advice, and fellow farmer adoption in that order.

- Purchases are mostly on credit basis.
- The maximum dosages of granular pesticides in most of the cases are: Cartap and Phorate upto 6 kg/ hectare, Carbofuran upto 10 kg / hectare and Reagent upto 8 kg /hectare.
- Cartap application procedure is perceived as a difficult one by many farmers.
- Pests are to be available between 10 to 60 days after sowing of the seeds.
- In case of pesticides, farmers are influenced by promotional campaigns and incentives. Dealer relationships, farmer education and relationships, jeep campaigns, wall paintings/posters, pamphlets, etc., are currently adopted measures.

QUESTIONS

1. Suggest a suitable positioning and product launch strategy for 'KILLER'.

Credits

Vinita Kumari, MBA(Final) and Mrs. Nandhani Murali, Assistant Professor, MOP Vaishnav College for Women, Chennai.

CASE

13

Devil or Angel ?

The General Manager (Marketing and Sales) of Sri Hatcheries Ltd. is perturbed by an article that appeared in one of the leading, Tamil weekly, *Kumudam*. It dubbed broiler chicken as a devil. Already the industry is hit by recession, foul play of traders and heavy competition. What should be our reaction to this propagation of negative attitudes? Is this an academic exercise in public interest or a bad publicity by competitors (of substitute products)?

ABOUT INDUSTRY

Poultry sector is one of the fastest growing sectors in the country. India is the fourth largest producer of eggs and eighth largest producer of poultry broiler in the world. The poultry industry overall is growing at a rate of 15–20 per cent per annum. The broiler farming which started very late in early 1970s has picked up very fast. In 2000, 750 million broilers were reared at various farms across the country. Number of broiler-hatcheries too have grown from just 77 in 1980 to more than 750 in 2000. Presently, poultry industry in toto has set a target of achieving a total turnover of Rs. 27,000 crore by 2005. Of the total production of eggs and broilers, states of AP, TN, Maharashtra and Punjab combinedly contribute more than 50 per cent.

INFLUENCING FACTORS

1. *Feed Prices*: The poultry industry is highly dependent on feed industry. So any price movement in the feed industry directly affects the prices in the poultry industry. Also, any shortfall in the Indian supply of feed leads to an import of feed. The prices of birds also get affected in a cyclical way due to periods of excess supply. Unfortunately, the quality of feed in India is still far below that of international standards.
2. *Less Support from Government*: Poultry sector is neither considered as an agricultural sector nor as an industrial sector. Thus, the governmental support is very less as compared to the two sectors. However, the government does fund research activities related to the sector either directly for poultry breeding and health maintenance or indirectly through APEDA (Agricultural and Processed Products Exports Development Authority) for providing infrastructural support and subsidies for poultry exports. The government also supports this sector by assisting the National Egg Coordination Committee (NECC) for promotion of egg marketing and consumption.

Governmental support for the sector has increased from Rs. 55 million in 1998–99 to Rs. 62 million in 1999–00.

3. *Growing Consumption*: The per capita egg consumption is in the range of 36 and that of poultry meat around 850gms. In urban areas, the per capita consumption is 100 eggs and 1200 gms of poultry meat per annum while in rural areas it is 15 eggs and 150 gms per annum. But with an increase in the income at disposal, the per capita consumption is expected to rise. NECC has set a target of increasing the per capita consumption to 180 by 2015.
4. *Towards Processing*: Even today, more than 90 per cent of poultry is slaughtered at the delivery shops to give fresh products to consumers, but with the fast growing fast food chains, the concept of processed meat has started picking up and this will lead to, a greater amount of poultry meat sold in processed form. There are five major poultry processing modern plants that are catering to this processed poultry market. These plants belong to:

   - Venky's
   - AgriTech Hatcheries
   - Peninsula Processed Foods
   - Shiraz Foods
   - Swift Foods

5. *Towards Integrated Farming*: Most of the poultry meat is sold by the unorganised sector. The concept of organised and integrated working has started gaining momentum with the establishment of modern abattoirs. India's broiler industry is highly unorganised specially in North India though in South India the players of the industry have come together for integrated operations. However, Layer industry is totally in the hands of unorganised sector.

Ethical issues involved in the poultry industry

Some of the major ethical issues involved in the poultry sector are related to the treatment of chickens for getting higher egg produce and also to the treatment of spent hens. These issues are:

- *Feeder space* Putting more number of hens in smaller cage leading to bruises on their body and feather loss.
- *Debeaking* Cutting their beaks which involves cutting their bone, cartilage and soft tissue.
- *Fatty liver syndrome* Making hens work to lay more number of eggs makes their body extremely weak leading to accumulation of fats in their liver.
- *Osteoporosis* Laying of large number of eggs leads to loss of a lot of calcium from the body leading to bone breakage, paralysis and death.
- *Spent Hens* After a year of egg production, hens are sent to slaughter houses for their meat.
- *Molting* This involves starving hens for 18 days in the dark leading to a loss in weight and they enter into another egg laying cycle due to shock leading to their death.
- *Crushing / trash canning* This involves crushing of live chickens.

THE ADVERSE PUBLICITY

In the article published by *Kumudam*, senior researcher and scientist of natural sciences, Prof. Nammalwar observed: "The broiler chicken can be called mobile killer rather than mobile protein. The country chicken lays eggs after eating worms and insects in the backyard of the house. But the broiler chicken never sees mud or mother nature from birth till death. Moreover, it is given injections to make it disease resistant. Because of this, many chemical reactions take place in its body. A few years ago, egg powder was exported from India. It was rejected in the foreign markets saying that it is adulterated. But nothing was added to the egg powder or packaging. In fact, the adulteration was due to the irritants already existing in the raw unprocessed eggs.

It is not safe to eat broiler chicken which are given heavy antibiotics. Even the feed of the broiler is not natural and contains chemical mixes which contaminates its flesh. It is for this reason that even the excreta stinks without decaying these days.The synthetic feeds, over dosage of injections, etc., given to chicks may cause impotency among men. For this reason many commercial advertisements are given to reduce impotency".

Dr.Ramesh, Veterinarian wrote," In the United States, a Department of Food Safety and Inspection Service (FSIS) is created. In this, a hot line service is given through which any side effect after consuming chicken can be communicated. FSIS collects the samples of chicken from those companies and there are incidents where harmful chicken are destroyed in bulk in many poultry farms. Why can't the same be done in India? If broiler is safe, it can be regulated and distributed to public. This should be the responsibility of the Government. Almost all the countries in the world face the problem of broilers. The concerned governments have started regulating this industry. The Department of Agriculture at Washington has conducted in depth research about broiler chicken and published a list of probable diseases humans can get after consuming broiler chicken: Our head reels if we read the list".

WHAT TO DO?

The General Manager (Marketing), is toying with the following ideas to counter the article.

1. Publish a counter article in the same magazine.
2. Release advertisements highlighting how safe broiler consumption is.
3. Refer the matter to industry association.
4. File a suit in the court of law for damages as the company's sales may be adversely affected.
5. Ignore the article.

Meanwhile, he has gathered the opinions of a few doctors to substantiate his view that "Broiler birds are mini angels and not devils". He listed the following points.

- Broilers cannot attain a marketing age in 10 days. It takes 38–45 days to grow them to the market. They are given three injections only.
- Hormones are not used in broilers.
- Amoebiosis is not a result of consuming chicken since it is a protozoran disease and Indians consume chicken after fully boiling it. This denatures chicken and it is left with only an edible protein.

- An average Indian consumes only 1 kg of chicken per year against 50 kg of American, 52 kg of Burmese, and 36 kg of Saudi Arabian . The men in these countries are more potent than the average Indian men.
- Sex hormones are secreted only after 18–20 weeks of age. Broilers are sold in the age of 6–7 weeks. Since the birds are sexually immature, there is no chance of impotency.
- Girls attaining puberty at an early age is also not true.
- Cartisones are never given to birds. If they were administered, broiler chicken would cost Rs. 300 a kg.

QUESTIONS

1. Will the information in the article disturb the consumers, particularly the rural ones?
2. What would you do if you were the General Manager of Sri Hatcheries ?

Source

1. *Kumudam, Tamil Weekly*, 16th August, 2001, pp. 138–140.
2. www.Indiainfoline.com—Report on Poultry.

PART

5

Price Strategies

- Rural Treasure Hunt
- Price Battle
- *Chavi Gumao Radio Bajao*
- The Pricing Dilemma
- Price Points Strategy

CASE

14

Rural Treasure Hunt

It's there, but just a little bit out of reach and focus. Indian FMCGs, who hit the dusty roads out of the cities to chase the great Indian rural marketing dream, are finding out that the pot of gold at the end of this rainbow isn't easy to find.

HURDLES

Companies like Procter & Gamble, Nestle, and Cadbury, after an exploratory safari or two, have come scurrying back to city slickers, and decided to stay away from the rural markets. Mr. Rajeev Bakshi, Managing Director of Cadbury India is on record saying that rural marketing is not for Cadbury.

HLL officials admit that a significant portion of its sales come from the rural markets, and with the downswing in agricultural growth, volume has been affected. HLL has recently phased out Lipton Tea–a 2-year old low priced rural tea brand with one of the highest recall values in the branded tea industry—following competition from loose tea.

CMIE is lowering its estimates for agricultural growth to 1.3 per cent against the 4.2 per cent projected earlier. It is going to hit FMCG companies, analysts feel. Adi Godrej, Managing Director of Godrej Soaps admits that the slump in agricultural growth has hit the purchasing power in the rural markets.

There is also a question of population shifts (people moving from one region to another), and tough competition from local brands in the rural market. But the first roadblock is getting there. Very clearly, products cannot be sold in these markets because they can't be easily reached. Harsh Mariwala, Managing Director of Marico Industries admits that FMCG companies have not even scratched the surface of the 'real rural' markets. "The main reason for this is that neither companies nor their channel partners find it economically viable to penetrate the rural markets directly. Low purchasing power leads to low demand, which in turn leads to low sales value and has an adverse cost-benefit", he says.

The costs incurred to make the products available, especially products with a shorter self-life, to the real rural markets call for huge spends, which is not being balanced by adequate volumes. Once a brand reaches a market, there are the local brands to contend with, lower trade costs and lower price points. This situation has begun worrying analysts who feel that with the saturation in the urban markets in addition to competition, the real volumes have to come in from the rural markets. Also, product pricing in such markets has to be realistic, which means the companies would have to operate on extremely low margins to build up volumes.

STRATEGIES

A lot of initiatives have been taken to ride over the slump.

PRODUCT

Unlike in the past, companies like HLL, Colgate and Marico are now coming out with products aimed specifically at the rural market at rock bottom prices and in sachets or pouches. FMCG companies have begun launching shampoos in sachets, low unit packs of biscuits, flexi-pouches of oil and small packs of toothpaste and toothpowder and soaps. HLL has just launched Clinic Plus shampoo in Rs. 0.50 and Re.1 sachets, which were earlier available at Rs. 2 per sachet. "The price was reduced to enable higher rural penetration", an HLL spokesperson said.

DISTRIBUTION

FMCG companies are trying to get their distribution system in place. They are investing in their distribution channels by way of subsidies with a view that the channel becomes viable in future. Companies are leveraging and developing the feeder channel in order to maximize the indirect reach in these areas. Alliances are being formed and costs are being shared with 'like' companies addressing the same target markets and rural purchasing power through community development and micro credit programmes along with governmental and non-governmental financial institutions.

QUESTIONS

1. Identify the reasons for the withdrawal or limited success of the FMCG companies.
2. Examine the strategies adopted by the FMCG companies to ride over the slump.
3. What additional steps do you suggest to the FMCG companies?

Source

Kala Vijayaraghavan and Anamika Rath, FMCG's Find Rural Treasure Hunt Tough, *The Economic Times*, December 15, 2000, pp. 1&3.

CASE 15

Price Battle

Tara had to fight many academic battles in her class room. She is also very much alive to the fact that she has to face competition one day or another. She did not expect it would happen so soon. When Tara graduated in business management, she found that there was a vast market potential for skin care products particularly in the economy range. 'The middle and lower income groups' she says, 'are in a state of despair not able to afford the high priced, high quality products offered by large domestic companies and MNCs'.

She teamed up with three of her class mates and set up Hopes India Pvt. Ltd. Hopes manufactured and marketed, Sri Raga skin care products using herbal secrets, priced affordably, and supported by persuasive and educative campaigns, in the urban areas and door-to-door selling with the help of self-help groups (SHGS) and DWCRA (Development of Women and Child in Rural Areas)groups in the rural areas. The product garnered substantial market share in a span of three years. In Andhra Pradesh and Karnataka, it has become the market leader in the herbal segment. Table-1 compares Sri Raga with other similar products.

Table 1 Price Comparisons

Brand	25 gms	50 gms	70 gms
Fair & Lovely	26.50	49.00	70.00
FairEver	28.00	50.00	--
FairGlow	25.00	46.00	--
Sri Raga	20.00	38.00	--

Sailing cannot be smooth in life or business. The slow growth rates of urban markets and intense competition in high-end markets has turned the attention of new entrants to the growing low-end markets. Even the established brands like Fair & Lovely have targeted at rural markets.

Sensing the evolution of competition, Tara called for a meeting of her key executives. The discussion considered various aspects pertaining to markets, competitive brands and strategic options. The members felt that Sri Raga's target market is mostly young married housewives in the group of 25–40 years. On the other hand, the fair brands attracted the teenagers and just married girls. The possible reasons for patronizing Sri Raga are: its low price, herbal-base and healthy skin promise. The fair brands claim a change in complexion whereas Sri Raga emphasizes on 'Give Life To Your Skin'. It asserts, "Why change your natural complexion? Give new life to it? Look bright always". The mature young woman appreciated the message and patronized it.

"I am sure, we have no threat from the existing products . A product similar to ours at a lower price or with high promotion blitzkrieg may destabilise us", said Tara. At this point, she got a fax message which read as follows, "French Cosmetics, the new entrant is launching Fair Always at Rs. 20 (50 gms) and Rs. 39 (100 gms) with heavy promotion".

To hold the market leadership, Tara considered the following alternatives.

Market	Tactics
Urban	1. Maintain same price and quality; increase promotion expenditure. 2. Improve quality of product and offer at same price; maintain same promotion hype.
Rural	Price cut.

In case of urban markets, the impact of marketing-mix variations are difficult to gauge as it involves understanding preferences of the consumer for a foreign product offered at popular prices. The price-cut in rural market is considered as a preemptive measure. Already low price offerings are on the rise in the rural markets. A Re.1 shampoo is now sold at 50 paise.

Tara was aware that prices should not be set out without first examining what will happen to profits. It is difficult to make a separate cost-volume-profit analysis for rural demand as the two plants (roughly equal capacities) set up in Andhra Pradesh and Karnataka cater to both urban and rural markets. Since, her sales are equally divided between rural and urban markets she decided to use the cost figures of one plant to arrive at a decision. Table-2 shows demand at various prices and corresponding costs. It is obvious that Hopes cannot lower its price below Rs. 17. Based on the information Tara and her team members have evolved three decision options proposing price changes taking into cognizance the competitive reactions. Table-3 depicts them.

Table 2 Cost–Volume–Profit Analysis

Unit price (Rs.)	Demand Units (Lakhs)	Total Revenue (Rs. Lakhs)	Unit Variable Cost (Rs.)	Selling & Administration Costs (Rs. Lakhs)	Profit (Rs. Lakhs)
20	10.0	200.0	12.0	14.0	28.0
19	11.0	209.0	11.5	16.0	27.5
18	11.3	203.0	11.0	17.0	19.9
17	11.6	197.2	11.0	18.0	7.2
16	11.8	188.8	11.0	19.0	0.0

Table 3 Decision Options

Option 1 Maintain price at Rs. 20.

If price is maintained at Rs. 20, there may be a fall in sales by 20 per cent due to craze for foreign company products. Variable cost is Rs. 13 per unit.

Option 2 Reduce Price to Rs. 19.

(a) Given a 40 per cent probability that competitor will not react. Sales will rise by 5 per cent.Variable cost is Rs. 12 per unit.

(b) Given a 30 per cent probability that competitor will reduce price by Re. 1 and sales will remain the same. Variable cost is Rs. 12 per unit.

(c) Given a 30 per cent probability that competitor will lower price by Rs. 2 and sales will fall by 5 per cent. Variable cost/ unit is Rs. 12 per unit.

Option 3 Reduce price to Rs. 18.

(a) Given a 40 per cent probability that competitor will not react. Sales will rise by 10 per cent. Variable costs per unit is Rs. 11 per unit.

(b) Given a 30 per cent probability that competitor will reduce price by Re. 1 and sales will rise by 5 per cent. Variable costs per unit is Rs. 12.

(c) Given a 30 per cent probability that competitor will reduce price by Rs. 2 and sales will remain the same. Variable cost is Rs. 12 per unit.

Advice Sri Raga.

CASE

16 Chavi Gumao Radio Bajao

The Rs. 1,666 crore Philips India has currently a sales turnover of Rs. 45 crore in radios and a market share value of about 58.3 per cent in November 2001. The market share has registered a growth of 13.6 per cent over the previous year. In the FM radio segment, it sells over one lakh units of FM radios per month. Mr. Rajeev Karwal, Vice-President (Consumer Electronics) says; "We aim at moving to Rs. 60 crore in sales turnover of radios by 2003-end.

BATTERY FREE RADIO

In a bid to trigger brand penetration in the rural markets for the audio segment, the company is planning to launch a new range of battery free radio across the nation. It runs on a small dynamo that has to be charged by a winding key.

JUSTIFICATION

This is a mass market brand with a primary focus on the rural audience. According to Mr. Suresh Sukumaran, Senior General Manager (Marketing), there is still 55 per cent of the rural households who can be the potential audience for radio. This is the core consumer base the company would proactively target. Mr. Karwal explains: 'Philips as a market leader in audio segment needs to drive the business and pioneer new concepts to grow the business and also enable consumers to see innovation and authority in the brand'. In radio segment, Philips competitors such as BPL and Videocon made an entry but have lost interest in the segment as volumes is the key here.

PRICING

"With the burst of FM radio stations, we believe the usage of radios in the day is bound to increase. With a product like this, with no recurring cost on batteries, consumers are bound to see value and novelty. 'Philips battery-less radio will enable consumers to save Rs. 1200 per year, which he would otherwise have spent on batteries. Value-conscious Indian middle class will definitely see the advantage of this product'.

A quick market survey revealed that consumers are willing to pay a price around Rs. 1,000 expecting that it would go down over a period of time. However, a positive observation is–the lowest end of the market segment's annual earnings has shot up to around Rs. 24,000. The high incomes combined with a low cost of living in the villages has meant more money to spend.

PROMOTION

The company is planning to launch the radio through the trade at all distributors' meet at Jaipur and showcase the product in all other launches during the year. The company will also be launching a new campaign targeted at both the semi-urban and rural consumers with the catch line '*chavi gumao, radio bajao*' in select states. The key message would be the world's first battery free radio. "In smaller markets, given the erratic electric supply and the cost of batteries, we feel that there is an inherent need and benefit which this product delivers and hence makes their lives better", says Mr. Rupam Ganguly, General Manager(Trade and Consumer Services).

QUESTIONS

1. In your opinion, what should be the price of the battery free radio? Justify your answer.

CASE 17

The Pricing Dilemma

Jagan is deeply concerned with new product choices. The market has become dynamic and competitive requiring innovations. The rural market is no longer a residual proposition. He is preparing a preliminary marketing strategy for the proposed launch of a new toothpaste for Kashmir Products Pvt. Ltd..

TARGET MARKET

The target market is the middle and low income segments of rural and urban market. Particularly those who are concerned with gum care and receptive to 'Always Fresh' concept. The new brand of toothpaste will be positioned as a powerful, economy, family product for those who dislike frequent brushing.

MARKETING STRATEGY

The product will be offered in three standard pack sizes at low prices. The paste will be in sky blue colour with mint flavour. It will be distributed initially in Andhra Pradesh through its existing whole sale-retailer chain in urban areas and by van marketing in rural areas. Free samples of 10 gm toothpaste will be distributed door-to-door in rural areas. The media will be vans, wall paintings, and pamphlets in rural areas and local newspapers in urban areas. The advertising themes will emphasise benefits of brushing once in a day for freshness throught the day and lasting health.

PROFIT GOALS

The company intends to capture 5 per cent market share in rural areas which requires an after-tax return of 15 per cent. To achieve this, price will be kept at the same level, quality improvements in product and package will be worked out. Promotion expenditure will be boosted each year by about 20 per cent. Emphasis will be on communication and freebies for children. Table-1 shows the projected sales and costs.

PRICING

Since the product aims at sweeping the rural side it decided to keep the price lower than the existing brands. "The low price will not only hit the competition but also expand market by converting the users from powder 'to paste'. We can do this because our costs are low and we are focusing on local market" said Jagan enthusiastically.

"We are considering two options in pricing (Table-1), along with different promotion efforts. We have to decide which will give us more advantage" said Jagan thoughtfully.

Table 1 Pricing Options

Size	Option 1	Option 2
50 gm	Rs. 10	Rs. 12
100 gm	Rs. 19	Rs. 23

The cash flows are given is Table-2 and 3

Option 1

Table 2 Projected Five Year Cash Flows (Rs. Lakhs)

S.No	Aspect	Year 0	Year 1	Year 2	Year 3	Year 4	Year 5
1	Sales revenue	0	50	70	100	150	200
2	Cost of goods sold	0	18	25	34	52	70
3	Development costs	3	--	--	--	--	--
4	Marketing costs	0	32	35	40	46	56
5	Allocated overhead	0	4	4	5	5	6

Option 2

Table 3 Projected Five Year Cash Flows (Rs. Lakhs)

S. No	Aspect	Year 0	Year 1	Year 2	Year 3	Year 4	Year 5
1	Sales revenue	0	40	60	120	170	230
2	Cost of goods sold	--	19	26	36	55	75
3	Development costs	3	--	--	--	--	--
4	Marketing costs	--	50	7	90	110	130
5	Allocated overhead	--	4	4	5	5	6

If market discount rate is 12 per cent, at which price do you advocate introduction of the product?

CASE

18 Price Points Strategy

Samsung is considering the launch of a new brand of CTVs aimed at the lower income rural and semi-urban buyers who are buying their first TV or upgrading from black and white sets. This is the fastest growing segment of the colour TV market in India, expected to account for over 65 per cent of the overall increase in colour sales this year and more than 75 per cent next year, according to industry estimates.

MARKET SHARES

The television market in India is segmented into black and white and color TVs. B&W TVs still constitute the majority of sales. With several MNCs setting up shop in the past two years, CTV sales have shown a sharp rise. This growth has necessarily meant a fall in the share of B&W TV sales. After years of dominating the CTV market, domestic majors are steadily losing out to multinational brands. A major part of the incremental sales has been of TVs produced by companies such as BPL, Onida, LG and Samsung. The MNCs (excluding the foreign brands marketed by domestic companies) have an approximately 35 per cent market share with domestic companies holding the rest. The Korean companies are growing higher than the industry average while others have shown a slow growth soon after the world cup.

According to market researcher ORG-GFK, BPL is the largest selling brand in the country with a 15.6 per cent market share, followed by Onida with a 13.6 per cent share. The Mumbai based Videocon International Ltd. is third with 10.3 per cent followed by LG Electronics Ltd. of Korea with 10 per cent. During 2001–02 the 14" size category accounted for 24 per cent of the total CTVs sold. The demand in this segment has witnessed a marked growth every year for the past two to three years. The reason being preference for this category among the lower middle class and multiple set buyers.

DEMAND DETERMINANTS

Demand elasticity and price sensitivity are prominent characteristics of consumer electronics industry. For an average Indian, a 21" CTV costing about Rs.12,900 would mean twice his monthly income .

Income Levels

With the rising levels of disposable income and the consequent change in aspiration levels, branded durables have become proud possessions, especially for the emerging middle class. The most surprising revelation is the increasing percentage of the rural rich who are willing to pay for a good quality product. The rural rich who have fewer options to buy branded products are willing to pay the price charged for any premium model. The industry majors have always assumed 'the rural' and 'the poor' as synonyms. However, a lot of rural communities are earning good money from agriculture. Several of these rural markets have flourishing businesses like exports of handicrafts, etc.

In fact, most of the consumer financing options provided by the companies have found more takers in the urban areas while the rural buyers have made cash-down payments. The new Onida KY series (29" and 21") and the LG's premium Golden Eye Series models have found takers in places like Jodhpur. In small towns, preference for branded products has increased. As an example, rural customers are opting for branded gold products to the traditional goldsmiths.

Availability of Financing

Expansion of hire-purchase schemes is one way of making the price-sensitive consumers spend. With financial institutions and commercial banks vying for the attention of consumers, staggered payments lead to increased discretionary purchasing power. Around 60 per cent of durable purchases in the market are hire purchase-led. Taking this into account, BPL, as a part of its promotional strategy, tied-up with ICICI, Standard Chartered, Instabuys, Transamerica and Bajaj Consumer Finance to facilitate the financing of purchase of its goods through various schemes.

LG for instance, has started a zero per cent interest scheme, which has helped in the penetration of CTVs. The company has tied up with financial companies, including Countrywide Finance, for financing schemes for its products.

Price

The CTV industry is very price-sensitive. The market has witnessed already a surge in the demand for CTVs vis-à-vis price cuts. The price of 21" CTV has fallen from Rs.16,500 to 12,900 in 2000. Akai, for eg., sold its CTVs at an unbelievable price of Rs. 10,000 to lure price-sensitive consumers. In spite of the rising cost of inputs, CTV manufactures have not increased the CTV prices as increasing the prices directly affects volumes.

With companies, both foreign and local, going all out to wage a price war and fresh competition coming in the form of a liberalized import regime, players need to guard their turfs. The entry of cheaper products have forced companies to reduce prices in spite of high input costs, high quality and superior technology products. Pricing has been the main weapon for companies to compete so far; however, in the long run, the level of sophistication offered will influence consumer preferences a lot.

Low Penetration Levels

Low penetration means huge opportunity only when the rural economy develops. NCAER statistics show that rural markets have grown faster, at a rate of 8.8 per cent between 1992–93 and 1995–96 compared to 5.3 per cent between 1989-90 and 1992-93. Despite this, and despite the increased share of rural purchase in some areas, the penetration rate remains abysmally low. Rural penetration levels remain lower than in urban areas. Perhaps Indian companies need to follow the African example. There, the consumer durables market witnessed a boom when companies introduced fans, refrigerators and TVs that ran on kerosene and batteries!

Table 1 Penetration of CTVs (per 1000 households)

	Urban	Rural
1989–90	123	9
1992–93	160	16
1993–94	178	19
1995–96	212	26

Marketing effort

Growth in the CTV industry is not due to government incentives, but primarily because of innovative marketing strategies and cost-cutting exercises adopted by various companies.

Due to cut throat competition, various players have been using a variety of strategies to push sales. Be it pushing the dealers, providing gifts, finances, high level of technology or luring the customers with hefty discounts, the companies have tried all the tricks to attract customers.

The increase in demand may as such be attributed to the brand building exercises adopted by the companies, improvement of the distribution system, quality perception, product competitiveness, etc.

Replacement Demand

Indians have a mindset which prevents them from throwing away old items, especially items like durables, which cost a big amount. However, if an individual can replace it for a new one, he/she will readily do so, for eg. items like garments are exchanged for utensils. Akai's huge success story was scripted largely because it tapped the latent demand for replacing existing TVs in the early 1990s. With the entry of satellite TV in the early 1990s, most TV sets in India had turned obsolete. They did not have the S-band facility to receive the large number of channels. What Akai did was to push the replacement cycle forward by taking back old TV sets. Their exchange schemes broke the inertia and the sense of guilt that exists while disposing of an old TV set that works. The old TV sets were supplied to the rural market at prices ranging from Rs.2,000 to 4,000. In time, they formed the new replacement market.

In an India Today-IMRB survey on consumer spending, among 2,045 people spread across six cities, about 20 per cent of the respondents admitted to having replaced at least one durable product in the past three years.The NCAER's Consumer Market Demographic Report of 1998 estimates that 21 per cent of the 4.7 million B&W TV owners are willing to replace them with newer models. The replacement market in India will remain active due to wide income disparities, which exist in the society.

Event-driven

The sale of TVs tends to be event driven. When the Cricket World Cup was on, CTV sales recorded a phenomenal rise of 40–50 per cent.

CHARACTERISTICS OF A RURAL CUSTOMER

- A rural customer though not well educated, has good common sense and is wise and sharp in many ways. He/she is very conscious of 'value for money'. He/she does not always look for cheap products but wants good quality.

- Rural customers sense a patronizing attitude and erect formidable barriers to protect themselves. It is not easy to introduce new products for them. They are bigger brand loyalists than their urban counterparts.
- The rural brands are mostly recognized through symbols, logos and colour.
- There is a very high degree of involvement in the purchase of any product, more so of expensive consumer durables. A typical rural customer checks and rechecks the expensive product he/she is buying. A rural customer cannot be pushed too far as there is no urgent requirement for the product.
- Inter-personal communication still accounts for 80 per cent of the rural communication process in villages. This means that word-of-mouth recommendation by users and sheer familiarity influences rural folks in their purchase decisions. During a study conducted by Anugrah Madison Advertising Pvt. Ltd. for Philips in Tamil Nadu, it was found that almost an entire village owned a single brand of TV such as BPL or Videocon.
- Very often, dealers act as consultants and so their influence carries a lot of weight at the point of purchase. Decisions regarding the brand of consumer durables are taken by the men in the household, in consultation with others in the community.

RURAL MARKETING LESSONS

With purchasing power on the rise especially in the rural market, Onida has adopted an innovative arrangement to widen its reach in the mofussil areas. The company has approached rural co-operative societies (tea garden societies in Assam, sugar co-operatives in Maharashtra and coffee plantations in Tamil Nadu) and sold them TVs at marginal prices. These societies then sell them in villages. The TVs sold are mostly B&W with certain modern features including 100 channels and an on-screen display facility in Hindi. A special remote function to help explain the operations is also available. Such a move forms a part of Onida's long-term strategy to gain the confidence of the rural market before the expected onslaught of the MNCs.

LG Electronics launched *Sampoorna*, India's first TV with a *Devanagri* script on-screen display. Priced at Rs.12,900, it was affordable, consumer-friendly and aimed at semi-urban and rural India. This has set the rural mind at ease and paved the way for its other products in the rural areas. LG Electronics has also tried to cash in on the festive spirit by launching a special discount scheme during the *Durga Puja* and *Diwali* festivals in states like West Bengal, Orissa and the states of the North-East. The reason—these festivals are treated as a special occasion for buying new household items. Customers were lured with loyalty rewards on the purchase of any LG product. The reward would enable them to get a discount of 10 per cent on their next purchase.

Samsung has drawn up a blueprint to expand its penetration in India with a special focus on rural markets. The company has earmarked a separate budget branch-wise, especially for rural markets. It expects more than 10 per cent of its sales to come from the rural markets in the year ending Dec. 2000. Finance packages have been designed with zero percent loans on specific product categories to push volumes in these areas. Rural vans have also been introduced in each region to tour states. This van will display all Samsung products and thus enhance brand awareness levels in the rural areas. The company has also tied up with local distributors to showcase the Samsung range in local *melas* and fairs.

However, the consumer electronics market has seen their rural marketing strategies going awry. All these years it was felt that the rural markets could not afford premium products, but models specially designed for the rural markets have found more takers in the urban markets while premium models have sold more in rural areas. Rural buyers have made cash down payments ignoring the financing options available in places like Jodhpur.

LG's Golden Eye and Onida's KY Thunder have found more takers in the rural areas while *Sampoorna*, which was launched by LG mainly for the rural areas are seeing more buyers in the urban markets. Companies are finding the concept of rural markets being poor to be wrong.

NEW STRATEGIC MOVES

Recently, BPL and multinationals have begun plugging holes in the Rs. 20,000 crore market addressing all price points by launching a wide range of models in all the product categories. By offering more affordable models, the multinationals are now trying to take on the smaller brands in the lower end of the market.

Onida, in fact, launched a mass brand early this year, called Igo, to grab volumes in the lower end. The Igo sets which range in price from Rs. 7,000 for a 14 inch set to Rs. 10,000 for a 2-incher are expected to touch a sales figure of 2 lakh in this year.

LG has benchmarked its volume growth with growth in the Chinese market. "If the market does not grow at the top, then we will grow at the bottom", said Mr. Pradeep Tognata LG's Vice President (Sales and Marketing). LG officials clearly stated that entering new price categories during January–April 2002 has enabled them to increase sales. "We sold around 3 lakh CTV's during the period out of which the 14 inch, 20 inch and 21 inch Cine plus models contributed more than 30 per cent", said Mr. Tognata. According to him, the company has taken a conscious decision to have a model to suit every wallet this year. "If there is a need for Rs. 6,000 priced model we will launch one—we may even take on consumers of black and white televisions and offer a CTV at that price", said Tognata.

Having established its image as a premium brand Sony is now leveraging its brand strength to push volumes in the lower end. It will no longer offer conventional televisions from its stable. However, its 21 inch version is available at Rs. 16,000.

SAMSUNG'S DILEMMA

The Company started its Indian operations in December 1995, and made its maiden profit of Rs. 50mn on a turnover of Rs. 5.4bn for FY1998. Samsung spent a huge Rs. 90mn for its six-week long 1998 Soccer World Cup campaign. It was also one of the official sponsors for the 1998 Asian Games and sponsored the Indian contingent. The company believes that in this way, they would convey the message: 'Like a sportsman, Samsung is also pushing old boundaries by developing new technology and products'. Hence, its ad-line 'Challenge the limits'.

A year later, the company declared a phenomenal increase in profits of Rs. 320mn on a turnover of Rs. 8.5 bn. The volumes so far have been less because it had neglected the mass market of the base line 21" CTV earlier. This range is now launched in the form of Metallica, available in 20" and 21" screen sizes. In future, it intends to focus on introducing new models in every category of a product line, some of them with a unique selling proposition. Samsung currently has a market share of 9 per cent, which it hopes to step up to 11 per cent.

Samsung has the following questions before it.

- Should we launch several models in the market to suit every price point?
- Should we sell entry-level sets under a separate brand name to protect the quality image of premium sets?

- Should we compete on 'price' or 'features'? Should we have a certain premium pricing with innovative features in the mass models? Or alternatively, should we offer the models at lower prices with features similar to the competitive models?

Advice Samsung.

Source

1. *The Economic Times,* May 28 & 30, 2002.
2. www.indiainfoline.com Report on Colour Televisions.

PART

6

Promotion Strategies

- Ruralfind
- A Tale of Tiles
- Ethics in Advertising
- Protecting Savings
- Gunny Sack Race

CASE 19

Ruralfind

"Last week, you told me that we should have a website of our agency. I could not look at it so far because, I was busy with the product launch of our client Aurati Ltd. Meanwhile, I have downloaded the web copy of 'Rural 8' for your perusal". Saying this, Dr. Srinivas handed over the copy to Mrs. Rukmini, his business partner.

Dr. Srinivas and Mrs. Rukmini together founded 'Ruralfind' in 1990 at a time when very few corporate enterprises were interested in rural selling. During the last decade of their operations, Rural find built up a rich database and served corporate major like Colgate, HLL, Dabur India, Mahindra & Mahindra, Nagarajuna Fertilisers and Britannia. They have ten fully equipped video vans that go into rural interiors to do selling, advertising, and relationship building. They have ten drivers and ten technicians to go with the vans. Their main strength is their young team of eight creative personnel who have to their credit outstanding achievements in advertising, research and merchandising.

Mrs. Rukmini, after a brief consideration of the copy said: "I find this copy interesting; the agency is much similar to ours. However, we need differentiation. Why don't you put the MBA project student on this job?"

Dr. Srinivas, accordingly, summoned the MBA project student and assigned him the work of preparing website copy. He gave him the 'Rural 8' copy (Exhibit-I) and instructed him to work independently making decisions on the type of information to be included, the size of the text, the style of presentation, the background, pictures, colours and boarders, etc.

Exhibit–I

RURAL 8

Rural India—the new El Dorado for marketers, who intend to stay ahead of competition. The potential is limitless for those who get in early, and those who do not, do so at their own peril. Rural India is Rural 8 territory. Get on our bandwagon, and establish your own niche, many have already done it.

Clientele

Bajaj Electricals, Khaitan Fans, Rallies India Limited, Shaw Wallace, Bajaj Auto, Population Services International, Parke Davis, Mahindra & Mahindra, Population Services International, Colgate Palmolive, HLL, Apollo Tyres, etc.

The Uniqueness of Rural 8

Rural 8 offers a fleet of comprehensively equipped video vans that criss-cross the markets in the East, South and West to add sizzle to your marketing efforts. Very soon the entire Northern region, too, will be covered by the Rural 8 network. Allow us to unfold the Rural 8 profile ... every single service can be customised to suit your exclusive requirements.

Entertainment and Advertising Videos

Rural 8 offers you a unique package of marketing support services. One - Rural 8 has the largest captive library of feature film videos in Indian languages. Two - Rural 8 has complete in-house facilities, entertainment software and experienced professionals to meet your total communication needs.

The Advertising Opportunity

For screening of entertainment, advertising or sales promotion videos, Rural 8 vans are equipped with 6' X 6' screen, large enough for an audience over 200 people. The vans have complete audio and video projection facilities.

The Retail Outlet on Wheels

Rural 8 vans can be your mobile retail outlets–for spot sales against cash in *bazaars*, *melas*, festivals and *mandirs*.

The Merchandising Option

In case rural shops need to be decorated or if a stall has to be put up at a fair or festival, full merchandising and showcasing support is available. The outside surface of the vans can be covered with blow-ups, cut-outs and other similar items featuring your current advertising themes.

The Sales Promotion Support

Your mobile retail outlets can be instantly transformed into a superb sales promotion van–fully decorated with display material, special promotion packs for discount offers, free sampling for a new product launch, demonstrations and test marketing. You may even plan contests and games of skill guaranteed to draw a crowd, all interested in knowing more about your products and wanting to participate in the schemes.

The Research Matrix

Each Rural 8 van can transport three persons–the driver, the technician and a marketing person who could undertake research into the soul of rural India, to draw keen insights and assist in strategy planning and marketing programmes.

The Impeccable Lineage

What gives Rural 8 a cutting edge is its parentage. Rural 8 is an independent enterprise of Channel 8, the trailblazer in the field of television production and marketing ... a leader backed by the sheer weight of its own achievements.

Rural 8 and you

With Rural 8's extensive support services, your marketing programme can get into the fast track. Because no one else can help you in rural India better than Rural 8. Rural 8...for that rural edge.

QUESTIONS

Assuming yourself as the project student prepare an ad copy for Ruralfind website.

CASE

20 A Tale of Tiles

Tiles India Ltd. (TIL) is a well known company manufacturing floor and wall tiles. It saw opportunity in the vast low income housing commitment of the government and embarked on the manufacture of low priced tiles. TIL has got a break when its indigenous low cost tiles received a big order from Maharashtra government when it was engaged in rural reconstruction after the earthquake at Latur. Now TIL is wondering how to expand its market all over India.

PRODUCT

The tiles are scratch proof and fire resistant. The ISI certification, testifies its quality. The main competition for this is from the locally manufactured terracotta tiles, which are not scratch proof and are fire resistant only upto a certain level of temperature. The tiles of TIL have another advantage, they could be reused even if there was a fire accident. TIL tiles come in two standard sizes; Large (10 inches X 10 inches) and small (5 inches x 5 inches). The local tiles are, however, of small size only.

PRICE

The large tiles of TIL were priced at Rs. 7.00 and small tiles at Rs. 4.50. The local tiles were priced at Rs. 3 only. The company decided that the target profit be Re.1 per piece irrespective of the size. Taking into consideration the margins necessary to meet distribution costs, the prices are fixed at Rs. 4.50 and Rs.7 per small and large piece respectively. The cost-revenue data are as given below:

Selling Price	4.50	7.00
Manufacturing Cost	1.12	4.18
Target Profit	1.00	1.00
Marketing Costs	2.38	1.82

TARGET MARKET

The potential buyers of the company include the middle and upper income groups in villages. Another important segment is the government and institutions as the tiles are cost effective and good in quality, they may be preferred for rural housing as well as institutions like hospitals, schools, etc.

DISTRIBUTION

The company is planning to distribute the tiles through company stockist. The retail outlets can be those which sell cement and hardware. Figure.1 depicts the distribution.

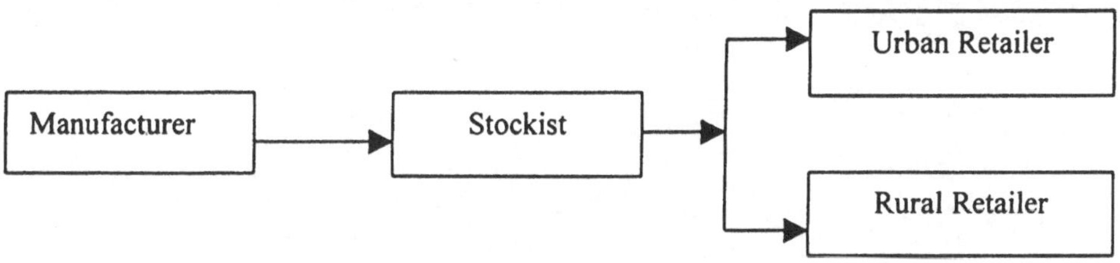

Fig. I Distribution Channel

The only snag in the distribution is the volume of purchase. The optimum lot which may consist of tiles of any size is 10,000 units. For this lot, the transportation cost works out at Rs. 0.01 per tile upto 100 kms of distance from the stockist. Even though the stockist clubs several orders during delivery, the transportation costs are charged based on lot size of the order, which will be higher when the order is less than optimal lot. A small order as such results in cost disadvantage to the retailer. Since the manufacturers of local tiles are small scale operators, there are no stockists and delivery facilities. Retailers have to make their own arrangements and bear the cost of damages if any in transit.

Promotion

Promotion is limited to wall paintings and POP material at the outlet of company stockists.

Problems

The irritants in the way of expansion of sales are:

1. The company tiles and the local tiles are of the same colour making identification difficult for the rural consumer.
2. The rural consumer, not able to differentiate between the products is wondering why he should pay more for a similar product.
3. The transportation costs are high for the rural retailer as his requirements are never large (10,000 units). Besides this, the retailer has to meet his operating costs. Put together, the costs may result in losses for the retail outlet as the end prices are fixed and retail margins are low.

With these problems, the penetration of the tiles of TIL has been low.

QUESTIONS

1. **Do you advise the company to lower the price to expand sales?**
2. **What kind of promotion strategy do you advocate?**

Credits

V. Shanti Latha, Doctoral Research Scholar, School of Business Management, Sri Venkateswara University, Tirupathi. Shantimouly@yahoo.com.

CASE

21 Ethics in Advertising

SITUATION 1 *BELOW THE BELT ADVERTISING*

The battle for sachet market share has been growing more suspenseful every year according to April 2002 ORG-MARG (A.C. Nielsen) Retail Audit. In volume terms, Chik has 21.19 per cent (15.18 per cent in April 2001) share of the 32,000 tonne/year (Rs. 1000 crore in value) shampoo market threateningly close to clinic's 22.95 per cent (29.19 per cent in April 2001). This and the fact that Chik went national this April (earlier available in Andhra Pradesh (AP) and Tamil Nadu (TN) appear to have generated considerable insecurity for HLL. This has culminated in the company resorting to blatantly provocative banner ads outside rural retail outlets in TN and AP. The banners show the Chik sachet (which has the Chik model Chitrapooma Banarjee on its cover) as an inset, with the caption ordinary shampoo. The Clinic model is shown with greasy, entangled hair and a glum face when she uses this, '*Ordinary shampoo*', *"which other than not removing oil properly, also does not give best cleansing"*. This is juxtaposed with the same model, now with radiant expression and silky, shining hair. Now the inset has changed to Clinic Plus mini shampoo and the catch line reads *"Other than removing oil completely, it also gives the best cleaning"*.

SITUATION 2 *UNIQUE PRODUCT DEMONSTRATION*

When it was reported that 40 per cent of the total sales of Maruti cars of some dealers in Andhra Pradesh constituted of rural sales, the dealers became aggressive. However, one dealer facing stiff competition from Santro of Hyundai Motors, displayed 'Santro' along with the Maruti models. The intention was to show off by on the spot demonstration, the superiority of Maruti models. Hyundai dealers were visibly annoyed by this demonstration. "It is a question of ethics. We have lodged a complaint with the dealers association" said a Hyundai dealer.

However, the Maruti dealer was unfazed by the controversy. "The question of ethics does not arise here. It shows the confidence we have in our product. We are saving the decision making time to the customer. Further, there is no such clause in the agreement which says we are not supposed to display the products of our competitors".

SITUATION 3 *HURTING CELEBRITY*

After appearing in just one film, the young Bollywood actor Hrithik Roshan, with rippling muscles and the vulnerable look, a cross between Sylvester Stallone and Leonardo Di Caprio, has become India's No. 1 heartthrob. So, it was only fitting that the world's biggest soft-drink company, Coca-Cola, should grab him as a local pitchman. But when Coke released its Hrithik commercial, it soon found itself rudely upstaged by arch-rival Pepsi, which aired its own TV spot poking fun at Hrithik Roshan. In the Pepsi ad, a Hrithik look-alike wearing braces on his teeth is spurned by a pretty girl, who instead kisses Shah Rukh Khan, a Bollywood star who has appeared in Pepsi's cola ads for the past few years. Hrithik, clearly hurt, shot off a letter to Pepsi claiming, with unconvincing modesty, that he was a newcomer who needed encouragement, not a put-down. His fans, meanwhile, wrote angry letters to local newspapers and even organized a street demo in Calcutta. His father, Rakesh Roshan, a prominent Bollywood filmmaker who produced and directed Hrithik's smash-hit debut 'Kaho Naa ... Pyaar Hai', complained publicly that Pepsi was "ridiculing" his son because it had lost the bidding battle for Hrithik.

The sizzle over Pepsi's mischievous 60-second spot underscores the fierce battle raging between the two multinationals for dominance of India's $1 billion soft-drink business. Pepsi has been selling in India since New Delhi opened the market to foreign companies in 1991. Coca-Cola, which was forced to leave the country in 1977, returned with a bang in 1993, buying out the leading local cola, Thums Up, and grabbing a big slice of the action. But the worldwide leader's cola drink still ranks No. 3 in India, behind Pepsi and Thums Up. "The more the competition, the more the noise!"

QUESTIONS

1. What are the ethical considerations in each of the above situations?
2. What kind of action do you suggest in each case?

CASE

22 Protecting Savings

The rural communities in developing countries are not able to protect their savings and contribute to economic development. This has become a concern of FAO.

THE PROBLEM

In rural areas, people have been traditionally reluctant to put extra money in banks. Some prefer to invest it in livestock. Others hide their cash in vulnerable places such as in jars or under mattresses, or, worse, carry it in their pockets. Banks, many inconveniently located in distant cities, have inspired little trust in rural investors, who consider them cold, unfamiliar and primarily "for city folk".

Yet the untapped potential of rural savings could provide a tremendous boost to local economies in developing countries. A large percentage of the developing world's population lives in rural areas. Savings mobilized by efficient and well-managed local financial institutions could finance increased levels of development investment in rural areas.

THE INITIATIVES

The vital importance of not only encouraging savings but also of protecting deposits, specifically in the rural communities of developing countries, is the message of a new video from FAO, 'Safeguarding deposits -protecting savers'.

The 15-minute video takes a look at the problems facing small banks and individual depositors in rural communities. It outlines measures to ensure the safety of deposits, including proper institutional structures, sound management and investment, and external supervision. It also outlines the general principles of the safety of deposits, describes the problems unique to rural banking and offers inspiring case-studies of successful small banks in rural communities:

- In a remote area of Tanzania, villagers decided to open their own local bank instead of keeping their money at home. The depositors at the Marangu West Savings and Credit Co-operative are not only the bank's customers, but also its owners and managers. Membership has grown from an initial group of 60 to nearly 2000.

- In Madagascar, an ambitious bank in the busy coastal town of Toamasina targets a local market by offering a unique customer service. It employs one of the stall owners to collect vendors' deposits right in the market thus saving them a trip to the bank. The service instills trust in the system through careful record keeping.

Many rural people are unaware of how banks use their money, so trust is important. Successful small rural banks inspire depositors' trust by observing the same rules as larger banks in urban areas. Transparent teller windows, for example, allow depositors to observe transactions. Access to adequate technology is also important. Banking software developed and distributed by FAO has helped many small rural banks to maintain accurate records. With the software, managers and tellers feel more confident, a feeling which they in turn communicate to customers.

QUESTIONS

1. Analyse the efforts of FAO in promoting trust in banks?
2. What kind of future promotional effort do you suggest for reinforcing the trust?

CASE 23

Gunny Sack Race

Asha Fertilizers and Chemicals Limited (AFCL) is one of the leading fertilizer companies in South India. It has a widely distributed marketing network well connected to feeder markets and godowns. Farmers are familiar with the entire product line of AFCL and have appreciated its quality and price fairness. This, along with the prompt delivery to local marketers, frequent visits of AFCL officials to villages, and also their effort to eliminate any imitations of their products, has earned the company a very large segment of brand loyal farmers.

Recently, AFCL was approached by both FMCG and industrial goods manufacturing companies to use the free space (on the back) of their fertilizer bags for promotion purposes. AFCL markets its fertilizers in HDPE sacks. On one side of the sack the details of fertilizer and manufacturer appear in a plain single colour print. The other side is without any print and it was this space that the firms wanted to use to print their multi-colour ads.

The price offered by the companies was quite good for a relatively unused space. The catch, however, was that the company wanted the background for its multicolor ads to be white or pale grey. The problem was that all fertilizer bags are not white or pale grey. Each product in AFCL product line was marketed in a different colour bag (DAP – Yellow, Urea – Green, etc.). The companies requested that AFCL market their fertilizers in white or at the most light grey HDPE bags. AFCL had a strong reason behind the use of coloured HDPE bags. This was not just a different promotional measure, but also an easy way to identify and eliminate spurious imitations.

The offer in terms of revenues is like this. The FMCG companies will print on greater number of bags paying Rs.5 per bag whereas the industrial products companies print on lesser number of bags but pay more–Rs.8.50 per bag. AFCL is expecting a lead time of 6 months before the competitors follow the suit. The revenue per advertisement/bag is then expected to drop down from Rs. 5 to Rs. 2 in the case of FMCG and Rs. 8.50 to Rs. 5 for industrial products. In the first six months, the company is expecting a profit of Rs. 16 crore just from advertising (as it was to be launched in the mid crop season). After one year from introduction of this promotion technique, there will be less benefits as every one will be advertising. Also, plenty of alternative companies will exist as message carriers.

The change in the colour of gunny sacks, however, may lead to confusion among the farmers which may result in an initial loss of about Rs. 20–30 lakh but not more than a minimum of Rs. 1 crore (due to brand switching and promotion of new products). From the second month, due to promotion efforts the sales are expected to return to almost the original level. The impact of this advertising on the company's image is not worked out. Then, of course, there is a problem of spurious products and loss of its USP.

Advice AFCL on its future course of action?

Credits

Ms. V. Shanthi Latha, Doctoral Research Scholar, School of Business Management, Sri Venkateswara University, Tirupati-517 502. e-mail: Shantimouly @ yahoo.com

PART

7

Distribution Strategies

- Silent Revolution
- Road to Success
- Viability of Agri Value Chain
- Choosing the Right Horse
- Marketing, Not Modernisation

CASE

24 Silent Revolution

Rallis India Ltd. has been the undisputed leader in the Indian agrochemicals market for more than a decade. The Rs. 1430 crore company is a part of the US $ 8.4 billion Tata group, India's oldest and most respected business house. It has also a significant presence in the pharmaceuticals, fine chemicals and export sectors. Agrochemicals and fertilizer distribution generates nearly 80 per cent of the revenues of the company.

Rallis is a company whose performance is clearly dependent on government policies and climatic conditions. Three consecutive years of erratic monsoon and drought conditions in Western and Central India led to a contraction of agrochemical demand. With net losses of Rs. 31.93 crore, and threats from MNCs like Aventis Crop Science, Rallis India's immediate concern has been how to turnaround.

THE JOURNEY BEGAN

Rajiv Dubey, the CEO of Rallis India said, "Rallis has embarked on its turnaround journey. To meet the challenges of the market place we have, over the last one year, commenced on a comprehensive restructuring and re-engineering drive with the objective of enhancing market share, margins, productivity and consolidating our presence in core areas. We see new horizons for growth as a result of the change initiatives that we are driving".

The company has initiated a programme to focus on:

- Sharpening its business and product portfolios
- Improving cash management
- Introducing new products
- Reducing costs throughout the value chain
- Strengthening controls and business processes, from procurement through manufacturing, logistics, marketing, sales and distribution
- Greater focus on R&D
- Human resources/people orientation

AGROCHEMICALS DIVISION

The company's product range includes insecticides, fungicides, herbicides and intermediates. The company is one of the largest Indian pesticides manufacturer, with eight factories having a combined capacity of around 18,000 tonnes per annum of technical grade pesticides and 40,000 tonnes of formulations per annum. Production in agrochemical industry is essentially a conversion job. Raw materials and labour are the major cost elements. Environmental concerns have resulted in high regulation for this industry. The industry is basically generic in nature with nearly 70 per cent of the molecules off patent. Among off patent products, wide distribution network, strong brand image and superior product quality act as entry barriers.

The Market

The world market for agrochemicals is primarily dominated by herbicides, which forms 46 per cent share followed by insecticides at 29 per cent and fungicide at 17 per cent. In sharp contrast, insecticides have the lion's share of 76 per cent followed by fungicides with 13 per cent in the Indian agrochemicals market. Herbicides have a share of only 10 per cent in the Indian agrochemicals market. The low consumption of herbicides in India is on account of cheap labour available for weeding operations.

The Indian agrochemicals demand is cyclical in nature with peak months being July to November and the consumption pattern skewed with regard to crop usage. Cotton crop accounts for 40–50 per cent of the pesticide consumption while other main crops using pesticides are rice, vegetables and wheat. The consumption pattern is also skewed in favour of certain states like Andhra Pradesh, Karnataka and Punjab. The Indian agrochemical market is highly fragmented due to the presence of a large number of formulators. The impact of globalization and GATT will mean that the consumption pattern of Indian agrochemicals industry is likely to gradually move towards the international pattern. The industry is currently going through a bad phase on account of factors like low pest pressure, unfavourable climatic conditions and decrease in acreage.

MARKETING STRENGTHS

Over time, the company has consolidated its competitive position through market penetration and introduction of new products. Significant investments have been made in research and development and in establishing a world class research centre at Bangalore, India. With over 200 qualified and experienced research scientists, this centre focuses on development of new molecules and toxicology studies. The centre generates data on soil, residue, bioefficacy, toxicity, eco-toxicity and the environmental fate of pesticides and pharmaceuticals to evaluate their efficacy and safety. The laboratory has GLP accredition from German and Dutch health authorities.

It has one of the most extensive distribution networks in the Indian agroindustry, spread across the country consisting of over 4,000 distributors and a sales force of approximately 2 lakh with over 80 per cent penetration of the country's districts. The 8 regional offices, 28 area sales offices and 24 depots are manned by highly experienced sales managers, field officers and field assistants.

It has been leveraging on this strength with initiatives such as the Rallis *Kisan Kendras*–one-stop-shop for agricultural inputs–which provide counsel to farmers on food farming practices. The company provides farm management services to benefit farmers by offering a customized package of practices suited to their land and environment. The company has set up Pesticides Efficacy Advisory Centres (PEACE) in various agro climatic zones of the country with the objective of spreading farm education amongst farmers and advising them on current developments in farming practices to increase farm productivity.

The Problem

Rallis launched Contaf—a product developed by its R&D department to combat sheath blight on paddy. It was a technologically advanced and good product which was initially marketed through dealers, agricultural fairs and by salespersons travelling from village to village in jeeps.

Farmers using it noticed that their yield was higher and the grains were of better quality. This made the product very popular among farmers. However, the usage of Contaf was restricted to the paddy crop (*kharif*) which meant it had a short product cycle from July to September. With increasing competition in the pesticides market, the company was keen to introduce products which could be used throughout the year, for different crops. Another related concern was how to create brand awareness in the minds of the farmer.

Market research suggested that the most effective way to achieve this goal was to work at the grassroots level and be there with the farmer through all his activities. In short, set up a one-to-one contact with the farmer and focus on selling a 'basket' of Rallis products.

NEW STRATEGY

A strategy is evolved based on the market research findings. The philosophy is to create a bond and develop a relationship with every farmer. The association should be complete with the farmers' lives from sowing to harvesting. "To be his partner in business and to be a part of his family".

The aims identified are:

1. To establish Rallis as a 'brand of first recall' in the minds of the farmers.
2. To encourage appropriate usage of pesticides.
3. To create a new usage pattern by promoting use of sprays, etc.

The salient features of the strategy are:

- Reducing dependence on jeeps and increasing the number of people.
- Selecting people from nearby villages of the target market.
- Training people for the jobs.
- Ensuring that at every stage of the crop and for every problem, there is a Rallis product as a solution.
- Liaisoning with organizations and government departments to give the farmers complete and updated information which would help them in growing their crops.

THE PROJECT

It decided to test the strategy in South India. The name "Silent Revolution" was given to the project because the strategy involved talking directly to the end consumer–the farmer–without making a noise.

Focus on Paddy

In South India, the main crops cultivated are paddy, cotton and chillies which are traditional crops. Tea, coffee, mango, groundnut, etc. which are niche crops, require less amount of pesticides and give high returns to farmers. It was decided to focus on paddy because in the last few years, the price of cotton (once a very lucrative crop for the farmer) has fallen and is not a profitable crop any more. Paddy is a safe crop, remunerative and more importantly, Rallis had an effective product-mix for this crop.

The Region

The cultivated areas in the region were divided into districts and each district was subdivided into *mandals* consisting of a group of villages. From these *mandals,* only the high-revenue yielding ones were chosen—those with a potential of 70–80 per cent volume sales.

Training Assistants

Every Trained Farmers Promotional Assistant(TFPA) had to touch base with his supervisor every day and once a week meet him to give a weekly report. Each TFPA was given the goal of covering seven villages in six months. It was hard work, but there were deserving rewards for achieving objectives such as maximum and most effective demonstrations, highest weekly sales and innovative marketing initiatives. The highest award was the 'Task Force Award' given to the TFPA who achieved a major change in a specific area, such as increasing market share of a product.

The TFPA's role was to educate the farmer while promoting Rallis products. He not only knew every inch of the farmer's land, crops, cultivation cycle, product usage, but also knew every member of the farmer's family. On a typical day, the TFPA would contact five farmers and hold two demonstrations and a farmers' meeting in the village. The demonstrations were the focal point for creating awareness about the benefits of Rallis products as the farmer could see these benefits for himself. After this, the TFPA would call or meet his supervisor to update him on the day's activities. His last task for the day would be to meet the dealer and check on that day's product sales.

RIGHT PRODUCT MIX

The Rallis 'basket of products' are changed according to the area's needs based on crop, farmers' usage pattern, etc. This included Marshall, Contaf, Fujione, Koranada, Furudan and Astaf–each fighting and preventing different crop diseases and giving the farmer a rich and healthy crop, increasing his yield per acre and adding to his wealth.

RESULTS

Silent Revolution was a success because there was continuous learning.

1. Twenty lakh farmers were contacted in six months by 700 TFPAs – through personal contact, village meetings and *mandal* meetings—and 2,10,000 Rallis product demonstrations were given.
2. Silent Revolution succeeded on two fronts – Rallis substantially increased their product sales and the farmer was able to double this yield.
3. Silent Revolution also created a new usage pattern by promoting the use of sprays, thereby increasing the total market for fungicide products.
4. Rallis has now created a strong customer loyalty. The farmers rely on its products from seed to harvest. It is perceived as a wealth creator for the farmer, as their well-wisher, and supporter. This goodwill of the farmers forms a strong base for the sale of all future products.

The success is celebrated in many ways. The Guntur sales office, for instance, used printed coloured postcards to record the goals achieved. The villages were designated as Ralli Yellow Village, Ralli Blue

Village and Ralli Green Village, according to the level of success achieved. In a district in Tamil Nadu, the villages were designated as Ralli Baby, Ralli Child, Ralli Man and Ralli Mega village.

FUTURE PLANS

The success achieved by the Silent Revolution is now planned to be replicated in other states in South India as well as some areas in the north. The goal is 'every field should be sprayed with Rallis products'. The task is considered difficult by the fact that in India, each area or district has different crops and the farmers also have a different mindset. Says B. Sivaprasad, the General Manager (South) of Rallis, "Therefore the need is to think global and act local". The initiatives for each area had to be specific to that area according to the local mindset of the farmers. The company is also planning to expand into related fields such as crop insurance, *kisan* credit cards, contract farming and credit points–a scheme which gives farmers buying Rallis products points which can be redeemed against future purchases.

QUESTIONS

1. Why did Rallis launch 'Silent Revolution Strategy'?
2. Can it be replicated in other parts of India?

CASE

25 Road to Success

When Sri Krishna approached me for advice, I was unable to say anything with conviction and good evidence. He got an interview call letter for the position of sales manager from a reputed agrochemicals company in South India. The job involved working in rural areas to promote pesticides and related products. Sri Krishna was in a dilemma for a good reason. He had neither science background nor rural exposure.

Ureka!, while surfing the internet lazily, almost aimlessly, I had a surprise finding. It was the interview with Aruna Bhinge. In this interview, she talked to Sujatha Agrawal about the twists and turns on the road to success.

The excerpts from the interview are:

"I was always interested in science and wanted to do an MS-PhD programme in the United States. Instead, I got married, moved from Pune and decided to do an MSc and then a PhD in Mumbai. It took me nearly five years to get my masters in science (by research). Luckily, I was working with the Maharashtra Government's Department of Science and Technology at the time. But the research experience was quite de-motivating.

I also discovered that I did not like staying in one place, a laboratory in this instance. I believe I am analytical, an independent thinker and good at getting things done. I also like to travel and talk to people. So I decided against a career in research. My husband suggested that I do a management course if I wanted a good corporate job. I was not confident about getting through the entrance test (it was almost 10 years since I had studied formally, though I was always a topper at school). He encouraged me by saying that if I did not pass only he and I would know about it. I did get into the Narsee Monjee Institute of Management Studies. I guess I was lucky, but it also shows what determination can do. I ended up topping my class in marketing. You don't really have to study marketing; it is logic and common sense, though my analytical ability and household experience helped enormously.

ANZ Grindlays offered me a job in corporate banking after a campus interview. It was a good break, with a fantastic salary. But I was keen on marketing products and felt a bit sad that my years of scientific experience were being wasted. To me Grindlays was a golden cage. When I got an offer from Merind I was quite happy to move on though the money was not that good. Merind was a fantastic experience and for that I must give credit to Mr. Nawshir Khurody, the company's then Managing Director. I was involved in setting up the diagnostics division and there was a tremendous amount of learning involved. I understood how to handle different business issues; dealing with suppliers, pricing, setting up a sales force, establishing a distribution network. In five years, we launched 25 products. I left the company only because its future seemed uncertain, since the Tata Group was not looking at pharma as a core business area.

I also worked briefly with Lifescan, an American company that was launching diabetes monitors in India. But I wasn't happy with their marketing strategy (they wanted to talk to doctors, not patients). And the scope of work was very small when compared with what I had done in Merind.

Fortunately, at that time Rallis was looking for a marketing person for agrochemicals. Though I did not know anything about the pesticides business, Mr. Vijay Rai convinced me about the job by saying that it was essentially a marketing function, of which I did have knowledge. Rallis has been an enriching experience. The marketing of pesticides involved visiting remote places, holding meetings with farmers, understanding their problems and psychology, creating marketing strategies to improve their knowledge level—it was an exciting period in my career.

I think farmers are wonderful people. They are receptive and they believe and trust you very easily. And they value and respect you. I had been dealing with doctors previously; it was so much more refreshing to talk to farmers. I believe that farmer contact is the key to success for Rallis. The farmer wants you to, for instance, guide on the correct pesticide usage. Some of them cannot even recognize the diseases or pests harming their crops. They simply take the affected part of the plant to the dealer and he probably sells them a product that gives him, the dealer, the best returns.

Earlier our people were very dealer-oriented, but we helped change their focus towards greater interaction with farmers. You need to go to their fields to really influence them. Our farms are not like those in America, where you will see fields that stretch beyond the horizon, but not a single farmer. In India you will see a farmer every acre or two. And they don't mind spending half an hour talking to you. We would plan farmer-contact strategies in advance, and visit the fields before and during the crop season. I think the sales force appreciated this, and the farmers found it very useful.

It is important to design literature and material that educates farmers as well as promotes products. We designed flip charts which explained, simply and clearly, the diseases and pests, how to recognize and eliminate them. We also designed material which the sales person could carry as rolled-up charts on his back along with a stand. As he travelled through the villages he would stop wherever he saw farmers working in their fields and hold meetings. It worked very well".

Now based on this, can I advice Sri Krishna to attend the interview?

CASE

26 Viability of Agri Value Chain

TataChem, Vice-President (Sales and Marketing) Kapil Mehan says, " India Inc., is fast changing and we have to change faster. When the subsidies on urea go, we will have problem in reaching out to our farmers. We want to differentiate, therefore, we package it with value-added services and create a sustainable differentiator". To that end, TataChem decided to provide farmers with a host of agri-services that they would identify with the company.

MODEL

TataChem plans to have 800 *Tata Kisan Kendras*(TKK) franchisees in small *mandis* in UP, Haryana and Punjab—its natural markets. These would be supported by 40 mother centres (with soil testing laboratories, training facilities and warehouses for inputs). It has put 25 per cent of its planned network (215 franchisees and 15 mother centres) in place.

TKK–SOLUTION SELLER

TataChem conceived *Tata Kisan Kendras* (TKK) to offer farmers not only agri-products but also agri-solutions. TKK has acquired digitalized field maps that profile the farmer and his farm. TKK has created a Geographic information system (GIS) based data management system to provide farmers with specific advice. The GIS based data management system uses satellite images and field maps to keep track of key parameters relevant to farmers—weather, ground water, and soil—almost on real-time basis. Using soil surveys, TataChem has created a fertility grid of these villages that shows where the deficiencies are, it has super imposed satellite images on these maps. This allows for better forecasting of trends and pest attacks, and provides the exact status of a crop. A pest attack can be proactively arrested and farmer need not lament in future saying "My crop is eaten away by pests".

VIABILITY

The benefits realized include better relationships with farmers, and increased sales. "They want to build a long-term relationship with the farmer so that he sees value in the services they provide, rather than just looking at buying the inputs" says Brahmanand Hegde, Chief Manager, Agri Business group, ICICI.

TKK has its own team to advise farmers on the right choice of inputs for a crop. It may even advise the farmer to use less fertilizer and pesticide. Although it means lower sales in the short term, it would build trust that would help in the long run. Also, TKKs allow TataChem to cut out some links from the urea distribution chain. The company can now bypass large distributors (C & F agents) and wholesalers and reach a retailer directly. This helps in improving margins. In fact, in areas where TKKs operate, the market share of TataChem ranges between 25–30 per cent against an average market share of 10 per cent for the whole of UP. As a result of selling in nearby places, mostly there is savings on transportation costs besides saving in channel costs. But on the costs side, it has invested heavily in land and buildings for each of its Rs. 2–2.5 crore mother centres.

A TKK franchisee is slightly better off. He has to invest about Rs. 3 lakhs only. At a margin of Rs.5–6 a bag, he earns enough to sustain his business. A TKK franchisee can sell 20,000 bags a year.

DISCUSSION

The company is deliberating on how to improve the viability of TKKs and especially of the mother centres. What additional revenue streams we can add to the mother centres and TKKs?

- Like Rallis, should we think of tieing up with produce buyers like Food World and HLL? (See Annexure-I for details)
- Should we tie up with ICICI which extends rural credit and promotes its products?
- Can we think of providing agri-equipment to TKK, so that they can be rented to farmers like Mahindra Krishi Vihar, the solution centre of Mahindra Sulabh Services?(See Annexure- II for information)
- Should we follow Nagarjuna and set up info kiosks which provide connectivity to farmers, dealers and buyers. It needs Rs. 2 crore investment and a minimum membership of 25,000 farmers, to be viable?(See Annexure- III for details)
- May we think of the ITC *choupal* system to disseminate information and provide market access to the produce? (see Annexure-IV for information)

QUESTION

1. Recommend suitable action plan to TataChem to set up a viable agri-value chain?

Source

1. Ranju Sarkar, Gambling on Agriservices, *Business world*, February 4, 2002, pp. 20–26 and February 11, 2002, pp.40–43.
2. Farwa Imam Ali, Farming Success, *The Week,* November 25, 2001, p.58.

ANNEXURE–I

Rallis *Kisan Kendra* (RKK)

Rallis has presence in seeds, agro chemicals and fertilizers. It has felt the need to address the farmers' other concerns and provide market linkages, access to credit, quality inputs and knowledge. To that end, it has started Rallis *Kisan Kendras* (RKK). The marketing end is crucial as the farmer does not understand the market. Also, farmers had to give cuts from their earnings to a host of middlemen—the village consolidator, the commission agent and the wholesalers in Bangalore. Rallis gives efficient market access by buying produce and supplying to retailers like Foodworld and Hopcoms. The farmer is benefited by low transportation costs (as he sends his produce with those of other farmers) and reasonable commissions. He is assured of correct weights. All transactions are transparent. To provide credit facility, RKK tied up with ICICI in Pipariya in Madhya Pradesh and HLL for market access. Rallis paid farmers *mandi* prices for their produce after deducting the loans. HLL is benefited by getting quality wheat devoid of the mixing that happens at *mandis*.

RKK's revenues come from enrolling farmers (Rs. 200 per acre per year), retailing agri-inputs, charging an additional fee for channeling loans from banks and financial institutions, and commission on sale of produce (1–2 per cent). Rallis has kept initial costs down. It has spent Rs. 25–30 lakh per centre with the soil-testing labs worth Rs. 20 lakh a piece. The rest has been spent on training personnel and paying visiting experts. RKKs are accommodated in rented buildings.

ANNEXURE–II

Mahindra Krishi Vihar

Mahindra Krishi Vihars are one-stop centres for agri inputs and services to farmers. It not only sells inputs like seeds, fertilizers and pesticides but also offers farm advices and rent out farm equipment and implements like harvesters. It steps in with services like drying, grading or bagging of the crop so that the loss could be pushed below the current levels of 16–22 per cent.

Mahindra adopted a hub and spoke model to take the centre to the farmer. The spokes serve as order-capturing points and as delivery points. The extension services where the knowledge of new farm practices is taken from the lab to the farmer are one-to-one, not on a group basis. Unlike other one-off services offered either by government or by private players, Mahindra's initiative is more intensive and continuous. They charge Rs. 500 per acre, for a season.

It started as 74:26 joint venture with a local tractor dealer. It initially invested heavily in fixed assets (land and building alone cost Rs. 1.7 lakh). About 250-odd farmers enrolled and 1 per cent of market share of retail inputs was corned against the expected 2 per cent share. With the objective of gaining a 10 per cent market share in retail inputs, Mahindra scaled up the model through franchising.

The franchisee pays Rs. 5 lakh as a sign-up fee (Rs. 3 lakh initially and Rs. 2 lakh in the next 2–3 months) and pays a 2 per cent royalty on inputs sold through the outlets. Mahindra provides the expertise, and supplies inputs to the franchisees. To maintain norms and systems, a Mahindra employee mans the centre, but reports to the franchisee. It is streamlining the supply chain management to lower input prices. Aggregating demand of the retail outlets and channeling supplies direct to retail outlets to save transportation costs are some cost reduction measures employed by Mahindra.

The challenge is in providing market access to farm produce. For now, it is concentrating on the input sid

ANNEXURE-III

Ikisan.com

ikisan.com is meant to connect farmers, agri-input dealers and buyers. The dealers of NFL set up an information kiosk. They buy a PC and get a net connection and ikisan provides value added content as well as extension services. The content was in local language and provides extensive information on 16 crops in seven states. The information is unique being location-based.

The company has to generate annually Rs. 2 crore to break even. The revenue model has three streams.

* Transaction fee charged on output.	- 0.5–1%
* Share of registration fee from farmers (Farmers pay Rs. 150 and of this Rs. 50 is passed on to dealers)	- Rs. 100 per annum
* Registration fee from dealers	- Rs. 10,000 per annum

For the dealer, the economics are:

Revenues:		
	Commission on outputs	- 2%
	Share of registration fee from farmers	- Rs. 50
Expenditure:		
	Registration fee/year	- Rs. 10,000
	PC and net connection	- Rs. 30,000

The dealer will break-even when he has 250 farmers registered in his area.

ANNEXURE-IV

ITC-E Choupal

ITC's International Business Division started E-*choupals* to bypass the old *mandi* system and buy directly from farmers. This has become necessary to increase its exports from Rs. 700 crore to Rs. 2000 crore by 2005. By buying directly from farmers, ITC derives two benefits:

- It can source produce of a far better quality. This commands a higher price in the international market. At *mandis* the impurities are mixed.
- The farmer stands to gain by higher prices and fair practices of ITC.

ITC set up a battery- powered internet enabled Pentium desk top computer along with a printer. The *itcibd.com* portal carries the *mandi* prices across the state, which is fed in daily by each of the *mandi* commission agents who have joined the ITC as *samyojaks*. It also offers the prices that ITC hopes to buy at. The farmers, based on the information decide to sell to ITC or at *mandi*. Even when the prices offered by ITC are same or slightly less than *mandi* prices, farmers prefer to sell to ITC because it offers a fair deal.

Mandis are crowded. It takes two days to dispose off the produce. The cost of bagging (Rs. 15 a tonne) the cost of transportation (Rs. 15 a tonne)and on loading and down loading (Rs. 3 per tonne) are to be borne by the farmers. In evaluating quality, agents throw a lot of produce away. The weighing is by a small *tol kata* (weighing balance). At ITC, everything happens systematically and savings range between Rs. 400 to 500 a tonne for an average farmer.

ITC also provides information on weather, soil conditions, on-line diagnostics of pests and diseases, information on the crop status across different districts and a few advisory services, such as what fertilizers are best.

ITC appoints a lead farmer as the community leader for each *choupal*. He is known as *sanchalak*. ITC invests Rs. 60,000–80,000 on the IT infrastructure, while the *sanchalak* pays for the operations (telephone and power) and the local canvassing. For the sale of produce, he earns a 0.5 per cent commission. *Samyojaks* would get 1 per cent commission. *Samyojaks* not only provide information to ITC about *mandi* prices but also aggregate produce from far-flung villages and bring it to the ITC centre. For this, they get 1 per cent commission.

ITC is exploring to tap into the farm input market. It has tied up with Monsanto to sell seeds directly. It is now considering such tie up with other companies. ITC gets 2–3 per cent commission whereas a *sanchalak* gets 2–3 per cent commission and *samyojaks* receive around 1–3 per cent depending on the product sold. The *sanchalak* and *samyojaks* collect orders from farmers and place them on companies.

CASE

27 Choosing the Right Horse

Star Ltd., manufactures colour TV sets priced lower than the national and local marketers. It has created a name for it in the middle and lower segments of the market. The TV sets priced at Rs. 10,000 per piece give a margin of Rs. 2,000 over its manufacturing cost of Rs. 8,000 per unit. To keep the selling costs low, it goes for local advertising through wall paintings, hoardings and leaflets distribution through newspaper boys. Its advertising and promotion expenditure is in the range of 1-2 per cent of its sales revenues depending on the market characteristics and competition.

It is considering to route its sales through a marketing agency and obtained proposals from three such agencies. All the three agencies have assured minimum sales of 6,000 units per annum. However, the commissions, credit periods and ad expenditures varied. Table given below shows details.

Agency	Commission (%)	Credit Period (months)	Ad Expenditure (% of sales revenues)
Bhattu	10	2.0	2.0
Srinivas	11	1.5	1.5
Sudha	12	1.0	1.5

In addition to this, the profiles of the agencies are also obtained for consideration.

Aspect	Bhattu	Srinivas	Sudha
Year of Establishment	1990	1988	1995
Products Handled	Consumer electronics	Household appliances	Cosmetics, toiletries. Since two years radios and tape recorders
Turnover	2 crore	1.5 crore	2 crore

Sales Network	Large and capable	Expanding.Less capable.Training courses are on the anvil	Expanding. Capable
Rural Exposure	Moderate	High	Moderate

QUESTION

Which agency do you select?

CASE

28

Marketing, Not Modernisation

Sircilla was in the news when some of the traditional weavers and their families committed suicide. Though, the jet and automatic looms invasion has spelt doom for the weavers, they still want to continue the same trade. However, they are designing strategies to attract rural markets.

AGAINST MODERNISATION

The Director of Handlooms, Ms. Srilakshmi, announced financial assistance to the weavers for modernisation of the existing looms by converting them into semi-automatic ones. According to a survey conducted by the district administration recently, the trainers of semi-automatic looms have said that they do not want to go in for semi-automatic looms and neither are they interested in converting their present looms into semi-automatic ones.

The weavers want to produce the same grey cloth on the existing power looms despite severe hardship. The weavers say their business could be made economical and viable if the cost of power per unit is reduced from Rs. 2.30 to Re. 1 or alternatively, for 5 HP motor units, the electricity bill is fixed subject to a ceiling of Rs. 500 a month. The four per cent sales tax on cone yarn may be relaxed to ensure that the price comes down from Rs. 485 per 5 kg to Rs.470.

SUPPORT BY SELF-EMPLOYMENT

In view of the above situation, the district administration has written to the Government to provide at least one income-generating asset, as a source of income to the 2,500 BPL (below poverty line) families of weavers. The Karimnagar District administration sanctioned Rs. 33.10 lakh under PMRY (Prime Minister's *Rozgar Yojana*) and Rs. 2.7 lakh under the SJSRY (*Swarna Jayanthi Shahari Rozgar Yojana*) to provide alternative employment opportunities to the distressed power loomers in Sircilla town. The steps taken to provide support to the weavers in the districts are:

- Assistance to 97 families by providing financial assistance to their units.
- Training to 132 women and girls of weavers on *juki* machines.

- Employment to 50 women in Pochampally Apparel Park.
- A cell was set up with the help of a voluntary organization, Krushi, to act as a forum where power loom weavers could approach.

MARKETING

For marketing the traditional power loom cloth, the weavers are confident that they will do it, as was done previously, by going house to house or by tom-tom. For example, in Pulugurtha village handloom society,250 weavers are presently working. Their turnover is 50 lakh. Dastkar in Andhra , a non-profit organisation buys about Rs.3 lakh. Their major market is nearby villages. They put the stock at known place or in an auto. The publicity about the sale is given through Siti Cable and by doing tom-tom (*dappu*). On this they spend Rs.100,00 so that people from nearby villages come and buy. If the society asks them to bring stock for bulk purchase, they send it through a sales man who is given 3 per cent commission. Besides this, they are planning newer approaches to marketing.

The weavers have decided to appoint educated youth as marketing experts. These experts will gather information on schedules of shandies in the district and also neighbouring districts. They would also test the market in various villages through SHG (Self Help Groups) leaders and *Grama Deepikas* and CMEY groups. Based on the feedback from the SHGs on consumer preferences and movement of the product (whether shirting or towel) will be given to the experts, who will in turn brief power loom weavers from time to time and accordingly production will proceed.

QUESTIONS

1. Are the weavers right in their approach? Would they be successful?

Source

The Hindu – August 7, 2001, p. 4 and August 12, 2001, p. 5.

PART 8

Marketing Strategies

CASE

29 Leader Hits Back

At Colgate–Palmolive India Ltd. (CPIL), the question is how to fight back and take charge of the market that is nearly lost to Hindustan Lever Ltd (HLL).

GLORIOUS PAST

Till the late 1980s, it was pretty much smooth sailing for CPIL. Smaller toothpaste brands like Promise, built a strong franchise in the early 1980s and then began to flag. Others, such as Forhans and Binaca (that later became Cibaca, and is now part of Colgate), faded away into the background. Then came Lever. For decades, oral-care had been a single-product market with Colgate's white paste offering the twin benefits of dental hygiene and bad breath prevention (with its 'ring of confidence' pledge). Rivals such as Promise had not tried to change the market's basic rules; they had only tried to hew out niches for themselves.

But now suddenly, in the late 1980s, Lever wanted to change the very way the market was carved up. It was moving aggressively to segment the market into two distinct need areas, with sharply defined brands for each: Close-Up, a gel paste, for conveyable fresh breath (a youth need) and Mentadent for strong gums and healthy teeth (a task taken on later by Pepsodent).

With Lever's advertising, the very dynamics of toothpaste marketing started changing. Soon enough, the white paste was viewed as a boring paste for oldies, and CPIL had to counter each of Lever's brands with offerings of its own. The great toothpaste war had begun. Colgate matched Close-Up with a gel variant of its own, aimed at those who wanted to keep their partners happy (perhaps even attracted by their breath). Simultaneously, CPIL's regular paste turned up the volume on tooth-decay-fighting benefits. For both these campaigns, teenagers and children were the focus of attention.

Lever had a stronger distribution network to leverage, and its advertising blitz was paying off. What it had done to one-time leader Halo shampoo of CPIL, it was keen on doing in toothpaste. Its earlier forays, with Signal and Pepsodent, had been disasters. But this was the 1990s, and now with Close-Up leading the charge, and with urban youth more receptive to a proposition of getting up close with the opposite sex, the company was finally making headway. Over the early part of the decade, Lever made rapid gains in market share, rising from almost nothing to a fifth of the toothpaste market.

CPIL brought Colgate Total, a top end formulation of its US-based parent, to India, priced at 2.5 times its regular paste. The product failed to justify its premium to the consumer, this tartar-fighter was supposed to be the knight in shining armour, and its failure dealt a severe blow to CPIL's leadership of the market. Meanwhile, Colgate's advertising had become 'globally aligned' with US-based Young & Rubicam (which tied up with Rediffusion in India), and lost some of its local zest. Meanwhile, Close-Up even used the historical story of Salim's love affair with Anarkali. In fact, by the mid-1990s, FMCG market analysts had started looking up to Lever with a combination of awe and reverence. India's most admired FMCG marketer had managed to contain the challenge posed by Procter & Gamble (P&G) in detergents, and virtually demolished the P&G-Godrej alliance in the soaps market. The buzz now was that P&G wouldn't dare launch its toothpaste, Crest, for fear of Lever—rather than CPIL. No wonder market analysts were talking of Lever's ascendancy to the top in this category as an inevitability.

Colgate Fights Back

But CPIL saw the opportunity. The market expansion was to be done as the 90,000 tonnes, (Rs. 200 crore) toothpaste market had barely grown 3 per cent in 2000 (down from 6 per cent the previous year and 12 per cent before that). "There's been very little conversion to the toothpaste market," admits Vikram Kaushik, Marketing Director, CPIL. There is a need to raise the entire consumption pyramid's value.

Colgate's Product Strategies:

Segment	Brand	Price Rs. (100 g)
Top End	Colgate Total	36
Breath freshness Segment	Colgate Gel	35
Oral Hygiene segment	Colgate Sensitive Care	38
Regular Paste	Colgate Dental Cream	30
Natural	Colgate Herbal	23
Economy	Colgate Cibaca Top	16.50
Tooth Powder	Colgate Tooth Powder	19

At the market's apex , Colgate Total, relaunched at a revised price, has started doing well in the past two years. Total is a medically superior formulation that is big in high-awareness markets (such as Australia where it commands 12–15 per cent market share). "Ideally, Total should be the biggest sub-brand," says Samuel, who was earlier heading Colgate's Australian operations, "but since it is pitched at a therapeutically aware consumer group, it will grow only as consumers become more aware". Indeed, Total seems just the perfect product to stimulate upgradations, for it satisfies oral needs on a higher plane by assuring the consumer bacterial-free mouth for 12-hours after brushing and clambering into bed.

Importantly, Total can upgrade users of gels as well as protective pastes. The strategy is expected to undo the 1990s' segmentation by harmonizing the two different needs (of partner-satisfaction and oral hygiene) that remain split into two segments in the zone one rung below the market's apex. That too, in a more clinically effective manner (the product addresses the root cause, the germs that cause bad-breath and infections too). Does it stand a chance? It is hypothesized that people outgrow their teenage fixations themselves once they enter mature relationships. CPIL on its part could help with an advertising campaign that shows the value of transcending artificial market divisions.

The action in the economy segment is complex because of the presence of multiple brands. Balsara's Babool was already a success. Colgate acquired Cibaca and relaunched it as Colgate Cibaca Top in a modernized package. Colgate Herbal, is launched as a part of its flanking strategy against Aim, a *neem* toothpaste by Lever. Aim was a price aggressor, priced at Rs. 6 for a 50-gm tube almost half of Colgate Dental Cream. Colgate Herbal sells at a premium overseas. But it is priced to penetrate in India by providing a value-added option (it contains Indian ingredients such as *tulsi, neem*, clove and mint) to the conservative buyer of low-priced toothpastes who can't afford to move upscale yet. It is promoted as a toothpaste with the 'science of Colgate and the goodness of nature'.

THE REAL GAME

The real game is at the lower end of the pyramid. The challenge is to rouse the latent brand equity into action. Tooth powder users can be converted to the white paste, and below that, non-users can be converted to the powder. It is a market placed at 26,000 tonnes per annum growing at 2 per cent.

Adds Kaushik, "It's challenging that only about 4.5 out of 10 Indians use toothpaste. Only 6 out of 10 use either toothpaste or tooth powder. The other four use other stuff such as twigs or ash. The task, therefore, is to get people to start using a dentifrice product. With penetration still low in rural areas, where 73 per cent of India's population lives, only 35 per cent of the population uses modern dentifrices". In North India, Colgate's white powder, famous for its minty flavour, has a strong competitor in Dabur, which sells its red powder in highly fragmented states such as Bihar and Uttar Pradesh (UP).

RURAL MARKETING

Promotion and distribution are meticulously designed and implemented by Colgate.

Promotion

In 1976, Colgate launched "Operation Jagruti" programme, to create oral-hygiene awareness. Nearly 100 vans went deep into rural areas to generate trials through its 30-gm pack. While most of the FMCG products, reach only about 20,000 villages, Colgate reaches 60,000 villages and 18 million rural consumers. Overall, an important part of the education programme is CPIL's association with the Indian Dental Association (IDA). Over the past 25 years, CPIL claims to have reached out to 18,500 dentists (of India's total 30,000) in 1,280 towns and cities. Colgate also sponsors dental conventions and gives scholarships to aspiring dentists.

CPIL also runs a programme called 'Bright Smiles Bright Futures', which takes dentists to schools to teach children how to keep their teeth healthy. So far, it claims to have covered 33,000 schools and 15 million children from 112 towns across the country.

DISTRIBUTION

The philosophy of distribution is like this. A toothpaste is still not a high-involvement, purchase, and consumers can be easily swayed. Availability drives consumption especially in rural markets. Colgate's distribution strategy is a three-pillar one.

- Physical distribution reach, the width and depth of it.
- Customer marketing approach.
- Modernization of sales operations and enhancement of sales efficiencies.

Colgate tries to make its presence felt heavily in *'haats'* and *'shandies'*, as it finds these to be ideal locations to carry out promotions. But by and large, it's the regular system that must do the job. If it weren't well managed, it would be a logistical nightmare. Reaching out to every single village (width) and retail kiosk (depth) is a mind-boggling task. India has around 3 million retail outlets that stock toothpaste, ranging from roadside kiosks to fancy supermarkets. Colgate supplies stock which are 'key account holders', supplying supermarket chains and the like.

Directly, Colgate sells products to about 850,000 outlets. The customer approach is one that treats everyone involved in distribution as a customer who must be kept satisfied. Each stockist, for example, is part of Colgate's incentive plan, such as the 'Colgate *Dil Se'* plan for wholesalers. Says Hegde, "A stockist should earn at least twice the return that he gets from a bank deposit, since he's investing in our business". Retail margins vary by product category.

In an effort to modernize its sales operations, Colgate is automating its stockists, to try and track market data on a real-time basis. This would give it a better feel of the market pulse. As it is, it runs on a fairly well-oiled system, with speed to market (from factory to deepest rural retail outlet) being about two weeks. Products move from factory to a central warehouse in each state, and then to the stockists, who in turn distribute the stuff to retail outlets by vans. Since stockists are Colgate's redistributors, it's easy to track demand by watching their numbers. That's the basis for its forecasting, on a monthly basis. Once the entire system is automated, Hegde hopes, it could reduce to a weekly basis.

However, in the smaller *Kirana* stores (corner shops), the toothpaste wars take on a different hue. Here, it's a brawl for signage and shelf space, and Lever has the advantage of having a powerful portfolio of other products, which gives it a greater hold on shopkeepers. For larger retail stores, CPIL acts as the Colgate Shoppe program, which is a shop-within-shop concept. The company rents out the shelf space to display its products. For smaller retailers, POP material is made available.

GROWTH AGENDA

Says the Managing Director, "With our strategy in place, and the organization completely aligned with that strategy, we have created a more exciting environment at Colgate. We want to drive growth while continuously looking at reducing costs, especially in our supply chain. We increasingly have a team approach to our strategy". The fact that all CPIL employees have to undergo an in-house dental check-up twice a week is testimony to how seriously it takes its job of keeping people's teeth in good order.

Brand signage needs powerful product portfolio. In India, CPIL's product range is narrow. With its R&D centre in Mumbai, CPIL boasts of product development (and speed of hitting the market) as a key strength. It took the company only six weeks to respond to Aim with Cibaca Top. The main elements of its growth strategy are:

- Expand product offering—straddle varied segments, upgrade consumers.
- Improve efficiencies—enhance vendor management.
- Widen coverage—through rural, urban, new products and dental programmes.
- Partner dental profession—through grants, sponsorships and scholarships.
- Leverage technological leadership—faster speed to market through R&D.
- Empower and energize human capital—build a seamless organization.
- Strengthen brand building—renew advertising vigour.

QUESTIONS

1. Explain in detail how Colgate regained its hold in the toothpaste market?
2. Considering the growth agenda of Colgate, suggest appropriate measures to gain stronghold in rural markets.

Source A&Ms

CASE 30

LG Targets Rurals

LG Electronics India Pvt. Ltd. is all set to be a market leader in technologically superior electronic products, with focus on the high end products and impetus on quality, service and value for products. Managing Director of the company, Kwang-Ro-Kim, said that the company is consciously targeting the quality market and the value market with specific products. The targets, are etched on the wall—usurping the throne among consumer electronics and home appliances in 2003, and topping the Rs. 5,000-crore turnover mark by 2005.

Mr. Kim said the turnover of the company in the country the previous year was Rs. 1,000 crore, which has been doubled this current year at Rs. 2,000 crore. The company has already made a mark in the television segment and is all set to capture the home appliances market with refrigerators, washing machines, air conditioners and other appliances. It is deftly moving ahead of its competitors, Mr. Kim said.

TARGET MARKET

"The Indian market, especially the rural market is growing at a very fast pace and LG will target it with high technology products at a reasonable price, "said Mr. Kim, adding that the stress is on "reasonably" priced products and not cheap products. LG is also training its sights on the institutional and Governmental segment anew. The idea is to grow sales from the institutional segment from five per cent now to 10 per cent in the next one year. As part of its strategy to tap the rural markets, LG has initiated steps in Andhra Pradesh, Tamil Nadu, Punjab and Haryana, mainly targeting the rich and middle class of agricultural segment. "We plan to extrapolate our experience in these four states to the rest of the country over a period of time as we are confident of emerging a strong player even in the rural market," said LG's Product Group Head, Air-Conditioners, Mr. Salil Kapoor. A budget of Rs.10 crore has been allocated for rural marketing in the next one year. The target, outlines Kim, is to increase off take from the rural market by 20 per cent the following year, currently accounting for Rs. 900 crore.

COMPETITION

Apart from the technology edge, LG is banking on its grassroots-level marketing to edge out competing heavyweights such as BPL, Samsung, Videocon and Whirlpool, which are all breathing down its neck.

Meanwhile, industry dynamics have already claimed their first victim. The Chinese invasion that had threatened to turn the industry upside down with rock-bottom pricing has all but fizzled out.

According to Brand Scan 2001, a comprehensive study of consumer durable conducted by the Chennai-based Francis Kanoi Marketing Research earlier this year, what's worked in LGs favour is its positive image on the technology platform. Among refrigerators, LG has outperformed other brands on the status parameter since 1999 although on a small base, acquiring the status of the fourth most favoured refrigerator brand in the country. According to the study, LG has become the fourth most favoured brand among intending buyers, overtaking Videocon, BPL and Allwyn. On top-of-mind awareness, Kelvinator and LG were the only two brands that showed an upward movement on top-of-mind awareness with the category.

In the case of washing machines, while Videocon leads the pack, the one brand dominating growth is LG—from 46 per cent in 1999, to 67 per cent in 2000, to 78 per cent in 2001. The study adds that LGs penetration and perception is not restricted to just high-income segments, but villages and lower-income households too. But, on the advertising front, it is Whirlpool that outperforms LG.

And, while the study reveals that LG has been the fastest growing CTV brand since 1999, it's cracking the stronghold of the Bangalore-based BPL—the most preferred brand of CTVs among intending buyers, a title that LG is gunning for now.

PRODUCT

The Managing director said "human touch" is high on the company's agenda and the product image is based on human aspects and health. "We have the wrinkle free TV, The Golden Eye, which has colours changing according to ambience, we have the 'Preserve Nutrition System' or the PNS in our refrigerators with a moisture controller and the plasma conditioners with special features such as bacterial" filters in our AC's, he said. Keeping in view the high electricity tariff rates, the focus will be to introduce energy saving and eco-friendly products.

To retain tight grip on the volume segment, the low-priced Sampoorna TV has been relaunched as Cine Plus at a Rs. 5000–7000 tag and sub-300 litre refrigerators have just started rolling out.

In a move to design its products more congenial to the Indian taste and also for further customisation, LG has earmarked around Rs. 18 crore towards research and development, to be taken up in conjunction with the Indian Institute of Technology, New Delhi. While the company has made inroads into the rural markets with its colour televisions and refrigerators, it is now pushing its air-conditioners and microwaves, where it finds a phenomenal growth, according to Mr. Salil Kapoor and Assistant General manager, Sales and Marketing, Refrigerators and Microwaves, Mr Amitabh Tiwari.

PRICE

The newly defined mantra is cost-innovation—from implementing higher technology efficiencies, to reducing design-related frills, to purchasing cheaper components, to more effective HR policies. It requires a lot of skill to cut costs. "Without denting profits significantly, LG managed to cut consumer prices of air-conditioners by 20 per cent, and of colour televisions (CTVs) by 15 per cent", says Kim triumphantly. Pitches in Pradeep Tognatta, Head, Sales and Marketing, LGEIL, "We are preparing ourselves for another 7–8 per cent reduction in prices across all categories. On the immediate agenda now is the commencement of its digital management system (DMS), a cost-cutting technique that would lead to shorter assembly lines, higher productivity, and reduced manufacturing costs by 30 per cent". The implementation of DMS is expected to result in an additional five per cent reduction in prices across CTVs, refrigerators and washing machines at the least. The DMS exercise is a follow-up of the Six Sigma exercise LGEIL had initiated late last year, with the objective of cutting costs across processes other than manufacturing.

PROMOTION

LGs health-centered communication, too, may be taken forward to be given an eco-friendly tack. Also, LGs Sales Head, Tognatta, does not rule out reducing advertising and promotion budgets in the forthcoming months, currently hovering around Rs. 100 crore. Even if we do cut advertising expenditure, our sheer presence in the market would see us through. We have crossed the minimum threshold required for advertising pull, says Ganesh Mahalingam, General Manager, Marketing, LGEIL.

The company will launch a series of 40 road shows in the four Southern states targeting small towns. The road shows will showcase the entire LG range of products and will cost Rs. 3.5 lakh per town. These marketing initiatives will span a period of 45 days.

DISTRIBUTION

Another recent move towards broadbasing penetration has been setting up area offices in 50-plus regions across 83 territories. Also, the next one year will see another 15 LG Shoppes (exclusive outlets), up from the current 35. Mr. Kim said their products are successful also because of quality marketing and swift after sales services offered by the company. "We have quality dealers and quality services and therefore we have quality consumers. This is our dealers' and consumers' perception and not our own. We respond to our customer's complaints within 24 hours in 95 per cent of the cases, "Mr. Kim said. The company already has about 100 service centres in the country to cater to the consumers and it intends to open two more service centres in Gujarat apart from the four centres that already exist in the state.

QUESTIONS

1. Is LG over ambitious in its targets?
2. Is there market for LG products in rural areas?
3. Develop a clear-cut strategy for rural penetration.

CASE

31 Fighting the Fakes

Ms. Sailaja is worried by the increasing menace of counterfeits in the urban and rural markets and is wondering what to do. Her company markets mosquito coils in both urban and rural areas. There are cheap imitations and fakes and due to them the company is losing around 15 per cent of its sales every year. When she expressed her concern to her friend, Mr. Raghu, he sent her a clipping which presented a research study on the subject.

RESEARCH STUDY

An urban pilot research study by A. C. Nielsen indicated that the FMCG segment in the country incurs a loss of about Rs. 1,800 crore due to counterfeit products. The survey of Marketing and Research Team (MART) showed that the phenomenon is rampant and much more virulent in rural markets than in the cities.

FAKES

The look-alikes sport a colour scheme that resembles a popular brand, but the brand name is totally different, for example, Shagun for Lifebuoy and Lalita Amla for Dabur Amla. The second category are the spell-alikes where you will have a `Viggo' for a `Vicco' or a `Pomes' for a `Ponds' and the packaging looks similar. The third variety are the exact duplicates which carry the name and address of the genuine company, but the product inside is spurious.

The researchers found that most look-alikes (also known as pass-offs) are manufactured by local players who have put in adequate investment. Many of them have their own manufacturing units and operate on a smaller scale exactly like the established manufacturer. They even have appointed stockists and distributors to make the product available in the rural market.

The look-alike manufacturers' strategy is to piggy back on the advertising campaign of the larger player and establish their own brand in the region. The researchers found that the look-alikes business is not a clandestine operation. Promotional campaigns such as wall paintings and display stalls are used and the manufacturers have no qualms about displaying their manufacturing units' name and address on the product wrapper. The product too is always of acceptable quality. However, the look-alike product is priced

10–15 per cent lower than the established brand, with margins offered to wholesalers and retailers higher than what established companies offer.

However, it's not the same case with spell-alikes and duplicates. The manufacturers involved in both these obviously intend to cheat. Such spell-alikes generally have the genuine product's MRP rate printed on them, but the retailer willingly brings down the price after a bit of bargaining. Most spell-alikes have an extremely vague manufacturer's address on the packaging that is impossible to trace. But duplicates have the established manufacturer's address, as the packaging is usually bought from the *raddiwalla* route and filled with a spurious product.

In terms of quality, MART found that spell- alikes and duplicates have very poor quality and the consumer realises that he or she is duped after using the product. In fact, the Nielsen report revealed that eight out of ten customers who purchased such products were cheated unwittingly.

Another interesting observation is that FMCG counterfeit products only come in the smallest size of packaging. In the rural segment and slums where fake products thrive, the consumers' low purchasing power makes sachets of 25g and 30g packs popular. And it is in the case of these small packs that consumers are duped more easily as the quantity is not large enough for the buyer to discern its quality. This is specially so in sachets of shampoo, hair oils, detergents and so on.

REASONS

What makes things worse ?

The marginal penetration of the genuine product into the rural areas. For instance, according to the MART report, in the traditional village *haats*, the main selling locales of rural India, the researchers found that the absence of original branded FMCG products was 100 per cent. "What would help even more than legal action in the crusade against counterfeits is companies increasing their presence in the rural markets. If they build a better rural distribution network, manufacturers of fake products will have to flee the scene," says Pradeep, as he gives the example of Colgate which has such a high rural penetration that its fakes are hardly to be found.

In fact, the MART study suggests that the demand-supply gap is fueling the problem in this sector. Distributors appointed by companies stick to the villages closest to their town, while tiny shops and *paanwallas* are serviced by mobile distributors on cycles who stock counterfeit products.

Besides, in particular seasons the manufacturing of fake products rises and reaches the retailers much before the genuine brand can. For instance, during summer, fakes abound in cold drinks and talcum powder, while in winter it's cold cream and Vaseline.

But in the case of Coca Cola, the company disagrees that there is any demand-supply mismatch. In smaller towns, rural areas, at bus stands and railway stations where consumers are in a hurry, spurious cold drinks are rampant. "They manufacture for less than a rupee and sell for Rs. 10," explains the company spokesperson.

Duplicate products that are filled into genuine packaging are also available in a sporadic manner depending on when the *raddiwallah* makes available a large number of used packets of the same product.

Counter Actions

Several measures are found in practice.

Brand Protection Committee

About 50 manufacturers, legal experts and research company A.C. Nielsen together set up a Brand Protection Committee under the aegis of the Federation of Indian Chambers of Commerce and Industry (FICCI). Its members consist of prominent players such as Procter & Gamble, Hindustan Lever Ltd., Colgate, Marico, Glaxo SmithKline, Coca-Cola, Pepsico, Gillette, Britannia, etc. The idea is to curtail fake products in the country and to this end work with the industry, consumer associations, government vigilance wings and trade associations.

The Brand Protection Committee has put in place a four-fold strategy including a focus on enforcement and application of laws; publicising the negative economic impact of fake products; taking direct action against illegal manufacturers, traders, wholesalers and retailers; and enhancing communication among the stock holders.

To increase information on the subject, a Web site, fake-busters.com was also launched. The Web site provides information on companies and their crusade against counterfeits, including details of raids conducted and fake products seized. Besides, it carries a legal section which details existing laws on the subject and the legal remedies available to companies and consumers.

Legal Method

Procter and Gamble (P&G) has been most proactive for the past 18 months in its crusade to stem the fakes market and bring to book illegal manufacturers. According to the company spokesperson, a year ago, P&G's Health care division sales were impacted upto 15 per cent. An ORG retail audit revealed that for every 100 strips of genuine Action 500, there were 54 look-alikes. Vicks VapoRub and inhaler had about 20 clones. In the last year, P&G had got 55 injunctions against as many manufacturers. In fact, after one of the massive raids in Madhya Pradesh for Vicks, the company used the services of an elephant to destroy the counterfeit catch.

Surveillance

Coke has put into place another elaborate system. Across the country, they have around 48 Consumer Response Co-ordinators who work with their teams and redress consumer complaints directly, including overcharging and spurious bottling. Besides, they have a large network of Route Salesmen who have a one-to-one relationship with the retailers on their beat and keep their ear to the ground. "When they spot suspicious activity going on, they let us know. So though it's impossible to plug the hole totally, you can minimise it," says the spokesperson.

Upgrading Package

Upgrade packaging so that manufacturers of counterfeits find it difficult to replicate their products. Dabur is one of them that is making its packaging more sophisticated and capital-intensive. Its *Lal Dant Manjan*, at the peak of the problem in 1999, had eaten into about six–seven per cent of its sales. When Dabur replaced its *Lal Dant Manjan* plastic blow moulded container with a premium four-colour shrink sleeve packaging which had a grainy texture and water bubbles, the packaging was difficult to replicate. This resulted in a sales growth of 12 per cent in the original product.

Dabur's popular Amla Hair Oil has been facing an increase in counterfeits for the past year-and-a-half and the company is trying to work a way out of it. Though four raids have been conducted in the past six months and the company has replaced its glass bottle with a pet bottle, illegal manufacturing continues. Dabur finds that a subtle difference in packaging such as a gold foil stamping on the label or introducing holograms is not enough for home product consumers, specially the less educated who find it difficult to make out the difference between a genuine and a fake.

What should I do?

Till yesterday, Ms. Sailaja was toying with the idea of taking the offenders to the court.

However, several companies that have taken recourse to the legal method have bitter experiences. This strategy brings them negative publicity as well, with consumers avoiding the product because it could be a duplicate. Also, to actually find the manufacturer of counterfeits is very difficult as these fly-by-night operators easily change their locale of operations. Besides, even if a manufacturer is nabbed, getting bail is not difficult as the offence is non-cognizable. It merely halts the illegal activity for a temporary period. It's soon back at a different address, in a different garb. Now she is looking up for other ways of handling the situation.

QUESTIONS

1. What alternative measures may Ms.Sailaja consider to encounter fakes?
2. Discuss the pros and cons of the alternatives you have suggested to Ms. Sailaja.
3. Which course of action do you recommend to Ms. Sailaja?

CASE

32 A Cool Strategy

The refrigerator industry needs a fine tuned strategy to boost its sales in the urban and rural markets.

MARKET

The refrigerator market can be segmented by product and size. The market can be segmented into direct cool (DC) and frost-free (FF). While DC accounts for 85 per cent of the market, the FF accounts for the rest. Size-wise it can be categorised into three—(i) 165–184 litres (ii) 185–225 liters (iii) 270 litres and above.

The structure of ιhe market is given in Table 1 and the estimated market size is shown in Table 2.

Table 1 Refrigerator Market

Product	*Size (%)*	
	165–184	*185–225L*
DC	71	29
FF	50	50

Table 2 Estimated Refrigerator Market Size

Mn units	*1998*	*1999*	*2000*	*2001 (E)*	*Growth rate (CAGR)*
Total Market Size	2.95	3.07	3.24	3.5	4.37
Direct Cool	2.60	2.61	2.7	2.9	2.77
Frost Free	0.35	0.46	0.54	0.6	14.42

Source: CETMA

As per ASCON (Association Council of Confederation of Indian Industry), refrigerator sales grew by 4.5 per cent in fiscal 1999, 5.54 per cent in fiscal 2000 and decreased by 4.5 per cent in fiscal 2001.

THE MAJOR PLAYERS

The major players in different segments are:

DC —Whirlpool, Electrolux and Godrej together hold 70 per cent market share
FF —Whirlpool, PL, LG and Godrej together hold 60 per cent market share.

In the above 300 L category, MNCs like LG and Samsung control more than 80 per cent of the market share. The sale of the refrigerators company-wise are shown in Table 3.

Table 3 Total Refrigerator Sales

Players	*2000*	*1999*
Whirlpool	879441	715000
Electrolux	769000	723000
Godrej	525000	715000
BPL	187000	226000
Videocon	349650	400000
LG	261000	165000
Samsung	20000	10000
Daewoo	45000	26000
Total	3216091	3070000

THE CHOICES

Table 4 shows the size-wise choices of buyers. The 165–185 L category is the most preferred one. A large part of the refrigerator market comprises first time buyers and the 165 L model is their most preferred choice. Buyers of large size refrigerators are normally upgraders from small one in need of a larger space.

In the frost free segment, the preferred one is 185–225 L category. This segment is declining by 20 per cent. Large size segment (270L and above) which today constitutes more than 30 per cent of the market is growing at the rate of 25 per cent mostly by replacements.

Table 4 Size-Wise Sales (%)

Category	*Frost-Free (%)*	*Direct Cool (%)*
Upto 165 L	0.3	0.9
165L–184L	0.1	71.4
185L–225L	5.2	22.2
226L–270L	17.1	3.3
271L–310L	14.1	1.5
>310L	16.3	0.6

PROSPECTS

The following indicators help assess the growth pattern:

- The penetration in urban market is 30 per cent and in rural it is a meager 4 per cent. The penetration in total is 10–11 per cent. Compared to 35 per cent of China's penetration figure, it is much lower.
- There are some 8 million refrigerators that need to be replaced with the FF ones.
- New technology and features are expected to spur demand. The concept of refrigerators came into being in the early 50s in the form of conventional single-door model with glass wool insulation and with external condenser coils at the back. The concept of frost-free was introduced in the year 1994–95, which was perceived as a big shift in technology. Videocon was the first company to introduce frost-free refrigerators. Since then, competition has intensified in this segment. Now technologically advanced models with newer product features like door-cooling technology, biofresh technology, multi-purpose chillers, reversible doors, door-open alarm, bio-ceramic vegetable boxes, etc, are available in the market.
- The refrigerator is now being viewed by the consumer as an essential appliance.

WHY THE SLOW DOWN?

The important factors that led to the slow down of the industry were:

- After an impressive 8.2 per cent rise in agricultural production in fiscal '99 it recorded a negative growth rate of 1.5 per cent in FY 2000 and FY 2001.
- Price realizations of farmers had been quite poor. This means, there is less disposable income generated in the rural areas.
- Drought and earthquakes resulted in tight money position in the market.
- Price cuts created confusion in the minds of the consumer. It delayed purchases as consumers were anticipating further price cuts. With this view wooing the market, the industry has gone through a spate of price cuts in 2001. The average fall in prices for the refrigerators in the industry has been in the range of 5.6 per cent in the last three years.
- The segment is heavily taxed both by central and state government. The excise duty now stands at 16 per cent.

WINNING SHOTS

- The historical trend seems to indicate only one thing: The need for a decline in prices for an expansion in the market size to materialize.
- Other than this, there are a few avenues. The most important is for the Government to reduce taxes levied on this segment—excise, sales taxes, and import duties. These, however, may come down only over the longer term.
- The other way out is for competitors to band together and agree to a cut in marketing costs. Savings can be routed to reduce the price of the products and expand market size.
- Consolidation of market shares through closures or mergers and acquisition activity is the only way to reduce prices and grow the market at a time when the resource constraint is proving to be a big handicap.

According to NCAER, the penetration of refrigerators in urban areas is expected to rise from 335 per thousand households in 1998–99 to 717 per thousand households in 2006–07. In fact, ownership for refrigerators in urban areas is expected to rise from 16.4 million units in 1998–99 to 43.1 million units in 2006-07 (almost at par with CTVs). In rural areas, ownership of refrigerators is expected to rise from 4.3 million units to 9 million units during the same period. Total demand, however, will see a rise from 3.1 million units per annum in 1998–99 to 5.1 million units in 2006–07.

QUESTIONS

1. Sketch a marketing strategy for the refrigerator industry.
2. Do you advocate price cut as a promotional measure?

CASE

33 The Vim Challenge

The new challenge for Vim bar of Hindustan Lever Limited (HLL) is to take its imposed variation further to smaller towns and villages.

CONSUMER NEEDS

The Indian housewife is hard working and family oriented. If you ask any Indian housewife to name the most distasteful chores, washing dishes is always among the top three. It's only natural. It's a task that involves sitting down amidst utensils and scrubbing them—most often with soda ash, sometimes with laundry powders, occasionally with scouring powders. And then having to clean the area that's been used and it has to be done after every meal—else what would the family eat out of?

A situation ripe for a song-and-dance solution, the problem could be defined in another way: to get the consumer to switch from what she considered a no-cost solution to a product specifically aimed at that market. Traditional wash materials like ash cost nothing and with laundry detergents, the cost was already factored into her budget. The solution wasn't to sell the product; but what HLL defined as 'process relief'.

EARLIER EFFORTS

HLL realised that the most cost effective way of selling a synthetic detergent-based product is a bar, scouring powders in the market were bulky; had low active content, high packaging cost due to expensive polyfil and high transportation costs.

In spite of the bar being an ideal solution for both the company and the consumer, there were problems. Chief among them being the Indian housewife's aversion to an obviously convenient solution. Explains Sanjay Behl, Marketing Manager, "The Indian woman is all about guilt". Research revealed she'd rather spend on her family than be seen taking shortcuts in her duties. HLL was, however, convinced that an effective demonstration would convert her. A task made difficult by the fact that the targeted users spent little or no money on dishwashing agents. HLL kept the formulation cost low—the end consumer price being Rs. 6 for a 40 gm bar, "next to nothing", according to Behl. Buoyed by the process relief and an effective launch campaign, Vim bar gained volumes over the first four years.

However, the aura began to wash away for a variety of reasons. Consumer complaints began to filter in about the product being hard to use in colder parts of the country, especially in winter. While keeping things cheap was crucial for trial, HLL's "on the brink formulation", was difficult to maintain. Especially since local players had begun offering cheaper options. Since pricing was a weak point for HLL, it decided to go in for product improvement.

NEW EXERCISE

A large part of the upgrade involved making it different from a laundry bar. Changes included making the top softer, to allow for easy application of scrubbers and address the most common consumer complaint. The final formulation was one that lasted longer, performed better and had better sensorial. The second significant change was in the brand's communication: restricting product experience to a commercial wasn't good enough.

Enter the Vim Bar Challenge: a promotional scheme that offered consumers the chance to sample the product. If they weren't satisfied, HLL promised them a year's supply of their favourite washing powder. These encounters were filmed and converted into the brand's signature ad campaign. It was supported by the heaviest media spend ever on the brand. Money was diverted from the powder to increase ad spends on Vim bar by 50 per cent. HLL lowered costs by regionalising production, drastically reducing the cost of transporting ingredients.

After that, it was a question of sampling and more sampling. "We dreamt of every single urban housewife having at least one chance to use it", says Behl. The brand was cross-promoted with highly penetrated brands like Rin Supreme. Other promotions included distributing instruction leaflets and nylon scrubbers.

This aggressive market activation pushed the brand across the 100,000 tonne mark. It more than kept pace with market growth: "Whatever the market has gained, Vim bar has got", says Behl. With penetration between 15 to 25 per cent, he expects the growth to continue. And this in the face of stiff competition. Since the bar's launch, Nirma has had two offerings in the segment and Henkel-Spic has launched as well.

THE CHALLENGE

HLL hopes to hit rural areas, which calls for a different communication strategy. They'll focus on vans, demonstrations, road shows, but the strategy will remain the same—inducing trial. As Behl remembers the Vim Bar Challenge, "Not a single consumer said she would not go with it".

QUESTIONS

1. Explain the reasons for the success of Vim bar.
2. Suggest a detailed action plan for promoting Vim bar in rural areas .

Source

Malika Rodrigues and Ravi Balakrishnan, Where There's a Vim, There's a Way, Brand Equity, *The Economic Times*, November 29–December 5, 2000.

CASE

34 Healing Rural

The Managing Director of the Healwell Laboratories is toying with the idea of shifting the sales focus of its successful new pain balm 'Sanjiva' to rural areas. He has attended the one-day seminar on 'Rural Marketing for Competitive Advantage in Globalised India' organized by Anuragh of Madison Advertising, the rural communication unit of Madison Communications and Asian Media Information and Communication Centre at Chennai in the first week of October 2001. Recalling what he heard there and relating it to his problem, he prepared the following note.

THE WORTHINESS

Rural market is large, also it is less tapped. The latest census puts India's population at 102.7 crore out of which 74 per cent reside in villages. However, only 18 per cent of pharma sales take place in the rural areas. While the per capita drug expenditure in India is Rs. 151, in rural areas this figure works out to a meager Rs. 39 per person.

According to ORG-MARG figures, sales of Rs. 2,871 crore in rural India accounted for 18 per cent of the Rs. 15,534 crore domestic pharma market. MNC major Glaxo Smithkline Beecham (GSK) derives more than 24 per cent of its sales from villages while for Cipla, Ranbaxy and Nicholas, the rural contribution is in 17–19 per cent range.

The demand for healthcare in rural India can hardly be understated—according to a NCAER survey, prevalence rate of illness for men is higher in the rural areas at 105.5 per 1,000 population as against 98.2 in the urban areas. For women, it is at similar level in the urban and rural at 108.4 per 1,000 population.

The purchasing power is growing for three reasons: lower cost of living, absence of taxes and growing number of working members in rural families. The influence of cable and satellite TV channels has increased the extent of brand consciousness. The overall exposure to TV is 50.6 per cent in India. About 39.8 per cent of rural India has TV exposure as against 79.8 per cent of the urban. Villages are now becoming accessible. At all-India level 209,360 villages or 33 per cent of villages are connected by *pucca* or all-weather roads.

Coming to hospital facilities, 20 per cent of the hospital beds are in the rural areas. There are 12.76 doctors per hundred thousand of the rural population as against an all India average of 50.

The traditional segments like anti-infective and alimentary drugs, which are to treat digestive ailments, dominate the rural markets in line with the overall trend (urban and rural), but these show a faster pace of growth in the villages than the urban areas.

In rural areas, competition is mainly from alternative medicines and spurious products. The size of the Indian system of medicine is put at Rs. 4,200 crore plus. Alternative medicines compete fairly aggressively with allopathic medicines, more so, in the rural areas. The Rs. 1,500 crore spurious and counterfeit drugs market also has a predominant presence in the villages.

EXPERIENCES OF MARKETERS

Despite the key bottlenecks, namely, strong presence of alternative therapies, and inadequate rural infrastructure, physical and medical, some companies have gone rural. The modus operandi of marketing in most of the cases involves:

(I) Markets

States with better infrastructure are preferred, for example, the proportion of villages connected through all weather roads is the maximum at 57 per cent in the South zone and minimum at 20 per cent in the east zone. Almost all of Punjab, Kerala and Pondicherry are connected by *pucca* roads. States with considerably higher population density than the all India average of 324 like UP, Haryana, West Bengal, Punjab, Tamil Nadu, Kerala are also better bets. Most of these states have literacy rate higher than the all India rural literacy of 49 per cent except UP.

(II) Promotion

Promotion involves meeting rural doctors through rural penetration campaigns which are essentially taxi tours, meetings specially organized for registered medical practitioners, chemist awareness programs some companies have formed and contract sales force to increase rural sales.

THE SUCCESS OF THE LEADER

A few years ago, Amrutanjan realized that its 10 gm bottle was not preferred in the rural market especially in North India. It decided to repackage the product. Repackaging the product was not an easy task. A pain balm in a sachet had a risk of leaking or evaporating. To avoid this, the company used small plastic containers which were then put in colourful sachets. The mini Amrutanjan was priced at just Rs. 2. Thus, Amrutanjan became the first company to introduce pain balm in sachets.

The product was launched by carrying out an extensive mapping exercise through-out Uttar Pradesh and Bihar. The map had details regarding the type of road, the number of petrol pumps and the availability of shelter. Next came the Amrutanjan Rural Van Promotion. The promotion included a variety of activities. Films depicting the benefits of using the product were shown twice a day and free samples were distributed to the villagers. The company also involved local opinion leaders such as the *gram pramhuk* in this initiative. It also used mobile stalls to sell its products in various *shandies*. At the *Kumbh Mela*, the company put up a 16-feet statue of Lord *Hanuman* with a six foot dummy pack of Amrutanjan. In a few years, the company earned Rs. 4 crore from the rural markets.

According to P. Eshwara Prasad, Executive Vice-President of Amrutanjan, the key to its success has been the ability to understand the needs of the rural consumer. Value for money and convenient package did the miracle. Using van for sales and marketing is cost effective. Mapping exercise is also necessary to understand the practical realities of a large region. It is important for marketers to select the market and

concentrate on one geographical region. Local promotions and involvement from the local community are also necessary to make communication effective.

QUESTIONS

1. **Identify the rural market characteristics and strategies for successful marketing of drugs.**
2. **Suggest a suitable strategy for marketing pain balm of Healwell.**

CASE 35

Mobiles Ring Success

Rural India has become the growth driver for mobile operators. Rajeev Chandrasekhar, Chairman and CEO of BPL's Innovision group says:

> "It just amazes me. From Gondia to Latur, everybody wants to be impacted by technology. We receive letters from village *sarpanchs* on how the mobile phone is being used effectively in villages where there was a single PCO which too often never worked".

Marketing strategies are being reworked, lower tariff plans are being drawn up and there's a new glint in the eyes of cellular industry chieftains.

THE TREND

Operators across the country are seeing more than 50 per cent of all incremental growth in their cellular business coming from small town and rural areas. And this isn't the customary mobile-totting rich farmers atop tractors. Cellphones have reached the man on the cycle, the fisherman and the village *sarpanch* in not-so-prosperous villages and towns in India. So much so, that some operators say they do not even need to explain in detail what a cell phone is. The villagers know it.

BPL

Out of 540,000 total subscribers, BPL now has close to 2,00,000 subscribers in small markets across Maharashtra, Kerala and Tamil Nadu. Out of 204 towns outside Mumbai that it is present in, 160 are small towns and villages.

BHARTI

Close to 40,000 of the total 460,000 subscriber base of Bharti across circles is now from smaller towns and villages. This is keeping in mind that 270,000 of Bharti's cellular base is from Delhi. Anil Nair, Bharti's Head of Mobile Operations has an interesting story to tell.

> "Even in Delhi, we have seen carpenters and small time contractors on bicycles as mobile users. There was this carpenter we were trying to hire and he gave us a cell number to get in touch with. More importantly, a small contractor sees value as he can call someone for more material from the site itself", he says. He has figures to show as well. In Himachal Pradesh, more than 50 per cent of the total 8,500 subscriber base is now from areas apart from the two main towns of Shimla and Kullu Manali. "It's a hit in the orchards. As it is easier to create more footprints by placing a base station on the top of a hill".

Talking about the strategy, Nair says:

"Operators are now trying to work out new tariff plans to keep up the growth in the smaller markets on an upward spiral. Our average tariffs are lower in the smaller markets at Rs. 2.75 per minute as against Rs. 4 per minute in Delhi. This is possible because our investment in creating the infrastructure in smaller towns is far lower. We are also now taking the Airtel brand to all smaller markets through a multilingual ad campaign through audio-visual media which will hit the market shortly".

Hutchison

Hutchison, which recently moved into Gujarat by picking up a stake in Fascel, is trying to figure out how to expand the list of 1,850 villages and small towns where it currently offers cellular services. It, too, is looking at introducing localised tariff structures.

"The main town of the state, Ahmedabad, Surat, Rajkot and Baroda account for about 70 per cent of our business. We are moving into towns where fixed line phones are less than 1,000. The stunning thing is that we do not feel the need to educate people in these smaller towns about what cellular is all about. They already know about it from word-of-mouth or their experience when they visit larger towns", says Sandeep Das, Chief Executive Officer of Fascel.

"The fresh growth is almost even, although given the trade profile of the state, we are seeing a simultaneous rise in subscriber base in the main cities as well. About 30,000 of our subscribers are today from small towns and villages and we expect this number in absolute terms to rise sharply", adds Mr. Das.

QUESTIONS

1. From the experiences of BPL, Bharti and Hutchison, outline a marketing strategy for mobile operators.
2. What additional inputs would you like to provide to the marketing strategy to make it even more effective?

Source

Vivek Law, Rural India Rings a Bell for Mobile Majors, *The Economic Times*, Dec. 21, 2000, pp.1& 3.

CASE

36 Controversial Sales

Mr. P.V. Satheesh, of the Deccan Development Society says, "The issue is not purely a scientific one, there are social, economic and political dimensions, all of which need be to be debated and considered before any conclusion is reached".

MAHYCO REPORTS

Scientists at the Mumbai-based Maharashtra Hybrid Seeds Company (Mahyco), in which US transgenic crop giant, Monsanto, holds a 26 per cent stake discovered that GM cotton was grown on farms in Gujarat and informed the regulatory authorities. Monsanto holds a patent on the transgenic involved. Mahyco has been conducting field trials of the crop in India with a view to obtaining permission for its commercial use.

Early this year, the Indian authorities ordered an additional year of field trials for the genetically modified (GM) cotton or Bt variety to be conducted under the supervision of Indian Council of Agriculture and Research (ICAR). The authorities concluded that the data provided by the companies, Monsanto/ Mahyco were not sufficient.

THE SITUATION

It was found that farmers had been using 'Navbharat 151', a cotton seed supplied by the Ahmedabad-based Navbharat Seeds Pvt. Ltd., and sold by local traders with the assurance of a vastly better yield at considerably less expenses on fertilizers and insecticides. According to the officials in the Environment ministry, the company could be punished under the Environmental Protection Act (1986). Mr. D.B. Desai, Managing Director of Navbharat, declined to comment. He also declined to disclose where the seeds came from. But sources close to the company say, they were brought from the United States and crossed with an Indian cotton variety to produce the hybrid.

Going by the Department of Biotechnology (DBT) investigation, the company has distributed 10,000 packets of GM seeds. If 10 quintals of seeds are required for one acre of land and the price is Rs. 2,200 per quintal, the cost incurred on 10,000 acres of land would work out to Rs. 22 crore. The company would have to cough up this amount if its culpability is established.

The cultivation of genetically modified (GM) or Bt variety of cotton is not permitted in India as yet. Stunned by the revelation that a genetically modified (GM) or Bt variety of cotton has been grown in some

10,000 hectares of land in Gujarat without its knowledge, the Genetic Engineering Approval Committee(GEAC) has on October 18, 2001, ordered the Gujarat State Co-ordination Committee on Biotechnology to destroy such cotton grown on all locations (six locations according to GEAC). Subsequently, state government officials visited these farms and told farmers to uproot and destroy the standing crop. But the malaise had gone much deeper; the Gujarat government found to its dismay that farmers in 25 *talukas* of seven districts, have sown GM seeds on a large scale and some have already reaped the harvest. The Department of Environment and Forest (DEF), Gujarat, is now studying the total area under this crop, the total quantity already harvested and sold as well as the number of ginning factories to whom that cotton was sold.

THE CONTROVERSIAL PRODUCT

The Bt gene is introduced into cotton from soil borne bacterium Bacillus thuringiensis (Bt) through genetic engineering.

ADVANTAGES

- Bt cotton seems to be the most effective tool to contain the damages caused by the bollworms in India and elsewhere in the world.
- In India, it is estimated that Rs. 2,800 crore spent on chemical pesticides used in agiculture in India as much as Rs. 1,100 crore is spent on trying to control bollworms in cotton alone.
- It will improve the profitability of cotton cultivation by reducing the number of sprays and improving productivity.
- Many countries are using Bt cotton (see Table 1).

DISADVANTAGES

- The target insects of Bt toxin protein are the spotted, pink and American bollworms. In a country like India, sucking insect pest also causes substantial damage to cotton and needs to be controlled through insecticides.
- Resistance can decrease in sensitivity to a toxin in response to the use of the toxin as a killing agent. The bollworms may develop resistance to the toxin.
- The cost of Bt seeds may be prohibitive.
- Since all the Bt cottons developed so far in India are hybrids, farmers will have to go to the seed producers every year for seeds for planting.
- Efficacy of Bt toxin declines during the later stages of the crop growth and development.

Table 1 Bt Cotton Area in Various Countries

Countries	Area in 2000-01		Estimate 2001-02
	Million Hectares	% of total cotton area	% of total cotton area
Argentina	0.03	5	5
Australia	0.15	30	30
China (Mainland)	1.00	15–20	25
Mexico	0.02	25	30
South Africa	0.04	40	40
USA	3.93	72	75

THE CONTROVERSY

The issue has raged a big controversy. But the moot point is: who is responsible for this illegality—farmers or the seed manufacturer. Mr. Devinder Sharma, Trade Policy Analyst and Chairman of Forum for Biotechnology and Food Security says:

"Navbharat Seeds Company should be given exemplary punishment. In addition to debarring it in future, it should be asked to compensate the farmers for the loss suffered by them (through the destruction of the crop). At the same time, the company from whom it imported the seeds also needs to be made public and blacklisted. The country must give the right signal to the seed industry. If the industry cannot behave, it has no place in the country".

The Seeds Association of India, however, believes that the destruction of crop is no solution for a mere procedural lapse; moreover, this was not an illegal cultivation. Mr. Viswanath, Chairman and MD, Cotton Corporation India says: " The industry estimate places the total compensation at a whopping Rs. 150 crore. The government will have to compensate the farmers for the loss of the crop, if it cannot realise the same from the organisations responsible for this illegal distribution of the seeds to the farmers. Instead of destroying the crop at this late stage, it should be allowed to be harvested under government protection and use the produce after due toxicological studies".

Mr. Arvind Kapur, Vice-President of All India Biotech Association says: "Law abiding biotechnology companies will suffer unless the government imposed tighter control on the sale of transgenic seeds".

Mr. E A. Siddiq, Chairman of the Indian Department of Biotechnology Committee observes: "This is the fore taste of a frightening situation where transgenics will be out of control and over the place. To address the problem, India will have to spend Rs. 100 million on six national laboratories equipped to monitor genetically modified organisms more closely".

Manju Sharma, Secretary, Department of Biotechnology argues:

- It has been proved beyond doubt that the GM cotton being grown across thousands of acres of land globally has improved yield by over 35 per cent. Moreover, it is resistant to the dreaded bollworm pest.
- DBT has conducted multilocation tests on Mahyco's Bt cotton and has approved it for further large-scale field trials to determine its safety on varying parameters.

C. R. Hazra, Agriculture Commissioner counters:

- With India being free from transgenic crops, there is no other option but to destroy the cotton crops in Gujarat.
- If harvests were allowed, it will set a bad precedent, robbing the law of all sanctity.
- Seeds have already found their way into Punjab and Haryana. The matter should be dealt with a firm hand in order to stop the spreading of the menace.

THE ASSURANCE

Mr. Purushottam Rupala, the Minister for Agriculture, Gujarat says: "There are no reports that cultivation of Bt cotton is harmful to environment. So, what purpose will be served by burning cotton? The real culprit for illegally selling the seeds is the dealer. My government is planning an action against the dealer of those seeds".

QUESTIONS

1. **Analyse the situation.**
2. **Is this the issue of environment or of competition among private companies?**
3. **Should action be taken against farmers and Navbharat Seeds Pvt. Ltd."?**
4. **What should Navbharat do now?**

Source

"Gujarat in a Vortex of Controversy", *Fortune India,* November 15, 2001, pp. 54–57.

CASE

37 Spray of Misery

The villagers have turned to the judiciary for remedy. They have obtained a stay order from the Kasargod *munsiff* court against the aerial spraying. The petition will probably come up for hearing before the next spraying season in October. Meanwhile, they are looking up for help from the government and related bodies.

LAND OF SUFFERING

Life in Swarga, however evocative the name of the village, is far from heavenly. Nestled among areca and cashew plantations in Kerala's Kasargod district, it is a hellish land plagued by diseases and suffering.

"Strange illnesses have afflicted these villages and there is no thorough study on why this is so," says Dr.Kumar. "There are around 300 cases of various kinds of abnormalities in just this small area". An enumeration in January in the 4-sq km Padre village, home to about 400 families, showed three cancer patients, 23 epilepsy patients, 46 cancer deaths, 23 mental and 43 psychiatric cases, nine congenital anomalies and nine suicides—adding up to 156 instances of health problems. Another doctor working in the region, Shripati Kajampady, says, "We have seen a gradual deterioration in the quality of life here. There are more people struck by diseases here than in other villages. There is something definitely wrong".

WHO IS RESPONSIBLE?

Nobody knows for sure why this little pocket on the border of Kerala and Karnataka in the pristine Western Ghats should suffer like this, but most blame it on aerial spraying of pesticides, particularly Endosulfan, in the cashew plantations of the Kerala Government Undertaking, the Plantations Corporation of Kerala (PCK).

EVIDENCE

While there is no concrete evidence linking the pesticide to the health problems, areca nut grower and Endosulfan Spray Protest Action Committee (ESPAC) spokesman Shree Padre is convinced it is Endosulfan that is behind the misery. "These afflictions are caused by the aerial spraying of Endosulfan," he insists. PCK sprays the pesticide twice or thrice a year from helicopters to protect the hilltop cashew plantations spread over 4,700 hectare.

Endosulfan is meant to destroy tea mosquito, a pest that affects cashew yields. It belongs to the organochlorines class of compounds, which has been classified as one of the persistent organic pollutants (POPS). There is a world wide campaign to ban POPS as they are carcinogenic, affect hormonal balance and the immune system and cause genetic aberrations. Unlike other POPS, Endosulfan tends to linger in the area of its use. The World Health Organisation (WHO) classifies Endosulfan in Category 2 among the moderately hazardous pesticides. The US Environmental Protection Agency classifies it as Category 1b (highly hazardous) pesticide. It is readily absorbed by the stomach, lungs and the skin.

Endosulfan is banned in Denmark, Germany, the Netherlands and Sweden in the West and in Singapore, the Philippines, Thailand, Bangladesh and Korea in Asia. In Kerala, however, it is not only being used but being employed without the necessary precautions. It is mandatory to cover all water sources like wells, tanks and other water bodies during the spraying of the toxic pesticide. "In one village alone, there are nearly 600 water bodies. How can anybody cover them?" asks Bellur *Panchayat* President, Chandrashekhara Rao Kallaga, who is now actively seeking a ban on the spraying of the pesticide. Numerous cases of occupational poisoning have been reported. Proper protective clothing (safety goggles, gloves, full sleeved garments and respirator) is needed to prevent poisoning when handling Endosulfan. Another concern, especially in developing countries, is that people with low-protein diets are more sensitive to the effects of this pesticide.

The Centre for Science and Environment in Delhi conducted tests on samples collected from the Padre village under the guidance of Padma Vankar of the Facility for Ecological and Analytical Testing at the Indian Institute of Technology, Kanpur. Vankar was shocked at the extremely high levels of pesticide residues in all the samples. "The figures were alarming, especially for human blood, fruits and animal tissue. This may have something to do with the high incidence of disorders of the central nervous system in the village," he says.

While the PCK cannot be immediately blamed for the afflictions, the symptoms noticed in the area do tally with those of Endosulfan poisoning. Yet this does not explain why only the region abutting Swarga is affected when cashew plantations in other areas are also sprayed with Endosulfan. Dr.Kumar, however, has a pertinent question; "Is Endosulfan necessary at all for cashew plantations? Why not organic farming?"

REMEDY SOUGHT

"Being located on the borders, we are a no-man's land. The Karnataka and Kerala governments have generally ignored us," says Dr. Kumar. "It is time the centre took a kinder look at us". Central agencies like the Indian Council for Medical Research should study the problem and find a permanent solution, he feels. The cash in cashew is probably too tempting for anyone to bother about the plight of these villagers. But surely, people are more important than profits.

QUESTIONS

Discuss the following issues relating to the case.

1. Social responsibility in marketing
2. Social responsibility of PCK
3. Role of government in protecting quality of life of the people.

Source

Stephen David, Spray of Misery, *India Today*, July 23, 2001, pp.68–70.

CASE

38 Right Marketing Mix

Venkat is examining the developments in marketing of hair oils. The Rs.10 crore turnover company is known for its 'Hair Silk' coconut oil which has a share of 2 per cent in the Rs.200 crore market which is growing at 5 per cent. The marketing team of the company has undertaken a survey in rural areas with a view to attain better rural penetration and thereby raise its sales from Rs. 10 crore to Rs.12 crore.

The survey identified the levels of awareness and preferences of the rural consumers. Around 80 per cent of the respondents are aware of the product. Of them, 80 per cent have tried the product. Of the triers, 60 per cent have favourable opinion about the product, about 25 per cent are indifferent, whereas the remaining rejected the product. Those who favoured the product appreciated it as a light, fragrant, non-greasy oil. The indifferent said it was similar to other products. The rejectors opined that it was high priced.

What should be the marketing mix, given the market feed back? What should be our emphasis? Table 1 shows the sales forecast and expenditures. Table 2 gives different marketing mixes evolved for considerations.

Table 1 Forecasted Sales and Expenditures

Last year sales	Rs 10 crore
Growth rate	5 per cent
Forecast of sales value	Rs. 10.5 crore
Contribution margin (70 per cent)	Rs. 7.35 crore
Fixed costs	Rs. 4.25 crore
Contribution margin to cover marketing costs & profits	Rs. 3.10 crore
Estimate of profit goal	Rs. 1.60 crore
Marketing budget	Rs. 1.50 crore

Table 2 Marketing Mix and Sales estimates

Marketing Mix	Product Quality	Price	Advertising (Rs. lakhs)	Promotion (Rs. lakhs)	Estimated Sales (Rs. Crores)	Contribution Margin per cent
1	Same	25	75	75	10.5	70
2	Same	24	70	100	12.0	70
3	Improve	25	100	80	11.5	65
4	Improve	26	70	120	11.0	65
5	Reduce	24	70	100	11.5	72
6	Reduce	23	70	110	12.0	72

Marketing mix 1 represents existing combination with expected sales. Advice Venkat.

CASE

39 Cola Wars

Jagadri is a dusty town in the hinterlands of North India in the state of Haryana, whose 60,000 citizens get by on a combination of farming and trading. This out-of-the-way place seems an unlikely forum for a marketing war between multinational corporations. But that's what has been going on there for the past 18 months. The combatants are PepsiCo Inc., and Coca-Cola Co., each of which claims over 50 per cent of Jagadri's soft-drink market.

THE CLASH

The soft drink market till early 1990s was in the hands of domestic players like Campa, Thums Up, Limca, etc. but with the opening up of the economy and coming of MNC players, Pepsi and Coke, the market has come totally under their control. Pepsi entered the Indian market in 1991, Coke re-entered (After they were thrown out in 1977, by the then central government) in 1993. Now Coca-Cola India leads the table with 54.7 per cent market share followed by Pepsi's 40.4 per cent. However, the two arch rivals are inundated by losses. While Pepsi suffered a Rs. 265-crore loss as on 31st December 2000, Coke too accumulated losses of Rs. 650 crore in the same period.

The figures look imposing despite the fact that Pepsi's figures do not include losses from Tropicana, a pure-juice drink. Similarly, Coke's figures have been arrived at after its Atlanta-based parent had written off $ 400 million in the first quarter of calendar 2000. Worth noting is the fact that losses have increased on a year-to-year basis. Thus, in Pepsi's case, its losses in the calendar year 2000 increased to Rs. 67 crore in comparison to Rs. 37 crore in calendar 1999.

MARKET SEGMENTS AND CHARACTERISTICS

The soft drink market can be segmented on the basis of place of consumption or on the basis of type of products. The segmentation on the basis of place of consumption divides the market into two parts: -

- On premise—80 per cent of the consumption of the soft drink is on premise i.e., restaurants, railway stations, cinema etc.
- At home—the rest 20 per cent of the market comprises of the soft drink purchased for consumption at home.

The market can also be segmented on the basis of types of products, into cola products and non-cola products.

- Cola products account for nearly 61–62 per cent of the total soft drink market. The brands that fall in this category are Pepsi, Coca-Cola, Thums Up, Diet Coke, Diet Pepsi, etc.
- Non-cola segment which constitutes 36 per cent can be divided into 4 categories based on the types of flavours available, namely:
- Orange (17 per cent)—Fanta and Mirinda orange
- Cloudy Lime (14 per cent)—Limca and Mirinda Lemon
- Clear Lime (3 per cent)—Sprite and 7 Up
- Mango (2 per cent)—Maaza, Slice and Mangola

There are some small local brands at city or regional levels. Most of these are either merging with the two big players (Coca-Cola and Pepsi) or they command a very small—less than 3 per cent, of the total market in their respective areas.

The consumer habits and practices are identified as follows.

- Soft drinks come under the low involvement category of products purchased on impulse. Product differentiation is very low, as all the products taste the same. However, changing life style, increasing urbanization, growth in rural prosperity and impact of liberalization has slowly and gradually started moving the market from occasion led to home refrigeration led consumption.
- Consumers prefer convenience. Consumers purchase soft drinks primarily to quench thirst. Therefore, people travelling and not having access to hygienic water reach out for a soft drink. This accounts for a large part of the sales. Availability in the chilled form affects the purchase decision.
- While there is no aversion to consumption of soft drinks by any age group, the main consumers of this market are people in the age group of 30 and below. Though the purchase decision is a low involvement decision, brand loyalty exists. Brand loyalty is high in the case of kids and people in the age group of 20–30 yrs.
- Consumers prefer economy products. They are sensitive to the outlay where the purchase of beverages is concerned. Hence, the market is price sensitive. Due to the high cost of soft drinks, a lot of times consumers prefer beverages like tea, coffee or other drinks like *sherbet* and squashes.
- The market preference is highly regional based. While cola drinks have the main markets in metro cities and northern states of UP, Punjab, Haryana, etc. Orange flavoured drinks are popular in southern states. Western markets have preference towards mango flavoured drinks. Diet Coke presently constitutes just 0.7 per cent of the total carbonated beverage market.
- Another skewness is in terms of the time of the year when the consumption takes place. Most of the sales of soft drinks take place during summers while just 5–6 per cent of total sales take place in winters. In summers, the high season lasts for 70–75 days which contributes more than 50 per cent of the total yearly sales.
- Per capita consumption in India is among the lowest in the world at 5 bottles per annum compared to 80 bottles in Thailand and 800 bottles in the USA.

- While 75 per cent of the PET bottle consumption is in urban areas, the 200ml bottle sales are higher in rural areas.
- According to NCAER survey 91 per cent of the total consumption of soft drinks in the country is done by lower, lower middle and upper middle class people.

MARKET SIZE AND GROWTH

The market size for FY02 is expected to be 8,000 mn bottles with an expected growth rate of 16 per cent.

97–98	4,920
98–99	5,670
99–00	6,480
2000–01	7,000

The market growth of 22 per cent till last year has got stifled due to high excise duty of 40 per cent leading to higher price of the end product.

PRODUCT-PRICE WARS

Pepsi and Coke are available in glass bottles, aluminium cans and PET bottles for home consumption. Fountains also dispense them in disposable containers at different price points.

When Coca-Cola came back to India, it launched itself in all major cities in the 300 ml size at the same price as Pepsi, which was then in 200 ml bottle. Pepsi was, however, prepared for Coca-Cola's launch in the larger bottle size and soon, in the cola market, in India, it was the 300 ml bottle which became the standard in most parts of the country, making the price a parity issue between the two brands. A few years ago, Pepsi launched itself in one litre and 1.5 litre non-returnable PET bottles at a discount in comparison to a 300 ml returnable glass bottle, the traditional packaging in this product category. This resulted in a significant increase in the depth of consumption; amongst the loyal consumers in the larger towns.

A similar experiment with Pepsi fountains where the soft drink was sold in a wax lined paper cup did not succeed because of the inability of the brand owner to ensure hygienic conditions; particularly in the water being used and also in the quality of the drink. Needless to say, Coke followed Pepsi in each of the above moves in order to reduce the cost per glass to consumer.

The soft drink majors also pioneered a 500 ml non-returnable PET bottle which was advertised almost totally on the cost of the consumer per 100 ml of cola. Of course, the great advantage of the PET bottle is that they not only encourage high level of consumers but increased home consumption which was small compared to out-of-home consumption.

'Think small, and keep the product simple' is the approach of Coco-Cola. Their model is the stolid Anglo-Dutch conglomerate, Unilever Group, which has enjoyed a century-long presence in India through its subsidiary Hindustan Lever Ltd. It was Hindustan Lever that several years ago popularized the idea of selling its products in tiny packages. Its Re.1 sachets of detergent and shampoo are in great demand in Indian villages—and in emerging markets throughout Asia and Africa. Sanjeev Gupta, Deputy President of Coca-Cola India makes no bones about whom he is copying. "We want to be the Hindustan Lever of the Indian beverage business," he says. Accordingly, Coke's newest weapon to gain an advantage over Pepsi is a smaller 200ml bottle of cola, which it sells for an affordable Rs. 5 in the town's small shops, bus-stop stalls, and roadside eateries. Obviously, Pepsi has not lagged behind.

DISTRIBUTION STRENGTHS

The companies have divided the country into various regions and established a franchisee in each region. The franchisees have their own bottling plants and manage all the day-to-day operations. However, of late, the soft drink companies have started setting up company owned bottling units and have been acquiring some of its franchised bottles. Coca-Cola has 8 lakh retail outlets whereas Pepsi has 7.5 lakh retail outlets all over India. While distributors get a margin of Rs. 8–9 per crate (1 crate= 24 bottles) at 3–4 per cent of MRP, retailers are given a margin of 10–12 per cent of MRP. The retailers are not happy with this as the cost of refrigeration is very high for soft drinks. To overcome this problem the companies are offering visi-cooler schemes to their main retailers.

A survey was conducted to study the retailers' views of the present market, future trend and the consumer behaviour patterns. The findings of the survey are as follows:

- Retailers stated that the consumers are loyal to a particular segment of the soft drink i.e., cola, orange or lemon. But as far as loyalty for the brands in each segment is concerned, it is not very significant.
- 43 per cent of the retailers surveyed told that in soft drinks, advertising is the key component in driving sales. While 32 per cent stated promotional schemes and 20 per cent brand loyalty as the reason.
- As consumers are not very brand loyal where the purchase of soft drinks is concerned, the retailer push becomes a critical issue. They usually sell the product in which they get the maximum benefit. For this, the companies try to offer them higher margins.

Recently, to make sure the distribution network was shipshape, Sanjeev Gupta, as he surveyed one Coke outlet instructed his staff to provide more display racks. Jagadri and thousands of towns like it are crucial to Coke's new rural marketing strategy in India. "Our hands are firmly in the dust here," Gupta says. "It's the only way we can capture this market." Not just this, aware of the power-starved Indian summer, Coca-Cola has found a unique tool for the Indian market. Metal boxes containing a base of ice, there by eliminating the need for electricity and at the price of Rs.6 for 200 ml. As many as 3,000 of such 15 kg carts rolled out in the dusty, pot-holed streets of the price-conscious rural markets of Bihar, Uttar Pradesh, Gujarat and West Bengal this summer.

PROMOTION WARS

Fierce battles setting aside decency are fought by the cola barons in terms of positioning and communicating for mind space. While Coke is targeted at teenagers and is positioned as refreshment for mind and body, it's, Thums Up brand is targeted at people in the age group of 20–29 years positioned as a thing for adventure-loving, successful and macho person. Pepsi's cola product is targeted towards the youth. With the Hrithik song-and-dance ad, Coke seems to be acknowledging that, in India at least, the youth market is where it's at.

Both Pepsi and Coke struggled initially in establishing themselves in the market, but finally it seems they have started understanding the pulse of the Indian consumers. Remember,Pepsi's Rs.49 lakh, 90 second launch advertisement was a failure. Critics opined, "Too much gas and not enough fizz". Its later struggles fructified when it took the clue from a market research in 25 countries which suggested that young today are restless as they are looking for more from life–more success, more entertainment and more glamour. Thus evolved the global baseline of Pepsi 'Ask for more' and it was launched in India in a commercial that featured Shah Rukh Khan, Rani Mukherjee, Kajol and Sachin Tendulkar.

Coke's oscillations between past generation and generation next seem to have finally found a median. Liberalising from the insipid nostalgia of 'share my dream' in 1993, Coca-Cola was tuned to the invigorated teenspeak of '*peetikya* Coca-Cola' and '*pyar mohabbat* Coca-Cola'. Finally realising that more than a third of India's 1 billion people are under 18, Coca-Cola has started talking about youth passions—Cricket, films, festivals and food. 'Eat Cricket, Sleep Cricket, drink only Coca-Cola', are the 'real refresher' ads.

Coke decided to fight Pepsi in any way, says a market watcher, "The Thums Up thunder series was a clear signal to the men in blue that Coca-Cola is not the goody-goody MNC in the Indian context. It's ready to be a street fighter". Both the companies have featured the most popular cine stars or cricketers in their life style advertisements. The ads are specific to regions. While PepsiCo's ad has been that of Amitabh Bachchan–Sachin Tendulkar's kite-flying jaunt, Coca-Cola's most popular commercial has been Aamir Khan's oafish '*thanda matlab* Coca-Cola' act in a pedestrian Mumbai restaurant.

Pepsi won the round of cola battle, beating both coke (Rank 20) and Thums Up (Rank 31) and raising to rank 14, the highest for a cola brand. The frantic advertising amongst cola brands seems to have worked in Pepsi's favour, no matter what Salman Khan (of Thums Up) has to say about it being a kiddo drink. The Amitabh ad has done well for it, and a Fardeen Khan starrer could be next. Can Pepsi aim to enter the top 10 next year?

A&M Brand Survey Ranks and Scores

	Coca-Cola	Pepsi
Rank	20(35)	14(27)
Score	31.5	33.0
Main Earner	33.8	33.7
Housewife	28.7	28.3
Young Adult Male	41.6	43.5
Young Adult Female	38.2	41.5

Hrithik Roshan, Aamir Khan and Aishwarya Rai have helped Coke to zoom ahead of its stable mate Thums Up but not Pepsi. But then, perhaps there's also some thing to Coke's finally getting a wide-angled strategy in place in the ever-so-complex Indian market.

BATTLES IN THE GROWING MARKET

The giants are lured to the countryside for a very simple reason: Economic growth in India's agricultural sector last year was over 7 per cent, compared with 3 per cent in the industrial sector. More growth means more income, and more income means more sales. "The rural market is a significant part of our marketing strategy which enables us to help the consumer link with our product" remarked Sanjeev Gupta, Coca-Cola's India Marketing Director. "The Indian market is constantly changing and is now fiercely competitive today. And in the process of understanding the market, we have segmented the rural Indians as a key factor. Primarily because that market is growing in a much larger proportion as compared to the urban scenario" said Deepak Jolly, PepsiCo India's Vice-President (Corporate Communications). Coke's rural strategy of selling small sizes helped sales jump by 34 per cent in the year 2002.

Mckinsey, which completed a study of India's food and beverage business in 1997, predicts that by 2005, the soft-drink market will grow to around $2.4 billion. India's per-capita consumption of soft drinks is still a paltry six bottles a year, compared with 15 in Pakistan, 22 in China and more than 600 in Mexico. "In India, drinking a cola is not an everyday habit," says Vikram Sakhuja, Coca-Cola's Marketing Manager for India. "It is reserved for special occasions—religious festivals, family outings, sports events."

There are other obstacles, though. With Indian per-capita incomes still relatively low, price matters. A small increase last year, for instance, stagnated soft-drink sales. And Indian taste buds represent a stumbling block: Coke and Pepsi are simply too bland to go with some highly spiced provincial cuisines. "We need more flavour, something distinctive and strong," says Ramesh Chauhan, a former soft-drink magnate who created the somewhat spicy Thums Up brand.

Since neither Pepsi nor Coke would ever countenance changing their sacred formulas, they'll continue to rely on stars like Hrithik to help win over young Indians. But it's a nasty battle out there. According to industry estimates, both the companies, put together, end up spending nearly Rs. 450 crore to Rs. 500 crore annually on advertisements. Then, there are heavy dealer discounts to contend with, will the companies cut out on their advertisement budgets, dealer discounts and other sales promotional activities? Apparently not, because as long as there is competition in the market, these strategies will have to be continued with.

QUESTIONS

1. In future, what course the cola wars may take? Comment on the consequences.
2. Suggest a suitable strategy for Coca-Cola to gain leadership. What kind of emphasis should be there in the strategy?

Source

1. *www.indiainfoline.com*—Report on Soft-Drinks
2. *India Express Magazine*, September 23, 1990.
3. Shuchi Bansal, Pepsi, *Business World*, June, 21–30, 1999, pp.32–34.

CASE

40 Integrated Marketing

"I am shocked to know that our poultry farmers are forced to migrate lock, stock, and barrel to other areas for livelihood. We have a responsibility to help them" Dr. V. Sundar Naidu, Chairman, V. S. N. Hatcheries Pvt. Ltd., said with great concern. His 'Operation White' team listened to him with rapt attention. He continued, " It is true that our company is losing because of the failure of poultry farmers in this area. But our revival plans should embrace the larger social welfare concept. We live and help others live. I want you to sketch plans with this goal in mind".

The words are still ringing afresh in the ears of Naidu, General Manager (Marketing). He is heading the 'Operation White' team. Today there is a meeting of the team to finalise the integration plan they chalked-out two days back. There will be a presentation by him followed by discussion.

THE PAST

V.S.N.Hatcheries was started as a private limited company in Chittoor by Dr. V. Sundar Naidu in 1989. It started production of day-old broiler chicks to cater to the requirements of poultry farms. Figure 1 shows the channel of distribution.

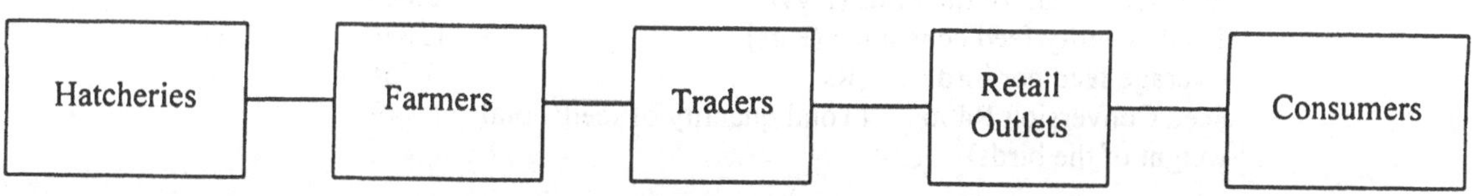

Fig. 1 Traditional Marketing System

The Failure

The individual broiler farming was forced to be abandoned primarily due to fluctuating prices of birds and the greed of the traders. The price of chicken is directly related to the following factors.

- Substitutes: The alternative food items are fish, eggs, vegetables and mutton. When the prices of these are high, people tend to go in for chicken. Thereby raising the demand and price and vice-versa.
- Seasonal habits: Generally the eating habits of people change with the seasons and these habits also play a major part in the fluctuation of chicken prices.
- Consumption variations
  - For example, people tend to spend less on meat food in May and June in order to save money to meet the academic expenses of children. So, the prices are naturally at the lowest.
  - If the consumption in one state is less due to various local reasons the cascading effect leads to a glut in the other states and prices fall down drastically.

THE SOLUTION

A brief of Naidu's presentation is as follows.

"After careful examination of the facts and estimates, we have decided to recommend 'forward integration' to be immediately implemented. The concept envisages adopting farmers to house the day-old chicks in their presently vacant sheds and rear them up to 42 days of age by arranging feed and other inputs and finally selling of the grown-up birds for table purpose.

The farmer is benefited because his job is only rearing the day-old chicks. The company will supply inputs, provide supervision and advice and pay him for his services. He is relieved of the agony of selling the grown up birds. As an integrator, we use the farm space and manpower of the owner of the vacant shed. We compensate him by paying him a commensurate amount linked to various parameters like cost of production, percentage of mortality and general up-keep of the flock, etc. Based on these, a Rearing Charges Chart (Table -1) is devised to arrive at the rearing charges payable to farmers. The procedure of arriving at production cost is shown in Exhibit -1.

Exhibit-1 Production cost details

Say,	No. of chicks supplied		3495
	No. of birds mortality		158
	Balance birds		3337
	Total weight of the birds (Kgs)		6940
	Average weight of the birds (Kgs)		2.083
	Total quantity feed consumed (Kgs)		12830
	Average feed per bird	(Rs.)	3.756
	Feed Conversion Ratio weight of the birds)	(Total quantity of feed/Total	1.849
	Cost of chicks @ Rs. 12/bird	3495x12	4190:00
	Cost of feed	12830x10	128300:00
	Cost of vaccine	12830 x0.36	2466:60
	Cost of medicine	12830 x0.05	316.80
	Total		173023.40
	Production cost/kg (Rs.)		24.93

As per Table 1, rearing charges will be paid in addition to production cost depending upon mortality percentage. If it is 1–5 per cent Rs. 2.55 is added to production cost of Rs. 24.93.

Table 1 Rearing Charges Chart

Mortality % / Production Cost	1 to 5	6	7	8	9	10	11	12	13	14	15& above
23.00	3.05	3.00	2.95	2.90	2.85	2.80	2.75	2.70	2.65	2.60	2.55
23.40	2.95	2.90	2.85	2.80	2.75	2.70	2.65	2.60	2.55	2.50	2.45
23.80	2.85	2.80	2.75	2.70	2.65	2.60	2.55	2.50	2.45	2.40	2.35
24.00	2.70	2.65	2.60	2.55	2.50	2.45	2.40	2.35	2.30	2.25	2.20
24.80	2.60	2.55	2.50	2.45	2.40	2.35	2.30	2.25	2.20	2.15	2.10
25.00	2.55	2.50	2.45	2.40	2.35	2.30	2.25	2.20	2.15	2.10	2.05
25.40	2.45	2.40	2.35	2.30	2.25	2.20	2.15	2.10	2.05	2.00	1.95
25.80	2.35	2.30	2.25	2.20	2.15	2.10	2.05	2.00	1.95	1.90	1.85
26.00	2.30	2.25	2.20	2.15	2.10	2.05	2.00	1.95	1.90	1.85	1.80
26.40	2.20	2.15	2.10	2.05	2.00	1.95	1.90	1.85	1.80	1.75	1.70
26.80	2.10	2.05	2.00	1.95	1.90	1.85	1.80	1.75	1.70	1.65	1.60
27.00	2.05	2.00	1.95	1.90	1.85	1.80	1.75	1.70	1.65	1.60	1.55
27.40	1.95	1.90	1.85	1.80	1.75	1.70	1.65	1.60	1.55	1.50	1.45
27.80	1.85	1.80	1.75	1.70	1.65	1.60	1.55	1.50	1.45	1.40	1.35
28.00	1.80	1.75	1.70	1.65	1.60	1.55	1.50	1.45	1.40	1.35	1.30
28.40	1.70	1.65	1.60	1.55	1.50	1.45	1.40	1.35	1.30	1.25	1.20
28.80	1.60	1.55	1.50	1.45	1.40	1.35	1.30	1.25	1.20	1.15	1.10
29.00	1.55	1.50	1.45	1.40	1.35	1.30	1.25	1.20	1.15	1.10	1.05
29.40	1.45	1.40	1.35	1.30	1.25	1.20	1.15	1.10	1.05	1.00	1.00
29.80	1.35	1.30	1.25	1.20	1.15	1.10	1.05	1.00	1.00	1.00	1.00
30.00	1.30	1.25	1.20	1.15	1.10	1.05	1.00	1.00	1.00	1.00	1.00

The consumer is benefitted because, he is relieved from the clutches of the traditional trader. There will be adherence to a strict pricing mechanism linked to that day's procurement rate. In effect, price does not vary much. As a result, he can consume more and regularly.

The retailer is benefitted. The company offers live chicken to the selling points and they can minimise in their shrinkage and mortality aspects. Ideally, elimination of the traders would be beneficial both to the producer and consumer. But to do so involves a gigantic task of opening and operating a huge chain of retail centres. Unlike Bata, which can have one outlet in a medium town and about 20 to 30 in the metropolis which are frequented by people at the most once or twice in a year, our outlets must be more in number and the frequency of customers would be on a daily basis if not weekly. So, the question of operating a chain of outlets is an option of the future. Presently, some of our competitors have entered into arrangements with Food World, etc., to supply chicken.

Now, we come to the last but the most important link in our marketing chain—the traders—to avoid exploitation by the traders, we have to eliminate them. But, we lack the necessary infrastructure, which entails heavy investment. On an experimental basis, we propose starting a few retail outlets and slowly expanding to other areas. The questions to be answered are:

i. How many retail outlets and where?

ii. How do we manage them? How much profit can be expected?

iii. What should be our plan of expansion, supposing the retail outlets are successful?

COMPETITORS

The major deviation in the thinking process of our company and competitors is that we are concentrating on rural areas targeting the potential of 70 per cent of our population, whereas our competitors are focusing on urban areas banking on their purchasing capacity. The modus operandi of one of our competitors is, lease a premise, model it to specification, install sophisticated machinery and let out as a frachise. The other competitor is transporting large quantities to major cities and arranging smaller vehicles to distribute the product to all the nooks and corners of the cities."

THE PLAN OF ACTION

After substantial discussion, the team came up with an action plan. The highlights are:

It decided to enter the market and has about 6 or 7 outlets to start with in the rural markets. Rural markets are preferred as a majority of population is in villages and the market potential is enormous. The logic is: "We offer quality products at reasonable prices and thereby increase the consumption in the rural area. Moreover, our products are produced in rural areas and there is no reason to shift it to urban areas." The proposed distribution is as shown in Figure 2.

Based on the recommendation, on an experimental basis, sales points were started at Punganuru, Puthalapattu, Penumur and Chittoor. They reported a net profit of Rs. 7,045, Rs. 24,823, Rs. 25,332 and Rs. 3,740 respectively in the very first month of their commencement.

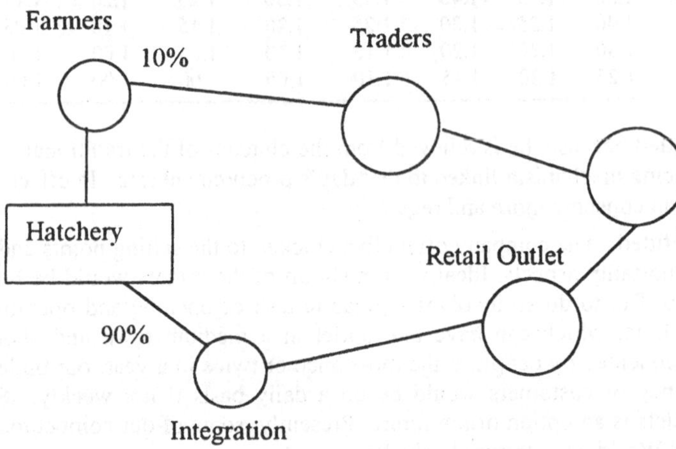

Fig. 2 Proposed Distribution System

QUESTIONS

1. Examine the proposed distribution strategy of 'Operation White' team. Discuss its merits and demerits?
2. Do you advise the company to start more number of retail outlets?

Credits

N. G. Naidu, General Manager (Marketing), Balaji & Hatcheries and V.S.N. Hatcheries Pvt. Ltd., Chittoor.

INDEX

D

E

F

G

H

I

N